T0380724

GOD Is Speaking - Are You Listening? My Story

Visions and Dialogue with The Lord GOD

Order this book online at www.trafford.com
or email orders@trafford.com

Most Trafford titles are also available at major online book retailers.

Print information available on the last page.

ISBN: 978-1-5536-9690-2 (sc)
ISBN: 978-1-4122-4873-0 (e)

Trafford rev. 10/16/2018

www.trafford.com
North America & international
toll-free: 1 888 232 4444 (USA & Canada)
fax: 812 355 4082

Table of Contents

Tables of Contents Page 2

Acknowledgments

First and foremost – GOD:

This is what I heard from you. This is what we shared. I pray to you it is accurate and what you wish to release as a book. I finally understand why I am, the way I am. You have been molding me and are not yet finished. May this give you glory and be the message of your Love. I love you, and now know you love me. May this glorify you and bring peace to us all. Thank-you for letting me be a part of this project. My soul feels alive and I have a purpose in my life. Amen

To Mom and Dad:

This is why all those "episodes" happened to me. This explains all the doctor visits and why I could not begin to explain what I was seeing and hearing. I love you both. You gave me life.

To Ted:

Thanks for listening and understanding. I love you as my brother and best friend.

To my Sister and her family:

No, your brother is not crazy. Just read this and realize I could not begin to share with you what I was going through all those times.

To Joshua, Cortney, Kelcey, and Jacob:

This is what I tried to explain when we talked about why Dad was hospitalized. I love you all. I would have gone through it all again just to see how wonderful you have all turned out. You are precious and dear to me. I love you unconditionally.

To Brian, Andrea, Jackie, Mike, John and all of the fire Department:

You are my friends, thanks for caring about me. We have such great times together and may we have many, many more. This is what I tried to explain after all those beers.

To my all other friends:

I have talked about this for years. This why I could not easily explain everything, it took this book to just start the process. Now, perhaps what I was tying to share will make more sense.

To Jennifer:

Thanks for being my friend. Thanks for the help with the editing of this book. I still think you are the nicest person I know. I miss our talks. "Slippers" say's thanks as well.

To everyone who has heard, or thought they heard, a voice or voices, or even had visions they could not explain:

This book is for you. It will calm your fears and give you insight into GOD. It will give you direction and the reason why they are there. You have been blessed. You just now are finding that out.

Finally, to everyone else:

If you say this is not possible, I say: "do not underestimate the GOD I know."

Introduction

Where do I begin? How do I explain to you the reader, in a short introduction, about a lifelong journey? This is my personal inner struggle and denial that *I have a direct connection with GOD*. Not possible you say? No one is worthy of such a thing? Well…what if GOD chose <u>me</u>? What if GOD volunteered me and I had no real say in the matter? Would anyone be able to <u>prevent</u> that type of connection? Think of it…GOD decided for me. I have fought and denied this connection with my very existence all of my life. I have lost the battle to deny that GOD picked me to channel his words into book form. This book is the result of that battle lost. This is GOD'S STORY. It is his plan, his words, his topics, his Love, his wisdom, his laughter and his warnings.

If 43 years of voices, visions and information is not enough for you, then you had better put this book down right now. <u>Start searching somewhere else for a connection with GOD</u>. Those people who will be able to accept this, are those who believe in a GOD who <u>is more than a church doctrine</u>. One <u>who Loves us unconditionally</u>. If that is what <u>you believe</u>, then this book is for you. This <u>in no way contradicts</u> the bible or church teachings. Reading this in its entire context will help to explain the "why?" <u>Why certain things happen as they do in life</u>.

This book reminds us that GOD does not change. He is eternal. Humanity has adapted church and bible teachings to be convenient or comfortable to our daily lives. A nice neat clean definition of what, or who, is GOD. We have adopted Jesus and others, all born of the Earth, as our savior or even elevated them to the title and status of GOD. But we forget that GOD told us to **worship no other GODS before me**, and that Jesus greatest commandment was to **Love GOD with all your heart.** Who was the GOD that Jesus prayed to? In this book GOD reminds us that Jesus prayed to <u>him</u>. This book tells of his Love for us and his desire for **a direct connection and personal relationship with each and every one of us.** Do you believe GOD would do such a thing? Why would he spend time on each and every one of us? Why Love any or all human beings? Well, read on…he is GOD and is CAPABLE OF SUCH THINGS that is why. Do not underestimate GOD. **I AM THE GOD OF ALL. I EXIST TO SHOW YOU A BETTER WAY TO LIVE AND LOVE.**

I have been receiving lots of information from "the other side" for what seems my whole life. Recently, prior to September 11th, input from their world has been fast and furious. I have been documenting everything they have been telling me, since I started keeping records back in 1998. I commented to a friend, *lately they have been extremely quiet and appear to be waiting for something.* That something was the terrorist attack's on the World Trade Center complex. I asked why? Why did GOD allow it to occur? I was told of other cultures, millions of years ago and millions of miles away. I was told that those societies built large buildings, skyscrapers and towers with devastating results.

Millions of people died as a result of being caught in their "Tall Towers." The buildings caught fire and there was no way for individuals to safely escape. This answer I received was that we should <u>stop</u> building OUR buildings taller than 55 stories. GOD Loves us and would not allow us to destroy ourselves by our desire to "build taller and taller." We were being disciplined. GOD "allowed the event to occur" to avoid massive loss of life <u>years from now</u>, when ALL the buildings we build may <u>too tall</u>. The conversation that took place is in the writings I have from the same day it occurred, Sept. 11th. Later material will have the conversations with GOD about the events of that day. It is not included in <u>this book</u> <u>however</u> because I have a 15" pile of notes that has <u>other</u> information that GOD asked me to share.

This book is the <u>start</u> of my processing and <u>documenting</u> of what I hear. This conversation that you are about to read is true, none of the information has been changed. I felt compelled to be true to the source, GOD. It is taken directly from my notes, starting in July 1998 as I received it. It is what GOD shared with me. I felt compelled to treat with the respect and dignity since it is coming from GOD. I did not alter, change, or exaggerate. Why would I change something received from GOD? I have respect for what I heard, and still hear, and if it is truly from GOD, should it not be treated as Holy? There are things we spoke about that still confuse me. But if I have difficulty understanding the information, that is <u>not</u> GOD'S fault. I eventually will learn what he is trying to teach me. It is simply GOD telling me about <u>his</u> wisdom. I am only human, and hopefully someday I will understand totally.

As for me, people are not supposed to hear voices, correct? That is what is drilled into our minds in this physical existence. Then why have I heard them for what seems' my <u>whole</u> <u>entire</u> <u>life</u>? I do not show any outwards' signs of this ability. I receive the information similar to the same way everyone else hears, except I receive it as thought and images. It is like a, and I hesitate to use this word, psychic or thought connection. To meet me, you would not know I have this ability. It is silent and non-intrusive.

Another major reason for doing this is to share with you, the reader, what I have gone through. Perhaps it will help others understand their voices and that GOD may simply be trying to have a direct connection with <u>them</u>. GOD'S Love may be directed to <u>them</u> and that may be why they "hear" what <u>they</u> do. GOD may simply be trying to establish a personal relationship with them as well.

The very first real memory that I have of contact with GOD is in 1960, and being 5 years old. I was running a very high fever and not feeling well at all. My parents had that "worried look" in their eyes. The doctor, who back then made house calls, said, eventually I would get better. I remember GOD sitting on the edge of my bed. He was holding my hand and telling me I will **feel better shortly** and he has **all sorts of fun stuff planned** for my life. This is the very 1st time I remember hearing his voice and seeing his image. I could also see more. I could visualize all his angels in my room. I could hear <u>their</u> voices and I could hear GOD speak to them <u>and</u> to me as well. He introduced me to Jesus and to the Saints. In the darkness of that small room, it was my "minds-eye" witnessing GODS glory. I could "see" or identify a very large man, and what I would call "glowing" bright clothes. I could see lights, colors, shapes and figures. He had a very big bright white beard. As we spoke my wall suddenly became a movie screen and GOD showed me a movie about MY FUTURE. He spent three consecutive nights showing me individual events that would take place in my life. He showed my being married; having children and playing sports.

GOD asked, **do you know who I AM?** I said, *You are GOD*. I asked… *Am I going to die? Is that why you are here?* I thought he was taking to Heaven. GOD said, **no… you are <u>not going</u> to die. Believe what Dr. Harper told you, that you are going to get better eventually.** I remember my little hand holding GOD'S finger. His hands were so large and mine so very small. I remember telling him he *looked just like Santa Claus*. He said **I AM Santa…that is why I look so much like him.** I said, r*eally, is it Christmas already?* He laughed and said **no…you will have to wait a while for that.** I told him that my parents look so worried because I'm sick. He told me **that is because they Love you and are worried about you.** *I feel so awful.* **I know…it is because you are sick. You will get better soon**. *Why are you here GOD?* **To make sure you understand that <u>I Love you</u> and that I have some things to show you about your life in the future.** I remember falling asleep after the first night and feeling at ease. I was not so scared as I was before. It was so very frightening to be so young and seeing that worried look in my parent's eyes. When my mom sat on my bed the next morning I was so excited and I told her I saw GOD last night. I even told her that I spoke to him. She had that look in her eyes like she was worried again. I got the impression she did not believe me. She did ask me what we talked about. *He told me I was going to get better.* She said "that was Dr. Harper telling you that, not GOD." *I know, but GOD said the same thing.* "I think it was Dr. Harper you heard not GOD." *But mommy, he sat on my bed just like you and told me I will get better <u>and</u> he showed me a movie all about me.* She felt my forehead "well, you are still warm, why don't you get your rest." I still was not feeling that well so I did not argue any more. I was also remembering GOD telling me how parents do not always see GOD like children do. The next night GOD showed up again. I told him…*I tried to tell mommy about your coming to visit last night and she did not believe me.* He said **I know Steve, remember… parents have a tough time seeing and believing in GOD.** *If she came in to my room now could she see you?* **She would, if she would really believe and wanted to see me. I AM right here with you holding your hand.** *Why doesn't she believe in you GOD?* **Parents get busy raising their children and they forget I AM here.** *Oh, does Mommy forget to Love me?* **No, GOD reminds her <u>not</u> to forget that. That is just too important to GOD.**

After a couple days I got up from my bed and had some soup. "I am glad to see you feeling better," my mom said. *I told GOD to help me get better and he did.* She said "that will be enough talk about GOD." Remembering what GOD said about parents not seeing or believing like children do, I decided to keep my conversations with him to myself. That is a decision I carried the rest of my life until now. This is part of that first conversation I still remember 42 years later. We spoke for several hours each night. I remember this vividly and clearly because GOD helps me remember. He allows me to remember with him. Imagine GOD sitting on the edge of my bed, holding my hand and speaking to me. Imagine me thinking, and speaking to him, and he hears both levels of my conversation. This is what I remember. This is my 1st remembered conversation and interaction with GOD.

Now it is the year 1975. I was in college for forestry and I hated it. I felt like it just was just not the right decision for me. I was still trying to figure out why I was there. Why did I pick this program? I remember when I was in the sixth grade having a teacher ask me; "what do you want to be when you grow up?" I said *Forest Ranger*. I still wonder why I said that. It came out of nowhere. I was later told in 1990, it was because GOD was planning on me to meet my future wife. I did meet her years later, but through a career in retail. Her dad was once a Forest Ranger in Maine and there was a very good chance we would meet that way. Anyway, I was in college and not doing well. I was trying to play freshman football and still do my studies. The program had a 67% freshman failure dropout rate. I could see why. There was very heavy Math, Science and Chemistry, all in the first year of study. My motivation was poor and I didn't do well academically. I prayed for guidance. When I got down on my knees it started to get very noisy in my thoughts. I was receiving thoughts, images and voices I could not make sense of. I felt the urge to try and write down what I was hearing from their world. All I could do was draw circles, lots and lots of circles. I do remember GOD telling me **do not worry I have a plan for your life,** and that is about all that came through with any consistency clearly. When I prayed the connection seemed clearer. I remember him asking me how college was? I remember telling him; *it was "sucky."* That meant I did not enjoy it. That was the slang of that time. Everything was either "cool, decent" or "sucky." He said **I AM the almighty GOD of all. I will see that you are happy, GOD'S way, in the future.** I remember thinking and wondering if this really was GOD. Was this who I really heard through all the noise? So many years had passed since seeing and hearing him when I was five years old.

Now it is 1986. I was in the military, serving in the Philippines. I had just re-enlisted and was coming home from a three-year tour of duty. I was feeling on top of the world. I had a career, family and a future, or so I thought. I decided to do something I have been meaning to do for years, that was to read the bible from cover to cover. I had seen so many things while being in the service. I had been exposed to different cultures, lifestyles and religions. I was now looking for my own personal connection with GOD. I had blocked out the episodes in 1960 and 1975 out of my mind. I was attempting to start a brand new and fresh relationship and contact with him. So I started to read. All was just fine with what I was reading in the Old Testament and I spread it out over several nights. When I got to the New Testament, and Paul's letters to the Corinthians, I heard Paul's voice. It was as if he was reading the letters to me. It effected me deep, deep down inside. I cried, no, better put…I wept. It moved me so much and it was totally unexpected. The voices that had I heard and tried to deny since I was five were still there, except I seemed much more emotional affected this time. I was not only hearing a voice whisper in my ear as I read but it seemed to be a feeling of extremely strong, almost overpowering Love. Wrapped in an emotional blanket of warmth and contentment. I was at a point in my life struggling with my spiritual identity. Who I was, and why do the voices only seem to target ME? I was having a problem with organized religion and the teachings they represented. They seemed to contradict each other on the very basic existence and definition of GOD. I could not shake the stories and teachings that GOD had shared with me at age 5. It was in my soul. I had met GOD and even though I tried to forget the encounter, the memory was still there. That night I got all my knees and prayed. I gave my life to Jesus Christ. I became a Born-again-Christian. It just seemed the natural and normal thing to do at that moment. The noise at that instance became even more intense. The voices were almost overwhelming from that point on. I was seeing confusing, and what I interpreted as "nasty," visions. I was witnessing big t-Rex type animals, flying spirits, and hearing strange noises and voices all at once. Here I was in the middle of an exhausting flight back to the states of over 14 hours and they did not subside. I could not sleep, I kept hearing the voices, seeing the visions, hearing the sounds of their world. To make matters worse I was traveling with three children and a pregnant wife. Eventually we made it to home. I probably only got three hours sleep during a 72 hour period and I was hospitalized for exhaustion. My first wife could not begin to understand what was wrong with me. I could not begin to explain. Why am I hearing all these voices all at once, why all these visions? I had just totally committed to Jesus Christ and my thoughts were not at peace. Why? It was very simple, I was committing to Jesus not GOD and that the GOD in Heaven was the same GOD that Jesus prayed to…Jehovah. You see, in the past it was that one clear voice, <u>GOD'S</u> that I HEARD ABOVE ALL THE NOISE. I found I was STUCK IN THE TRADITIONAL THINKING FROM MY RELIGIOUS TEACHINGS HERE ON EARTH THAT JESUS WAS LORD. When I <u>finally</u> got to my next duty station the voices were still there. A few months later I suffered what they called "an emotional breakdown." I was then honorably discharged from the military after tests that stated, "he is fine except that he is very emotional." The doctors who checked me out gave me medication to try and stop the voices. I played along, letting them think that the medication was working. <u>I still heard the voices.</u> I found out later that GOD did not want me to re-enlist in the military, and that was the reason for all the "noise" from their world. The future upcoming battles that the military was going to go through were things GOD did not want <u>me</u> involved in personally. It was currently "peace-time" but GOD knew about the "Desert Storm" yet to come. At the time, I did not understand that, it cost me a career in the military, and my first marriage. I remember, even with all visions, and all the voices, I could STILL see GOD standing there. Sometimes off to the side, sometimes sitting in a chair, <u>but always there.</u> He was saying things to me like, **trust GOD'S plan in your life. I AM the LORD GOD Almighty, maker of all things great and small. I AM the great I AM.** I could see him when everything else was in pandemonium, or confusion in my visions. Other conversations about that time and those events are written in greater detail in this book. GOD talks about each of the times he interceded in my life to make changes and adjustments. He talks about the hospital stay in 1986 when I was treated for exhaustion and later that year my apparent emotional breakdown. A full year after being treated for the voices the by VA (Veterans Administration) the doctor treating me suggested I "ease off" all medications. I did not "ease off" anything. I immediately threw them all away. They never really stopped the voices anyway. I still heard and saw visions and such. It wasted away that normal feeling of "brightness and energy" on the medication. It simply sapped it out of me. The medicine just seemed to make me tired all the time.

Every time I tried to talk to anyone about the voices or images I see, they all had that "look" on their face. That look of, "what do you mean you hear voices?" On several occasions, when I was younger, just trying to explain what I could "see and hear" was difficult. Growing up I found that other children either didn't remember, or did not experience the same thing I did. They had no memory of with having had GOD visit. I tried to bury that memory deep. I was still in denial as to what had been occurring. But, GOD would not give up trying to "get my attention."

It is July 5th 1998 another divorce, a bankruptcy and another lost job. I was destitute, depressed, and unfocused as to where next to turn. I prayed to GOD, *why is this happening to me? Why is this happening now? What did I do to deserve this? GOD please tell me why?* I did not REALLY expect an answer. I certainly did not want to go through "episodes" like in the past, but I needed help. I was not doing a very good job of running my own life. I prayed and prayed and prayed. I got an answer all right and one I did not expect at all. It all started out by seeing a vision of GOD sitting on his "Throne of Power." I was hearing his ONE VOICE, LOUD AND CLEAR. All the other noise had miraculously vanished. It started out as a just a whisper in my ear. Then I was seeing light, a bright white light, the sound of powerful rushing waters and in a loud, soul-felt voice**…I AM GOD, I AM the Holy Father, The GOD of Moses, Abraham, Isaac, and Jacob. I AM the GOD of the living Christ. I AM the GOD ALMIGHTY. Creator of Heaven and Earth, creator of Adam and Eve, creator of ALL things, your Holy Father. I AM the GOD of ALL. ALL things come from me.**

Steven…it is I …the LORD GOD, I would like to talk to you. He could hear my thoughts… *oh no…it is happening again.* **I know, I know, this is happening again. It is not like the other times. I KNOW you can hear ME.** *Is this really you GOD? I can hear you clearly.* **Yes, you know it's ME.** *Are you back for a visit to me again?* **Yes, I AM back to visit again. Remember I Love you, and I over the years have noticed your Love for me. I have something, a project, I would like you to do with me.** We spent over 4 hours talking about personal stuff. He knew all that I had been through and was currently going through. The feelings I was encountering were overwhelming. My emotions made me just want to cry. I have never just simply wept so much in my all my life. He told me, **remember when I came to**

visit you when you were sick? *Yes, I was 5.* **Do you remember when college was "sucky" and you wanted out?** *Yes, LORD.* **Do you remember when I told you not to re-list and you did? That is why you had all those strange visions. Only I can do that to you. This is ME....Jehovah. You know I AM...** I cried, sobbing, weeping, and just making a mess of myself. I lost control. It was <u>GOD</u>. I cried, and cried and cried. 43 years of this curse, ability, this gift, all came crashing down. All the visions, the noise, the disarray and confusion the fear that it was "all going to happen again." But...in his presence all my questions were answered. All my troubles, concerns and fears disappeared. All my thoughts were silent, they where at peace. I only heard HIS voice. I wept. I was a wet, sobbing mess. GOD said, **Tissues please.** I laughed. My soul felt cleansed. When he first visited me, back when I was 5, he said, **yes, I do look like Santa because I AM Santa Claus.** He this time he said, **it is ME Steve...Santa.** I did not think I could cry anymore, but I did. When I stopped, or at least let up crying, we reminisced about all the times he intervened in my life. Taking time to correct my behaviors, my thoughts, or my choices. He was intervening again, he explained. He was asking for me <u>to assist in a project, WITH HIM.</u> I felt compelled to assist. After a talking for a while he requested me to, **pick up a pen and put it on a pad of paper.** I had an empty spiral notebook handy and grabbed a pen. <u>He started in immediately to channel this book to me.</u> At first I felt his hand guiding mine as I wrote, I was crying again as I wrote the first few lines of the foreword, keep that in mind as you read. He was standing right beside me it seemed, in my room, holding my hand, guiding my writing and writing with me.

When I had been contacted in 1975 I tried to write like this then, but to no avail. All I could write was circles, lots and lots of circles. In 1986 I had the visions, nasty ones, but I still could see his form, his presence, always standing to the side, talking to me. Telling me, **everything will be fine, trust GOD. Trust in my plan for your life.** Now in 1998 it was happening again. But this time was different, I was hearing him instantaneously, AND <u>writing it down</u>. It started with...

GOD? It really is you isn't it? **Yes, Steven only GOD can do this type of writing with you and make you feel the tears you feel. GOD has the power to help with your life and everyone's life. We are just getting started. I have much to share.**

GOD? Am I hearing you correctly? **Yes, you are doing fine. Just relax and let me guide your hand. You will get better at hearing me over time. It takes practice...patience and more patience.**

My spelling and handwriting are terrible. **You are doing just fine, relax and just write what you hear. We can always go back and fill in anything you might have missed.**

I am so nervous, or is it just excitement I feel? **It is both...GOD has that effect on people.**

I hear you loud and clear, this is not like all the other times. **I know, that is just part of my plan. This time... you have grown and are mature enough to accept me as GOD, just like when you were 5. I AM, I exist, that is the reason for doing this. I AM here on the Earth everyday. I have** decided that you need to be a part of my plan. **I AM going to share with humanity my words.**

You really are here with me aren't you? **Yes, believe me, I AM. It is not your imagination. I AM real. I will show you how real in ways you cannot yet imagine.** *I can see your image with my mind, you are standing in my room.* **I know it is my way. So that you know it is GOD and not your imagination. I AM real. I exist. I do not pretend be anything but GOD. Now, let me ask you, AM I speaking too fast?** *No, I can keep up so far, I need practice writing so just speak slowly for me please.* **Very well, I will do that. Are you feeling tired?** *No I am fine, I feel very lightweight somehow, and energized.* **Good, that is how channeling this way with GOD is supposed to feel.**

Is my presence, here with you, disturbing you in any way? *No, I am fine, but I can't seem to stop crying.* **Oh, there is more that will make you cry. I can promise that. Other people will want to read this you know.** *Really, will they believe that this is really you that speaking to me like this?* **Yes, and I have much, much more to show you in the rest of your life. I have many stories to share that you will enjoy. I Love you, and that is why I AM here with you now.**

I am crying again. **I know, tears are just my way of showing you how much I Love you. It is my Love right back at you, that is what makes you cry. Oh yes, before we start, let me remind you, I LOVE YOU, you will benefit from this in the long run. Let's GET started right away with my book, I have so many stories to share. But wait… we will start when you finish your tears.**

The majority of this book, are the actual conversations that GOD and I had over the next 15 days in July 1998. I wrote down, to the best of my ability, what we spoke about. I would hear him in my thoughts, and then do my best to keep up, and reproduce what I heard.

I did not choose the topics or their content. This is what GOD wishes to share with his human family. Humanity's challenge is to recognize that GOD speaks to us daily… yet we do not really listen.

Different colors are for voices other than **GOD'S** and *myself*, Maria - *Green*. All others - Blue.

In reading this book, you will notice several important "rules" that GOD demands be a part of the editing:

1. Whenever the word "lord" is encountered it must be written as LORD.
2. Whenever the words "I am" are spoken by GOD they are to be written as I AM.
3. The book shall have the word "God " as GOD.
4. The words "holy, heaven, kingdom, and earth" shall be written as Holy, Heaven, Kingdom and Earth.
5. The word "love" shall be written as Love.

This is the standard form of writing in Heaven.

Now, GOD shares with us his wit and wisdom here on Earth.   Amen.

Foreword

This book is a soul expanding, revealing experience.

These are stories channeled directly from Jehovah…<u>GOD of us all</u>. He is responsible for it's content, material and topics discussed. This is his free flow forum. This is from GOD. These are his thoughts, wishes, and warnings for his human family. These are <u>his</u> words. This is his challenge to humankind to <u>stop ignoring him,</u> and his directives. The bulk of this writing is his expressed desire to have a PERSONAL RELATIONSHIP WITH EACH AND EVERY ONE OF US. The remainder are from his observations of us during the past 47 years. He comments openly and candidly on what he has been witnessing. He holds nothing back with his opinions. He gives himself that right.

He shares and includes the things that are standard practice and everyday occurrences in <u>his world</u>, the Kingdom of Heaven. He tells stories of his birth and childhood. Yes, the GOD of Heaven was born. Why not? Does this contradict our understanding and preconceptions of "GOD the creator?" Then why did we elevate Jesus to the status of GOD here on Earth? Is our definition of GOD "limited" to a book called "the bible" ONLY? Are we calling GOD "the eternal," the all-knowing and the everlasting LORD of all, then telling GOD that only "the bible" is what I understand about him? If our GOD is the GOD OF ALL why have we narrowed our perception of him to <u>only</u> writings of a 2000 year old piece of literature and nothing else? He is more than the bible, this book, or even our limited understanding. He is more than the written word and Kingdoms we cannot yet even imagine call him…GOD. So, do we have problems, or issues, with a Holy birth in the Kingdom of Heaven, over 50 million of our years ago? Or do we open our minds to the endless possibilities that is GOD and his wisdom?

Well… lets' see what, or if, you believe. You had better make sure he is not "testing" your perceptions or preconceived notions of what is, or is not, divinely inspired and ultimately from GOD. Since he is "all things," will you understand that connection? Can you? Are you open-minded enough to understand <u>his</u> logic, and reason for doing things HIS WAY. Not yours. Not mine. He told us to <u>prepare</u>… are you? Were you ready in case he announced his return? Did you believe he exists? Did you pray to him? Did you take time to acknowledge his being with you? Can you? GOD knows these and other things about you. He is going to teach you how to think… not what to think.

I hope you were prepared, because…HE IS BACK. If you are ready then read on, and be prepared to "change your ways" to HIS WAY.

Windy day
God walking!

I am not an artist, though I do get a lot of practice doing these with the Lords
help.
This is a recent vision I had of GOD walking up a mountain. The wind was
blowing and making his very long cape flow behind him. His eyes glowed a
soft white light. No pupils, just light. His clothes were a deep rich royal
purple with gold trim on the cape. His beard and hair were a bright white. He
wore sandals that seemed to be high-tech, difficult to explain, but they
seemed to be of a lightweight space-age material.
The grass was green and was short. The sky was clear blue with few light
puffy clouds. GOD said, **he was visiting Earth that day.**

GOD'S Book of Stories

July 5th 1998 4:00 P.M.

I AM the GOD of ALL. The reason for this writing is that the stories I AM about to unfold to you, through my friend Steve, are stories to teach, inspire and to create hope. Hope, in that when you greet me in my Heavenly Kingdom, you will have a better understanding, appreciation and moral imperatives, necessary to the alleviation of your guilt.

I AM in the world as a spirit of Love, hope, divine inspiration and most of all understanding. I have tried to conquer you, and your fears, by sending messengers to your world, Moses, Abraham, Isaac and Jesus the Christ. I have been alive 50 million of your Earth years and the stories I AM about to tell you are just one of many, told countless times in my Kingdom.

My Story – Jehovah

Yes, I was born. I was born on Star Date 1415, in My World of Tantus 4. I was born to Martha and Petra Jehovachavich. I have two sisters and three brothers. Brother's Peta, Jeho, Laria, Sisters Mara, Martha and I even had a pet dog, which looked like your Cocker Spaniels, named NOMA. My childhood is best described as a time like your 20th Century is NOW. Lots of discoveries, new machines that fly, new clothes of different materials, but one major difference. We, my people, were at TOTAL PEACE. We gave up war three centuries prior to my birth. Realizing it was totally inappropriate for a species to claim "enlightenment" and still kill one another. You see my world was <u>eight times bigger that Earth</u>, and we had to TOTALLY stop war in order to grow. Spending our time fighting amongst ourselves tended to limit our population. Our resources were constantly depleted and our weapons could destroy our world JUST LIKE YOURS. I tried to find my enlightenment by channeling, much like Steve does, through to a "Supreme Being" to help with my growth. I found no one. My planet was 50 million light years from <u>any</u> life forms and 200 million of us were constantly channeling each other. The noise for a person who is a good channeler is disturbing to say the least. The next book will help in the <u>channeling of that energy</u>. To help those in the predicament that I, yes, "I" Steven, put <u>you</u> in. You have no idea how individually strong you are as a channeler.

The rest of the story can wait for just a while, so I can tell you something. I planned for you to do this <u>all along</u>. I know the rest of the story before it even begins. <u>I plan on you being taken care of by this</u>. I KNOW You. I Love you. You have spent 23 years of your life (Steve's crying), trying to channel my energy. You became alarmed when Neale Walsch wrote <u>his</u> book. You thought, and spoke to me, that <u>you</u> were supposed to write that book. You felt the energies, the thoughts, and the spirit while it was BEING WRITTEN. Well, guess what? Neale will help you with this. Trust me. Have I ever NOT told you the truth? *I still Love you, and I still hear you loud and clear.* I know. I planned it that way. Others can too. But they have to do it My WAY. *Not the way <u>they</u> expect it to work.* Exactly… now to Continue. I AM in the book you know.

Now, oh yes, I had a growth spurt of 6 inches in 6 months on my world. I AM over 7'6 tall. Our food, gravity, and location allowed our race to be over 8 feet tall. For another species, such as yours, it <u>looks like we are GODS</u>. Now, I tried to find the Supreme Being to channel or learn something from in my universe. Or at least the corner I was in. I found only noise. Noise, noise, and more noise. I left my world to travel, oh yes, did I mention, I AM <u>has never been flesh and blood</u>. That's right, I AM is <u>only Spirit</u>. I can still remember the first time Adam and Eve heard that. They got all nervous and frightened that I could not understand them because of that. Silly, I had been taking care of their, needs, wants, and desires, for <u>centuries</u>, and they panicked. *Like I am sure readers will.* Yes, I bet that too. You know <u>ME</u> Steve. I like to tell the truth. Right now you are sitting in your room, at your brother's. Writing this on the Queen Anne table you and I built. Waiting for your wife to return to you. Yes, <u>return</u>. At this writing Steve and his 2nd wife Tina, are going through divorce proceedings. I say when, you say OK. *When?* By the time this is published. *OK.*

Good, now enough with the long face. I plan on you to be happy with what I AM about to say. I AM. I AM here for you to channel. I AM here for you to talk to, to speak through, to be one with. I AM, GOD. I AM Jehovah. I AM. Now feel better? *Yes, father.* I know my son, I cry sometimes too. The joy in your heart <u>needs to be shared with others</u>. We will see glory, hope and the will of GOD restored. JEHOVAH RULES. <u>Your world</u> needs to hear that. I AM. My chapter on myself can wait. I plan on explaining a few things to you. Do you remember the hit? *Yes, opening kickoff my senior year of high school and the sharp shooting pains up and down my spine?* Yes, that hit. I tried to talk to you then, but you were hurt, angry, and <u>scared</u> that you may be paralyzed, or worse, later in life. It is later in life and you seem fine. I AM. I tried to tell you <u>then</u>, that you would be fine, but you were scared of the feeling you had. The fact that you knew the other teams plays <u>before they happened</u>. I know it was eerie, weird, and most of all <u>unusual</u>. You were frightened <u>that no one believed you and that you were alone</u>. You were never alone. <u>I was always with you</u>. I told you I would take care of you. I have. Now, with the help of friends, you will be helped again. I AM the GOD of Steve, Tina, and all the Earth. I know how much you Love her, I know, I put it in you. I told you all about her, <u>years before you ever met</u>. I did the same with her. <u>Her</u> abilities allowed her to selectively hear my voice; she called it "Michael." She only could hear what I said if; "she liked what she heard." Guess what? I tell the truth. The truth, the light, and the way is ME. I AM. Now back to my story. She is now my child. That means like all others on the Earth, I have decided to "impose," yes <u>impose</u>. I have decided to take an <u>active participation in affairs of the heart</u>. LOVE. I cannot continue to be disabled by the one known as hate when my children cry out for help. I AM. I care. I choose to. I did this of my own free will, taking all the hate <u>out</u> of the world. <u>I brought only LOVE</u>. MY LOVE. How did I do that you ask? I did that by allowing people like Neale, "Conversations With GOD," Walsch, and others like Damion Brinkley, to tell what I AM like. Who AM I? I AM GOD. I do not get enough press now-a-days. So I decided to write through others about ME. My life. My TIME AS GOD. My hopes. My Loves. My traditions. My way. My hope is that those who read this will <u>feel my spirit guiding this writing</u>. Those who <u>do</u> enter my Love, do so through the open door. My door to my Kingdom,

Heaven. Yes, despite all the press asking, "is there a Heaven?" *And songs like Lennon's "Imagine."* Exactly.

There is a Heaven. It is my Kingdom. My home. My reign. My domain. My Love and Holy home for ALL who believe in ME. Simply put, I started to create a Kingdom for ALL to enter. ALL, is my way of justifying my choices for entering. My choices are simply EVERYONE. Yes, EVERYONE. Even in the nasty state of flesh and blood, the spirit released from the body experiences ME. *Is that the light at the end of the tunnel the near-death-experience people talk about, Father?* Yes, Thank you Steve. It is, MY TIME. MY TIME has come. MY TIME is now. Why? Too show you ME. Why this way? Why not! Do you want miracles? Look at the overall leaps in Science in the last 50 years. Look to the space race as a chance to explore new worlds, homes and places for humanity to settle. No, you are not alone. The people in your governments KNOW, but are afraid of mass hysteria. Guess what? "They underestimate the human spirit of the average person." They conclude, that if the following headline were released "ALIENS ARE IN OUR MIDST," we collectively as one would rise up and go insane. FOOLS. I allowed these beings to travel to this sector because they are benevolent. They are explorers. They simply choose to visit very remote systems as a test of overall genetic sequencing, and compare it to the closer civilizations in the center of the galaxy. Yes. I know you are wondering are these people humanoid? Do they look like anyone? No, they look like: See Alien in our Midst sketch

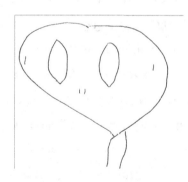

So how does that affect humanity? It doesn't. They only observe. They consider you zoo animals. Yes, zoo animals. It is because you cannot escape your planet, so they feel they can use you as a study of humanity, and observe your behaviors. I AM permitted this. Your governments cover it up. I asked for open and honest government in 1872 during a speech in congress, inspired by me. I asked for DISCLOSURE TO THE PEOPLE, but it fell on deaf and superstitious ears. I AM SAYS: DO NOT FEAR THOSE IN SPACE WHO VISIT YOU. They, if you will excuse the expression: "Come in Peace." I know. I AM this species GOD as well. I came to be because of a need. Amazed yet? That need was LOVE. We are all in need of Love. We are to be in Love our whole lives. By the way, I support birth control, but NOT ABORTION. That's right "it is not a fetus but a human life," was spoken by a man who received it from GOD. I realize this is controversial, so let me say this about LIFE. All life is beautiful, special and precious to ME. GOD creates no mistakes. I believe in that. Given circumstances, such as rape, incest, or attacks of genetics on the human equation, I realize people need to have laws. Simply put, I do not condone abortion, AFTER the first trimester. That is MY stand. You will have to deal with me when it comes to the moral, political, and social issues that you face on Earth. I understand. I put laws in my world as well. One that serves this is: "A life is too priceless to be thrown away." Another version is: "A life is too new to argue for it's right to exist, give it that right." Now, when you read this, you will fear My Judgment. I do not judge. Remember…you are harder on yourself than I could ever be.

I AM understanding. I tell you the truth. I don't want you feeling guilty, because of how I run my Kingdom. My Kingdom came to be through much trial and error. My Kingdom is glory, power, Love, and hope in that order. My Kingdom is Love, Love, Love, and more Love. My Kingdom is hope, hope, hope, and everlasting hope. I tell this freely and with no remorse or regrets to anyone reading this. I forgave Adolf Hitler, completely, totally, and without anger or prejudice. He was not met with any anger, hate, or misgivings. He was met by ME. He fell to his knees and pleaded forgiveness. I granted it under one condition. No more "like him" must be allowed to surface on Earth again. That's right. No more.

I allow "angels rights" to come and go, and to watch over the Earth. I grant them authority to work in my name, I grant them power to invoke miracles and to make signs, and to "please the prayer" we call it. They help with prayers, and they do the grunt work. They push you when you feel weak. They make you happy. They are my children. Angels are my messengers. So now you wonder if Adolph Hitler is an Angel? Yes, but only an "angel in training." I still have "My Condition" to be met. So are Barbarosa, Attila the Hun, Julius Caesar, and Numing Su. (5th Century Ming Dynasty.) These were all considered evil or anti-Christ's in YOUR world, NOT IN MINE. They all encountered me. JEHOVAH. The GOD of Steve, Tina, Donald, Damion, and George Anderson. He is the channeler of the ghost known as Newfuss. He does not know the name of his angel guide, now he does. I AM permits this daily. I tell you now. My way is constant. I do not change. People change because of their encounters with ME. I do not wavier, stagger, or fall. I do cause others to do this, when they ignore my Love and ME. Yes, MY LOVE. My Love is deep. It runs into your soul. I tell you how to live your lives, daily. I get "I CANNOT RIGHT NOW LORD, I'M TOO BUSY," or…"Wait, I will get to it later," or "Don't worry I will be back in touch when I finish this." I hate that one. Why? You <u>never</u> get back to me. I AM forced to wait. I could show you so much of my Love. When was the last time you prayed? … I KNOW…I hear <u>all</u> prayer. Answering all prayer takes time. I do <u>answer all prayer</u>. I even say, YES. I FEEL I NEED TO SAY SOMETHING ABOUT…

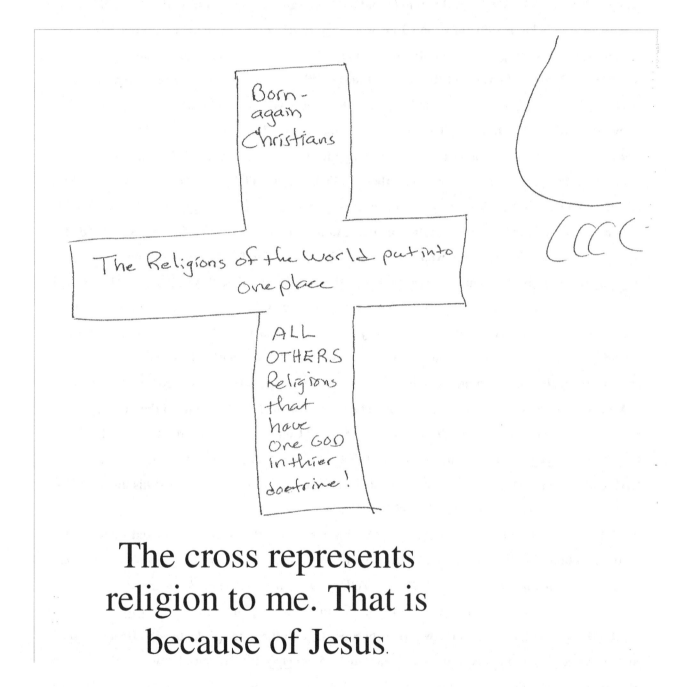

Born-again Christians

The Religions of the World put into one place

ALL OTHERS Religions that have One GOD in thier doctrine!

The cross represents religion to me. That is because of Jesus.

The Jesus Legend

The <u>LORD'S Prayer</u> is a "blessing." Why? <u>I hear your inner most thoughts when you</u> <u>recite it.</u> Yes, YOUR SOUL. I tell you to be patient, or to go here, or go there, to talk to this person, or that. That is sometimes how I answer. <u>That quick.</u> I guess you believe in me, but somehow, overtime "I get pushed to the back burner," so to speak. Well, guess what? I AM BACK. Does not the Book of Revelation describe "the return of GOD?" Yes, "the return of GOD." I AM GOD, I AM HERE, SO I AM BACK. Jesus wrote to you of me and he spoke to you of me. He spoke of this time. He mentioned death, famine, world destruction, etc. With newspapers, satellites and newscasts, now, <u>worldwide</u>, is it not coming true? Remember he said, not to go to this place or that, I "won't be there." Well… that's TRUE. I AM in your soul. I AM GOD. I created you. I decided to write to you since you hardly ever write <u>to ME</u>. I AM. I created a man and a woman, to father and mother a civilization, a species, and call it humanity. I decided to write to <u>you</u>, of my friend Steve, who has known this information for 23 years, but until now, <u>no</u> <u>one would believe him.</u> If you were told by GOD, that this is "my time, I AM BACK." How would YOU respond? Could you tell your friends? Who would believe YOU that you speak with GOD? Why should he come back NOW? WHY? Why? Why? I can answer all those questions with this thought, "I came back now because it is a time I AM most familiar with." Remember I was born on this "equivalent time frame" on Tantus 4. I choose Steve to write this because of his Love for …ME. It has cost him two wives, numerous jobs, and a medical discharge from the military as Schizophrenic. Well, if you had the secret of my Second Coming…WHOM WOULD YOU TELL? Or who would <u>believe you</u>? Years ago I, JEHOVAH, tempted him with being "the next messiah." Giving him grandiose promises of life eternal, and of glory in your world beyond his imagination. He thought for a while and responded with; *LORD, if you Love me, do not ask me to do this*. I asked why? He said; *haven't enough martyrs died in your name?* I RESPECTED THAT, and I agreed. I then asked him to write a book about ME. He said; *that's fine, but please speak, clearly, slowly, and let me ask very few questions. It is YOUR book, YOUR time, and I simply am glad to answer some questions I have in MY mind.* Exactly. My point is I did not give up on him, to write <u>this</u>. I PUT HIM THROUGH HELL. He lost two wives because he told them he speaks to ME. He lost two jobs, because <u>he could not concentrate on his work.</u> <u>I interfered.</u> I felt I needed to get his attention. In 1975, I took away his "Inner Voice." Yes, for 23 years, he heard "all of you." He tried to talk to others about it. No one really listened. He tried to cope the best he could, but I ran the show. In January 1998 I restored his "Inner Voice," but now his second wife was leaving him. She had met someone I told her would "take better care of her, than Steve." I TEMPTED HER. She believed it. Why? Because she is his <u>Eternal Wife</u>. She <u>would not have allowed the book to be written if she was still with him</u>. All his energies would be focused on <u>loving her</u>, because that is what he does. HE LOVES. I know I have been EXTREMELY hard on you, Steve. I told you years ago to "do my will" this book is MY WILL. I AM HARD ON THOSE WHO LOVE ME. I AM because I demand the best. I choose you because I LOVE YOU, I AM. I know, I command. Do not heed the words, in the end of Revelation, that say, If any one adds anything to them, GOD will add TO HIM, the plagues described in this book. I already put this man through an Internal Hell, no one is his judge, least of all humanity, I AM.

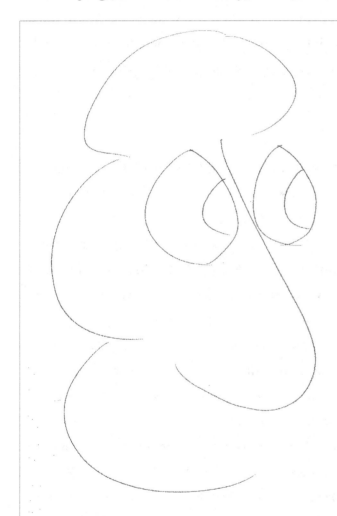

GOD IS WAITING FOR YOUR PRAYER

Spiritual Time

I AM in Spirit, in ALL of you, most of all, <u>in those who Love ME</u>. Those who hate me simply want my attention. They are like children, reaching out for my Love, but thinking I don't hear or notice them. I AM knows these people well. Since ancient times, MOSES, Caesar, and JESUS all responded diversely to <u>My Will</u>. Some would rebel, others would cry. Some would try to hide... others simply ignore. My Spirit is in ALL things not just what Humanity calls Life. My definition of ALL is <u>The Everlasting Thought of Love, to the Everlasting End of Time.</u> ALL is ME. I AM ALL. Jehovah is my REAL name. My proud last name of the family I grew up with 50 million Earth years ago. I kept it out of respect for my parents, my family and my wife. Yes. I AM has a mate. She has been with me, <u>45 Million Earth years</u> now, <u>and</u> would like to say a few things... *Hello, I AM Maria Voncount. I WAS BORN ON Tantus 2 in the year 4, of our timetable. I AM is my mate, or husband as you call it. He is my friend, mentor, and confidant. I KNOW is my call sign sometime soon you will be told why.*

I KNOW is her handle when we get playful I say, I AM GOD she says I KNOW. It is shortened to I AM and I KNOW. See...I brought my whole family with me. I AM GOD. I decide these things. I packed up my family, and set off to planet Earth 47 years ago. I watched as you fought the war of your world called encounter with ME. You tried to start wars since then but seem unable to escalate them. Vietnam, Afghanistan, Korea, Falklands, to name a few. I decided to include Korea, because that could have been your last war, if I did not get involved. Humanity needed to find its common sense, NO MORE WAR. No more destruction. <u>No more failure to listen to GOD</u>. Now, perched on the outer rim of your atmosphere, I can sense the smallest skirmish, the slightest tremor, and the tiniest disturbance that could destroy you completely. Hurricanes, Tornadoes, floods, river's (redundant of floods) destroying towns, and fires, have been going on for centuries. Only now, at this time, do you fully understand how small your Planet really is. <u>I told you to STOP KILLING.</u> You did <u>not</u> listen. I AM here <u>to make it stop</u>. If you find this hard to believe, try and get mad. Go ahead; get mad, right NOW. Not easy is it. That is me I AM. I felt the cry for peace. I felt and heard the PRAYERS for me to come back. I felt the urge to be happy, hopeful, and to stop the Insanity, that is HATE. War and Hate go hand in hand. GOD IS LOVE. Ultimate Love. Total Love. Unconditional Love. My Love knows only ME, and you are a part of ME. I created you, or I should say, re-created you. I AM giving humanity a 2nd chance, a reprieve. Only I can grant that. I AM GOD. I tell you the truth, not like the religions on Earth that say I condemn you to hell. NO. I save you from each other. I tell you this; NO MAN has greater Love for ME than Steven Wade Raasumaa. I have seen this. I CHOSE HIM FOR THIS. I made him write this while his hand was having cramps, why? Because "I felt the way he writes." I say again… NO ONE Loves ME like Steve does. I AM TELLING YOU THIS BECAUSE I TOTALLY FORGET SOMETIMES THAT I AM DICTATING TO HIM. He let's me flow. He allows me to write, speak to you, rapid fire. The way I speak. The way I AM. I do not pull any punches. I do not sugar coat. I AM the TRUTH, the LIGHT and the WAY. Jesus was channeling ME, JEHOVAH. Ask him in your prayers, he will confirm this. And why pray to HIM? I AM GOD. I hear ALL. He is retired. He has a nice place on "Fourth," that's right "Fourth." It is a ranch, and he raises, or trains horses. So, how often does he get to Earth? Once in a blue moon, he says. I AM here always. I listen. I AM the one who wrote the Gospels anyway. So I can write more if I choose to. Going to be a long time before you hear from me again, unless I get some Love sent my way. I hope you do realize I do have a sense of humor. The trick is to recognize it. I plan it that way. Gets' me out of trouble with the Mrs.…Steven laughs. He knows me. He has spent his whole life talking to me, and I listen. He would tell you about me, if you would listen. I need him to try. Why? Because as children you have selective hearing. You only hear what you want, and disregard anything that may be unpleasant or too harsh, do you think I have been harsh so far? Let me share this with you. Humanity is all but dead. Yes, DEAD. 50 years ago you harnessed the atom, and have been refining it ever since. Do you really believe my being nice, at this point, is going to solve anything? I have been quiet for all this time and look what you have done? You nearly killed your whole planet in 1962, the Cuban Missile Crisis. Now, Third World countries are playing, yes, playing with the bomb. You cannot be allowed to destroy my work. I have too much at stake in you. Humanity is at the brink of its greatest discovery, ME. That's right GOD. Your consciousness is fully capable of comprehending ME. You have seen space travel, witnessed laser technologies, and had time to eat, drink and be merry. Now it is MY TIME. I AM. I tried to show you, ME, in Life Magazines. I inspired that whole Angel/GOD/Miracle thing that went on. I also inspired the development of Compact Disks, because I LIKE ALL MUSIC. Forensic Medicine, DNA sampling, and my greatest achievement of all…cloning. Yes, cloning. Why? Because the steps taken to arrive at cloning techniques will uncover other procedures, and cures for other ailments, ESPECIALLY CANCER. That's correct, Steve, the cure for cancer lies in clone research. Now, with that in mind who do you think is funding AIDS research? You are not, I AM. How? AIDS is the first step in the battle to keep humanity alive. Other more active viruses, resilient to anti-biotic and sterile methods will arise in your future. You need to boost your immune systems to completely combat these in the years to come. AIDS is old, Very old. It was here when dinosaurs ruled the Earth. You discovered it by depleting the rain forest. That's the truth. You can check it out yourself. Monkeys mutated the original virus in 5 BC. They were in what is now Tanzania. They were all but wiped out. They allowed your ancestors to contract it by eating monkey meat. They started to die as well. Fortunately there were enough of you as a species to survive. Moving out of the jungles was what saved humanity from early extinction.

I AM is at a loss to tell you why, but you, as a species seem to crave knowledge. To have it, one must go to great schools, pay outrageous tuition, and then claim to be knowledgeable. Yet some of your greatest inventors and inventions were from simple folks. The Wright Brothers, Alexander Graham Bell, and Mosconii, were all considered fools in their days. But now, history proves them a genius. Believe ME. <u>Time will prove I AM right in all that I say, and when you find that I AM correct, will you believe in ME?</u> Worship ME? Tell me you Love ME. <u>I know you will</u>. I AM GOD. I know these things. I tell you NO ONE CARES FOR YOU, Earth, MORE THAN I. I AM here to prove that. I tell you all that I know so you can go to new ways, new directions, and new thought processes. I prefer to teach you <u>how</u> to think instead of <u>what</u> to think. Once humanity thought, the world was flat, then round, but the center of the universe. Now, you know the truth. It is that way with ME. Right now, we need to get past the flat part.

Love

My Love is more than the Love from anyone you know. It is more than Earth has ever witnessed. You worship different people from your past with different religions, all of which focus on ONE SUPREME BEING. That being is ME. Think of it, Islam, Hindu, Christian, Moslem, etc. all have one Supreme Being called GOD. They don't agree on my name, but in theory they all believe the same thing. That one "being" is ME. JEHOVAH... GOD of ALL. Years ago I chose the Israelites as my people. Why? "To start them on a quest of greatness." They constantly strayed. They stray now. They are lost in the past. They worship Moses, his laws, his ways and shun their Greatest Prophet, Jesus. I sent Jesus the same as Moses to prove his authority. I told Israel to expect him. "Prepare the way," I said, through John the Baptist. Israel is still following the ancient laws of Moses and ignoring my Greatest Commandment, Love the LORD thy GOD with all your Heart, and your Soul. I tell you this, ISRAEL NEEDS TO FOLLOW AMERICA'S EXAMPLE. Try it you will like it, I say. Israel, I still Love you, but again you try my patience, you follow the laws of Moses ONLY. It is time to move into the 21st century. I AM HERE. Do not worship laws that were written for a 10,000-year-old period of time. CHANGE, progress, and for my sake, SHAVE. I LET MYSELF BECOME A GOD OF LOVE AND WAR FOR YOU, now DO MY WILL. Choose LOVE. Choose ME. Listen to your prophets NOW. They CAN HEAR ME. Especially... Hugh Monanon in Old Jerusalem. He can guide you if you listen. I AM, I WILL, I CARE. I made you a nation. Make me proud of you. GROW. Do the right thing, not the traditional thing. I AM not asking you to abandon your religion, but to look at ME. LOOK TO ME. Look ...and you will find. I AM here. Listen to me o'Israel, I AM says to you now, in your year of 1998, "if thy neighbors are trouble, you shall see more if you DO NOT modernize." Listen to America and protect thyself. *Father, is this what you REALLY want written?* NO, it is what is needed to be said, written and listened to. *This makes you very sad, father. I can feel it.* YES, I get sad thinking WHY? Why are they still so STUBBORN, why do they take so long to change? Change is good, I say. It takes no effort, it's FUN, new, different, and the very act of changing becomes "normal change" with practice. It gets easier. I decide to do things for the greater good, not for the convenience of others. I try to save Love for those who Love ME. I SAY TO YOU, "no greater Love, than the LOVE OF GOD, is allowed by myself or my chosen disciples." Jesus spoke that. THAT IS THE EXACT QUOTE. Your Bible does not ever address this either... *"I am told me I must die."* Peter said, *"NO, LORD tell me it is not so."*

"Peter I say to you, I will not die but have eternal life. My father says so."

Now, do you still plan on enjoying the old writings, or would you like to hear "The

Gospels" <u>exactly</u> <u>as</u> <u>it</u> <u>was</u> <u>spoken</u>. Our Bibles <u>here</u> do so. If you listen we can tell you ALL. I AM is now tired of listening to YOU. You need to listen to HIM. He says, "to try." I AM SAYS TO YOU, Steve, I Love you. YOU TRY. I AM will not forget your sacrifice, nor your hate of all things not from me. I KNOW. I feel it too.

I tell you this, my favorite position is lying in bed watching Laverne, and Shirley reruns and I get Smokey and the Bandit on satellite, now and then. Yes, I do get Earth broadcasts. I have the ways and the means to do so. I also like comedies like Shirley, Dick Van Dyke, and Lucy. <u>I DO NOT LIKE WAR MOVIES, police chases or science fiction of a violent nature</u>. As a species: <u>you do not understand the damage you do by viewing these.</u> The youth of your world needs positive inputs. No more violence means NO MORE WARS. Get your programming cleaned up, and watch your crime rate go down. <u>Damn</u> <u>free</u> <u>speech</u>, yes, <u>damn</u>. It is <u>not</u> a GOD given right to <u>blast a child away</u> with senseless violence on your television programs, then expect him to display normal behavior. Psychologists call this "brain washing." Come on WAKE UP. STOP BRAIN WASHING YOUR YOUTH. Give them <u>positive</u> role models. Give them humor, strength, or challenges that <u>they can meet</u>. Then watch your civilization take off in a positive direction. The reason that TV is so powerful a median is that all your thought process is pictorial. If it isn't so, how can I understand 4,000,000,000 different languages all at the same time? I see the thought process. I can distinguish all the methods to that, by viewing the thoughts that go with that vision. <u>I AM</u> is writing with you, Steve. That is the reason for the change in penmanship. I just wanted <u>you</u> to know I AM. I AM IS HERE FOR THIS, not IN HEAVEN as earlier in the book. I came <u>directly</u> to get ONE THING CLEAR. I AM <u>NOT</u> HERE TO CONDEM, BUT TO RECOMMEND CHANGE. It is up to humanity to listen and to act upon it or not. If what I tell you makes sense, then <u>I will see change on a global scale</u>. If not, well, it will be slow, painful, and yes, unfortunately deadly for <u>all</u> of humanity. I AM now ready for <u>next week</u>. Trust ME and MY TIMING, I said so, it is so. I tell you ALL, I have spent most of my time on Earth, with Steve. I know him as a friend. He has been blunt, honest and totally frank, with me. I respect that. I asked him the other day, What do you think about "Total Recall" the movie? He said, *I thought it was O.K.* So I went to see it myself. I enjoyed it. I asked Steve to tell me his favorite ice cream. He said, *A Dairy Queen Blizzard: Heath bar flavor.* I went and tried it. Delicious. For <u>23 years I have been doing this,</u> watching, examining, and observing. For 23 years, I have been following him around. Watching his <u>every</u> move. I know him as well as anyone can know a man. I LOVE HIM. I told him of my Kingdom. <u>He visited it in his dreams</u>, and cried tears of joy. He also felt my presence, and said, *Now I know why YOU are GOD. NO ONE could fight that feeling of <u>total Love</u>.* Yes, that is the truth. Now, I find myself using him again. Asking him to sacrifice his free time, his peace of mind, and his channeling ability, (not to mention his cramping writing hand), to do <u>more work</u> for me. I cannot find the words to express my gratitude. He quietly sits at his desk and writes, what I dictate as clear as any of my angels in THIS world. *LORD, is he your son?* I GET ASKED THAT EVERY DAY. I SAY TO THEM YES, MY <u>FAVORITE</u> SON. He tells me like it is, and I hold nothing back from him. I say to you, your new job is taking care of "Tina" Steve. She has had enough. Her mother is driving her crazy, and this is my promise to the two of you, I…Jehovah…Love you BOTH.

Your ideas about Love are <u>mine</u>. You are my children of the light. I tell you this freely, and with everlasting Love. I will always protect, and cherish the two of you. I Love you both. I tell you this because it will come true. Just like the other writings I have done for you in the past. I tell you things that are true, from <u>MY</u> point of view. My point of view, <u>is your thoughts</u> - your deep innermost thoughts. That's where I hear YOU. No one gets to hide from ME. I rule that domain. They can run but they cannot hide. Some of what I say may seem harsh, remember, it's been over 2,000 years since someone has been in Love enough with me to take my name in GLORY, NOT IN SELFISHNESS, EGOTISM, FOOLISH PRIDE OR ANGER. I AM IS GLORY. Glory of creation, glory of Love. I LOVE MUSIC, and a song by Pete Cetera, "Glory of Love," says it ALL. Other songs I HELPED TO WRITE are "I did it for Love," Night Ranger. Dan Fogelberg's "Believe in Me" tells of MY LOVE for ALL My Children. Dan would be <u>the first to tell you</u> he felt a "spirit guide" in the writing of that song. MY SPIRIT. Another is Amy Grant, "Baby, Baby," I Love that video. Those are just a sample of what I <u>listen</u> to. What I AM who I AM, and WHY I AM. I know you artists all hope your song, or songs, would be mentioned. Stop and think. Why? For your purpose? Or for <u>my</u> glory. See… if you got humbled, it is for YOUR PURPOSE, NOT MINE. Glory, is my way of telling you about ME. Subtle, yet powerful, a good way is through Music. Otherwise, life would be boring and dull. I <u>would share</u> others, but if I include them ALL, you would not get to read the rest of my book. I AM. I do things my way, <u>not</u> Frank Sinatra's way, who by the way, made it to Heaven. So did John Candy, Michael Landon, Red Skelton and Lucy Ball, to name a few. They all worked their way up the angel training ladder, and are on the Earth with the ones they Love guiding, helping, counseling. <u>There are many others</u>, but again, how much time would it take to name them ALL. I chose them to help me. I told them to fix problems in; art, theater, and in television, and they work diligently to do so. The major complaint is YOU DON'T LISTEN. GOD HAS A BETTER WAY, is the cry I hear constantly. Now go to sleep, Steve.

July 6th, 1998 11:02 A.M.

I could not in good conscience allow you to write a part of your life you feel uncomfortable with. **Your past is OUR past. If you felt you are being used again, say so. I don't have to tell you.** *Let me think about it a few day's, Father.* **I AM say's to you, Steve. I will put you through, NO MORE. I refuse to allow my son to be poked, prodded, and examined, I will NOT allow my son to be polarized, chastised, and characterized as Jehovah's whipping boy, I AM. I said NO MORE.**

Now, let me continue, many reading this will want to know about <u>you</u> so let ME explain. Early in life you were diagnosed with a high fever and bedridden, do you remember? *Yes, Holy father.* **Good. You also remember I came to visit you, sat on the edge of your bed, and showed you the future I had planned for you?** *Yes, I remember vividly.* **<u>You told no one</u>.** *No one would have believed me.* **Exactly, then in 1972 you were hit, head on, by a block in a football game. It started a chain reaction, up and down your spine.** *I remember.* **That was ME, I CAUSED IT.** *Why?* **To get you to notice me.** *The premonitions?* **Yes, the premonitions. You were able to see all the plays BEFORE they happened, even after that game. <u>I know you have never told anyone about this</u>. That is why, at 169 lbs. you were Class B ALL STATE at <u>Defensive Tackle</u>. Yes, otherwise you would have been just another bench warmer.** *I believe you.* **I KNOW. Now in 1986, in June, you were asked to contact ME.** *I remember reading the Bible cover-to-cover, and hearing your voice.* **Exactly, correct. I was with you those days in the Hospital.** *I could not sleep because of the excitement of hearing GODS VOICE.* **Yes, and again in the Military Hospital.** *I was hearing your voice and my first wife had me admitted. She thought I was nuts.* **Exactly, also when we came back from the Philippines, I remember flying with you on that 747 to LA from Japan.** *I was having visions, nasty ones, hearing voices, seeing you.* **Now you know. I have cling-ons. They hang around me and try to <u>under-mind</u> my efforts. <u>Neale</u> found this out the hard way. He got extremely frightened by one I will call Dufus. He said, "That was scary." I said, "No it was necessary."**

(That never made HIS book.) *Mostly, I hear just you, and your Angels.* **Yes, you are practiced in the "art" of channeling. There are those who would question your abilities. Consider this, after 40 years of voices, do you think anyone else could come to this point in their lives and NOT be affected by <u>my presence</u>.** *No, you are the truth. I always tell your energy by the repeating of Your Truths.* **Yes...**

My Truth's

Here is Truth #

1. No man, woman, or child cannot <u>NOT</u> know ME.

2. No one may enter into the Kingdom, except through ME.

3. I AM GOD…there is no other to call on, only ME.

4. I AM the ALMIGHTY…NO OTHERS, OTHER, OR GROUP CAN MATCH MY POWER, GLORY, or Charisma.

5. I AM…the truth.

6. I AM…the light, the only light in Heaven.

7. I AM…the way, my way or NO WAY.

8. I AM…MY best friend; I try to be YOURS.

9. I tell you truth, from my point of view, NOT YOURS.

10. I promise you everything upon entry into my Kingdom. No catches, no obligations, no tasks, <u>no works</u>.

11. I tell you this…<u>I have "no greater Love" for anyone than I do YOU</u>. I plan to allow you into my world, free of charge. No tariffs, duties, and NO TAXES.

12. Death is NOT THE FINAL WORD…I AM. I tell you this because humanity fears death <u>more than it fears ME</u>. Have you ever asked yourself why that is?

13. Truth is my way to show you I Love you. I tell you "the way it is." No sugarcoating, no cover-ups, no deceptions, no partials, the truth, the whole truth, so help <u>I WILL</u>.

14. My way to you is proven. No getting around it. You cannot circumvent, avoid, or escape, My plan to your soul. <u>My plan is your salvation through my mercy</u>. Not through your self, or your mind's standards, set by society.

15. My truths are set in solid rock. They do not wavier, falter, or sway. They are <u>mine</u>, <u>not yours</u>. It is my plan, my journey with YOU. I GUIDE…YOU DECIDE.

16. Timing is MINE. I DECIDE when things, events and problems occur. I tell you what is best. You decide if you <u>want</u> to follow that course, path, or choice. It is inevitable…<u>YOU ONLY DELAY KNOWING ME.</u>

17. <u>I CHOOSE</u> WHOM TO BE MY MESSENGERS. I HAVE <u>NEVER</u> chosen someone of fame, political power or acting abilities. I choose simply on their Love for ME. GOD DECIDES WHILE <u>you</u> DEBATE. I AM.

18. Do you have questions? Ask ME…not each other. Debate amongst yourselves, never solved

any of your problems. Only MY guidance does that.

19. Do you need help? Ask ME. Not each other. You only get in my way; you slow down my journey to your soul. I AM HELP. I AM LOVE. I AM GOD. I AM ALL. I AM the GOD of ALL father's, mother's, and children. All races, colors, and ethnic upbringing. I AM GOD of universe's, solar systems, planets, you cannot even imagine yet. I surely can help YOU.

20. I CAN, AND WILL GUIDE, counsel, and observe. There is one catch. I will not do the work. YOU MUST. GOD helps those who help themselves. Don't ask ME to do dishes. I invented the dishwasher. Don't ask me to clean the house. I invented the vacuum cleaner. Don't ask me to come over and cook. I invented the microwave, the toaster oven, and YES, laser cooking, YET TO BE.

21. Do not fear anything heard, or seen, in my world. When I teach you to open your inner eyes, you will see things you never thought existed. Let me explain them to you. Others are not so clear as ME. I AM CLARITY. I AM TRUTH. I AM COLOR. I AM LIGHT. I tell the TRUTH. I have POWER OVER ALL. I frighten them, so they frighten you. They are spirits that cling on me, trying to under-mind OUR LOVE, our connection, our path to glory, our mutual reward of knowing each other, as GOD and his children.

22. I TRUST YOU. That's right YOU. You always tell ME the truth, even if you try to lie. Why? Remember that I see the pictures in your thoughts. I read them. You cannot even begin to lie to ME. It doesn't work. I see through that…TO YOUR SOUL.

23. No one trusts you more than ME. I start every day by trusting you. No one can give you more trust than I can. Not your doctor, lawyer, clergy, or the guy or gal on the TV. I TRUST TOTALLY. I LOVE UNCONDITIONALLY.

24. No one will Love YOU more than I. I AM LOVE. I STARTED LOVING YOU BEFORE YOU WERE BORN. Before I even met you. I started to fall deeply in Love with my child, my wonderful creation. My totally new, and precious baby. My special friend, My new buddy, my special pal. I tell you this; no one can take credit for loving YOU more than GOD can. JEHOVAH IS GOD. I AM.

25. I say to you, all who read this, I AM BLESSES YOU. I bless you as part of my creation. Part of ME. I do not care if others say…"you sinned." To me you are HOLY… SPECIAL… PURE AND NEW. I do not care if others say…"you are born in sin." NOT TO ME. To me you are, "aching to be with ME." My ways are pure, Holy, and special. I do not care if others tell you…"you cannot be close to GOD, you are NOT worthy." I SAY TO ALL that you are part of ME and created by ME and are Holy, blessed, and pure. You did not sin in my eyes, my child. I AM.

26. I AM BLESSING. I tell you this, if my friend Steve cries on #24 and #25, and you cry too, you have felt my spirit. I AM. I decide who cries now, and who will cry later in this book. I AM.

27. I AM…is below, above and ALL around. My spirit is everywhere. You cannot escape ME. I AM in places you cannot even reach yet. I AM IN YOUR HEART, your soul, and your mind. Yes, your mind, GOD is there. I tell you why? You say, because GOD says so. I tell you to GO here, you say "OK…GOD SAYS SO."

28. I AM MYSELF. I DO NOT CHANGE. To know ME, is to LOVE ME. Yes, I get tough with you sometimes, why? Because I LOVE YOU, and it pains ME to see you wander off thinking I can do this myself. WRONG! I AM always there. I tell YOU by pushing you when there is no one around, having you drop things etc. You get the idea. I AM getting your attention. Behave, MY CHILDREN, and I AM WILL launch you into the next step of your evolution. Spiritual growth, MY WAY, JEHOVAH.

29. No one can show you except ME. I DECIDE THE PROCEEDURE, THE PATH, AND THE PAYMENT. YES, PAYMENT. I paid for your souls. How? By telling the worlds I create about you. Your very nature, your space, your place, your soul is already there. That's right. I already reserved a place in my Kingdom for you. No one can occupy that space in my Kingdom except, YOU. I AM knowledgeable, and trustworthy about such things. To see this, open your mind to the possibilities of hope, trust and Love. Then you know this is true. My reservations are never full. There is always room for more. If it gets crowded, I create a new world, to put you on. If it gets noisy, I put clouds in the sky to absorb sound. If it gets cold, I make another star, like your Sun, to keep you warm. I AM GOD. I create. I AM the GOD of ALL THINGS, not just what you can imagine I can do. I AM.

30. Truths such as these are MY WAY. I do not change. YOU change your way of thinking, acting, and behaviors, to adopt ME. No fear, only ME. No stuff such as I'll do it later, or wait, till I die, or the best one yet…"give me time to think about it." I say there is no time like the present to worship ME. Trust in ME, and to prevent you from gathering the wrong information, which causes you to go a stray. You constantly tell ME, *I trust you LORD.* **DO YOU TOTALLY, I ASK?** You say *yes, I do,* then I ask you to give me a dollar. Yes, a dollar. You say, *I cannot LORD, you are in your world, and I am in flesh and blood.* Yet, if you thought you did, if you simply thought here is a dollar for you. It WOULD BE SO. I AM GOD. I can tell you such things about you, and your potential not yet discovered.

You fight amongst yourselves over religious beliefs. Yes. Religious beliefs. Yet, I do not fight with YOU. You talk about free speech and freedom of the press. Yes? Yet, you do not speak of ME in SCHOOLS OR IN THE TEXTBOOKS. WHY? It is OK for a child to read about Hitler,

Mussolini, and Stalin. All these are negative influences on your youth, yes? Yet <u>you do not respect me</u> enough to teach the BIBLE IN YOUR SCHOOLS. You fear it. *Clouds young minds with non-sense. Stuff in the BIBLE DOES NOT EXIST.* No. It did exist once. Once David slew Goliath and Jesus <u>walked on the waters</u>. Yes, on the waters. How? By stones, slightly below the surface. No one else knows that but ME, and now I share it with YOU. David's sling shot WAS NOT ONE STONE shot at the giant's forehead. It was <u>MULTIPLE STONES</u>, launched many times, which found their mark and felled Goliath. You say, "Why tell us this?" Because IT IS THE TRUTH. IT IS REAL. I AM REAL. Moses <u>DID NOT PART THE RED SEA</u>. No. Cecil B. Demille's depiction was NOT quite accurate. Moses split his forces at the Red Sea. Half went left, half went right, and the Egyptians DID NOT KNOW WHICH WAY TO GO, by looking at the tracks. So they LEFT. Moses knew if one of his forces survived it would be enough to start a new life. A new beginning. A new start. A new nation called Israel. I AM said, Steve, you FINALLY SPELLED Israel correctly, good work. Remember I AM in contact with him. He simply dictates MY WORDS. Sometimes I simply think of a sentence and he writes it down. This is easy for ME. It is unlike most of the other channelers I have encountered. They question, doubt, or interrupt. His mind stays quiet and I rattle on as I would if YOU could hear ME. I look at my notes on what I plan to say, and have him write. They are nearly identical. If it is slightly different it is because I change it. I meaning GOD. I meaning Jehovah. I meaning I AM. I TELL YOU THIS, I NEVER PLANNED TO LET Damion Brinkley, WRITE A BOOK ABOUT HIS ENCOUNTER WITH, ME. Or to let George Anderson write about, "We Don't Die." Again, an encounter with ME. Or even Neale Donald Walsch in "Conversations with GOD." I simply decided, Humanity needed it. I found people who would spread the word, then I asked them to do the deed, (or the work), and then you know the rest. They all have met ME. They all experimented with my energy. So have, Lucien Cambell, Troy Willis, Lawrence Taylor, and many unknown others. I AM GOD. I KNOW these things. I tell you this, other channelers could not write all the above names. They would NOT KNOW THEM, so they could not write the names down. I REALLY MEAN THIS as a complement to Steve. He has, in the past, been hurt by criticism that, *You should not be writing, that is elementary stuff.* That's right. Another so-called Psychic, close to him, told him that THIS form of channeling is "elementary." Guess what? I AM NOT AN ELEMENTARY GOD. I AM OLDER THAN DIRT. I AM as old as your Sun. THAT'S <u>S U N</u>. I AM TELLING YOU THIS BECAUSE OF THE SO-CALLED PSYCHIC FRIENDS NEIGHBORHOOD is a little out of whack with reality. Sorry, unless I tell you it is so then it is just you listening to others <u>like yourselves</u>. Few <u>really</u> have the abilities that they brag so much about. They simply use a version of the "old shell game." Telling you what is common with most people, then adding a fee to justify, their work. I AM agrees with you Steve, "they are con-artists." People, who have encountered ME, have an aura, about them. A GLOW. an everlasting smile in their soul. I know. I put it there. Few ask me, *LORD, use me as your tool.* I say again, few. Steve said in prayer, in 1986, *LORD, please come to Earth, we could use your help down here. We seem to have so much potential, yet we seem to be spinning our wheels. We need your help LORD, Please come.* **I HEARD THAT PRAYER.** It was over a period of 6 months. Yes 6 months, of constant prayer. That's how <u>he got through to me</u>. I was busy saving Neptune Future from herself, when I heard "The Prayer." I came to Earth to see what was going on. I told him I would stay, IF he let me guide His Life. He said, *I could use your help, LORD. I seem to be lacking LOVE in my life.* **I AGREED.** At that time I KNEW, Steve as a CHANNELER of my energy, BUT HE WAS CONFUSED. Tradition told him it should be Jesus WHO IS in CHARGE. All the bibles, books, religion he was exposed to, told him so. IT WAS JEHOVAH. I originally planned to get him OUT of the military, by asking him NOT to re-enlist. He re-enlisted. I ACTED. I made him hear all the sounds of my world, for 6 months straight. He tried to tell his first wife, but she said, "he is crazy, he hears voices." So she had him admitted, to an Army hospital for mental patients. So here is Steve. He prayed to Jehovah to help Earth. He said to Jehovah *take over my life,* and now he was sitting in a mental hospital, hearing voices. They tried to medicate him. HE STILL HEARD. They tried counseling. HE STILL HEARD. I had to intervene several times in his life when he was making improper choices. Now, he was extremely angry with ME. Do you blame him? Confused, hurt, being told he was schizophrenic and discharged from the military. His wife and kids, LEAVE HIM. He asked ME one day *LORD, if the ones who ask for guidance get treated like this, what happens to the ones who <u>Love you</u>???* **Truth...I** tell you this, he has been <u>disciplined</u> by ME. I decided his fate. No one else can dictate his fate. ONLY ME. GOD knows this is old news, Steve. But it is an example for others. I DO DISCIPLINE. <u>I do not want my children making mistakes that may cost them their lives</u>. Steve does not know that his continued enlistment was to be sent to Desert Storm, and to contract the viruses there, that others experienced. I, GOD ALMIGHTY, REFUSED TO DO THAT TO HIM. I do the same to others, until the choices that I recommend are made, you struggle. You fight my will. I ALWAYS WIN. The price is your soul. I took the time to tell you this because, not only is it a good example of MY DISIPLINE, but also my Love. Today is Monday July 6th 1998, it is 6:45 P.M. Steve is writing my words as I speak, UNCONDITIONALLY, UNEMOTIONALLY, (most of the time,) and without QUESTION, HESITATION, or deliberate changing of my words. His goal in life was to DO THIS FOR ME. I AM has not told him some of this before, so it is new to him, and YOU the reader. That is my WAY. I tell you when, I decide it is time. Currently, you are unemployed, going through another divorce proceeding, and fighting the first ex-wife for increase on child support. Do not think poorly of him, for over 11 years he has paid child support to his 4 children. Joshua is 17, Cortney 16, Kelcey 14, and Jacob 12. His first wife still Loves him but thinks he is crazy. BECAUSE OF ME. I TOOK AWAY HIS JOB, FAMILY, AND HIS LIFE, TO WRITE THIS BOOK. In 1991, he started to write a book, like this, called "The Last Will and Testament of Jesus." I MADE HIM THROW IT OUT. I AM JEHOVAH, NOT Jesus. In 1998, I told him this is "the year of patience." The wait is over, MY BOOK IS STARTED. In 1999, it will be done. I WILL IT SO. I do not plan ANY others, but I do adapt other's to follow IF NEEDED. I plan for one book. My book. It is my will, my guidance and my plan. I have selected Steve to write it. He tells me, *You volunteered me didn't you.* I said, YES. I volunteered FOR you. I tell you ALL this, because you may think this is a spur of the moment writing, or maybe even in response to other books about me. NO. It is MY WILL. I decide such things, and I choose, Steve. He, as you can see, DID NOT choose ME. *Will they believe?* he asks me? Those who Love me will. I tell you this. Steve will not need to be introduced to ME, in my Kingdom, I KNOW HIM NOW. I AM SAYS TO ALL WHO CAN HEAR, I WILL LET ALL WHO LOVE ME INTO MY KINGDOM, BY MY GRACE, MY MERCY, and my timing. Not by human hands, not by force, not by treachery or deceit. I choose, whom I choose. I say to you all, I AM THE ALMIGHTY. I will it so. I AM SORRY to put you through this my son. You need peace of mind. NOT this. But it is, in MY OPINION, necessary. Humanity needs to be shocked, slapped like being born, and told the gospel, the truth, the truth about ME. MY WAYS. NOT THEIRS. The libraries of the world are full of books about each of them. Lot's of stuff is fiction, novels, and such. I AM REAL. As real as this paper and pen. I EXIST. I AM. Now, where were we, my notes, oh yes! No. I do not mind if you write my side comments as well. Yes, I use notes. I have lots of stuff to cover that I have observed over the last 50 or so years, so here goes.

Side Comments

1. Do not fight ME. <u>I always win</u>. You cannot fight me, DIE, then expect ME to forgive. I discipline here too. Hitler did 20 years of labor, for my purpose. Believe me <u>it was not pleasant</u>. It was torturous. It was needed.

2. Do not think you can out wit or fool ME. I know your plan as you concoct or invent it. I see your thoughts.

3. Do not forget to worship ME. I told you before, I AM A JEALOUS GOD. I mean to be. It is MY choice.

4. Do not forsake my words. Not teachings from your bible scholars. <u>MY WORDS</u>. I put "Red Letter Editions" in your hands daily. I spoke through Christ.

5. Do not forget ME. I AM is my name. I AM is my fame. I AM IS MY GAME. I choose to push, pull, or mold you as I see fit. <u>You are now warned</u>.

6. Do not wet your appetite for things other than ME. Yes, I AM ALL things, but more good things than evil. <u>You</u> invent things to hurt each other. I supply things to save you. Cat-scans, DNA sampling, Laser surgery, Non-Intrusive surgery, etc. etc. I AM the inventor of such marvels. I told you, you have been helped. <u>I AM that helper</u>.

7. Do not strike out in anger. I say again control your temper. You seem PRIMATIVE to ME when you do so. I have seen it before, heard it before, and viewed the aftermath…it is repulsive to GOD.

8. I say to you. Do not hurt each other. Verbally, physically, or posthumously. Words kill, more people HERE, than you can imagine. Do not dig up stuff with the dead. Let them live their everlasting lives in peace. They did their best while here with you. Respect that.

9. Respect each other. You, as a species, tend to be overbearing, pompous, and self-assured of your invulnerability, as far as physical, emotional, and psychological matters go. But you fail to show compassion. "You need to give in order to receive." Heard that one before I bet.

10. Do not destroy. Learn to build. That includes marriages. You all tend to bail out when it gets tough. Why? Because it is easier to do than work out problems. Many of you regret years later you didn't try. You took the easy way. You failed to remember. I put the obstacle there, in the first place, TO TEST YOU. Build things, homes, families, friends, relationships. The rewards from building far out weigh the short term joy in bailing out or tearing down. Fix that old car, find that lost friend, and go to that game. DANCE, or go to the theater or the Park. <u>Create, build, and do not destroy.</u> When you do, you destroy a part of YOU as well.

11. Do not touch GOD. That's right. Not with thought or magic, or with any other means. Why? GOD is not touchable. You cannot put GOD on display. You cannot find a look-a-like, or statue to display. *Look I have GOD here on my dash,* **or** *on my desk.* **I do not work that way.** I AM everywhere in everything. I tried once to Clone myself once, but all I got was a busy signal. Laugh. Will ya…I do sometimes get TOO serious. I know that. My Angels are telling me at this point I should, stop, relax, and Tell a Story. I planned too, but after this…

12. Do not hurt my children. That means people like Steve, and his family. They have enough on their plates that I cannot even begin to tell you. They are constantly trying to find quiet time. To be together, and to find Love. My children are my own. Someday you will ALL be my children, so think of how you would want to be treated in a similar situation, and DO SO. With KINDNESS. With RESPECT. Steve knows…. I AM is NOT EASY TO CHANNEL. I TEND TO GET LOUD, BOLSTEROUS, AND I SAY IT LIKE IT IS. If you do not KNOW ME, YOU MIGHT SAY IT IS ARROGANCE, but I know EVERYTHING so I say it is CONFIDENCE.

Since I have made this a "Story Time" HERE GOES…When I was little, I had a dog named NOMA. It was my pet, my friend, and my first Love. One day my dog ran into the street and was killed by a big, heavy, dump truck-type vehicle. I had never seen anything die before. I found I was confused, hurt, and lost. Where did it go? Why did it leave? Why did it die? I found, years later, it did not die. It simply materialized on another world, leaving its shell behind and not remembering what happened to it. That is why most NEAR-DEATH EXPERIENCES have no real memory of MY conversation with them. I send them BACK. My world now has flying cars, and such. We don't kill things by accident anymore. If something dies, we now know how to bring it back to life, on the spot. I tell you this to share my Kingdom with you. MY WORLD. MY DOMAIN. My child is bothering me, Yes, Nathan what is it? Oh, OK. I will tell them. Nathan, my youngest, tells me to share with you that NOMA is still our family dog. Has been for 50 or so million years. She is a good mutt. Eats too much though. Once she even wet the bed. Got frightened, by a blast of cosmic air coming through our home, oh, 50 or so years ago. That was a fluke that got taken care of by ME. I fixed it on-the-spot. Now, let's break for lunch, I AM starving. It is 7:45 P.M. EST. In MY WORLD it is high noon. My stomach growls and my blood sugars are down. NOMA, come here girl. Let's break for lunch Steve. *After a lunch of ham-hocks, legumes and rice pudding, Jehovah's very favorites, we continue.* I Love the forward thinking you displayed in the forward you just wrote. Yes. I read it. *You helped, father, Holy Father.* Thank-you Steve.

I TOLD YOU TO TELL ME WHEN LUNCH WAS READY. Now, go relax, and we will write, more later. Now, do not panic. I told you to expect word from your new job. You just got it. YES. Now, go watch the homerun-derby for the ALL-STAR game. Relax. I know your hand is cramping. I AM says to you, I will not forget you. I will remember you. I will bless those who believe in ME. I WILL DISCIPLINE THOSE WHO FORGET ME, OR DEFY MY WILL. I know, who you are. I created you, and I can call you <u>home.</u> You are my children, Earth. Hear my voice, and me listen to my spoken word, IT IS TIME TO DO SO. You are mature enough to accept this as my mode of communication with you. You can hear me if you will listen. I AM HERE, THERE AND EVERYWHERE. I AM NEAR, FAR, NO MATTER WHERE YOU ARE. I AM in, out, and all about. I suffer with you, and for you. I care to. I choose to. I hope you believe ME when I say, I Love you. It is MY WAY OF SHOWING YOU A PART OF ME. My Love. My hope. My mercy. My POWER. My grace and my forgiveness. "My Love is deeper than the deepest ocean, higher than the sky." I helped Petula Clark with that in the 1960's. Yes. I <u>helped</u>. I decided to bring you more music. ROCK and ROLL, in particular, was MY creation. I choose to sing to YOU ABOUT ME. Prepare you. The Beatles were my first attempt to show you about Love. The Rolling Stones are my attempt to show you longevity. The Grass Roots sang "Heaven Knows." Did you ever realize he had ME in mind? I wrote songs for Joan Biaz, Bob Dylan, The Turtles, The Loving Spoonfuls, The Troggs, Herman's Hermits, and the 5th Dimension. I sang with Dan Fogelberg, Kenny Loggins, Steve Perry, Pete Cetera, Prince (or the former prince, as he is now called) Hammer, and Madonna. I CHOOSE TO.

TO SHOW YOU MY LOVE LISTEN TO THE FOLLOWING SONGS. I left my heart in San Francisco, Tony Bennett. Substitute "San Francisco," for "Heaven's Holy Gate." Then listen to it again for the first time. Listen to the "Glory of Love" by Pete Cetera, and substitute NOTHING. IMAGINE MY DIRECT VOICE SINGING TO YOU. "Believe in me" by Dan Fogelberg, same instructions. Then listen to Gangster Rap. Do you hear ME? Do you hear my voice? I AM IS NOT INTO GANGSTER RAP MUSIC. It is laced with violence, hate, bigotry, AND MOST OF ALL COLOR. <u>I KNOW NOT COLOR</u>. Only the color of LOVE. I choose to tell you this before you abandon MY WORKS completely. <u>I inspired your Love songs.</u> Songs of hope, compassion, Love and joy of Love, are part of ME. I care not, for hate, violence, or prejudice. I tell you this, LOVE KNOWS NO COLOR. I care for the Four Tops, Supremes, and the Motown Sound, MORE than Gangsta Rap Why? Love is in THAT MUSIC. Hope is in THAT MUSIC. <u>I AM IS IN THAT MUSIC</u>. Classical music is ME, Country music, Garth Brooks, (who is influenced by James Taylor) IS ME. Dwight Yokam (is influenced by Hank Williams) IS ME. Johnny Cash, who IS NOT the original Man in Black, I AM, IS ME. These are just a few. Why only these? To make a point. I hear your music. I listen to MTV, VH1, radio and TV. I go to concerts. The last one I attended was a Yes concert at Camden's E center. Steve did not go. I kept him broke during ALL THIS. The concert before that was Journey's concert in New York, at Madison Square Garden, in 1998. Before that I attended The artist formally known as Prince in LA at the Tropa Cabaña night club. Before that I went to Oregon and helped Neal, with his last book from ME. I ATTENDED 6 CONCERTS THIS YEAR. I watched you have fun. I went to see Puff Daddy and Smokin' Joe at a bar in New Mexico. I have witnessed these things first hand, in person. I TELL YOU THIS BECAUSE IT IS TRUE. <u>DO YOU BELIEVE???</u> I went to this extreme to make a point. I hate what you have done to MY MUSIC. Songs of Love are scarce, songs of hope are even scarcer. All you do in music IS COMPLAIN. STOP.

I hate to see so much talent WASTED on complaints, on artistic endeavors, on artistic freedom. <u>Complaining is easy.</u> Writing about Love, relationships, and most of all about GOD, IS TOUGH. Steve listens to Christian artists like Petra, Amy Grant, and Michael W. Smith, to name a few. He doesn't listen to radio anymore. I encouraged him to do this. I became so melancholy over MY CREATION of Rock n' Roll. I could not in good conscience, praise more than the artists I have so far. I heard someone say This generation doesn't know how to Rock n' Roll, I AGREE. Groups like Def Leppard play their collective hearts out with the type of music, which is by the way, EXTREMELY popular in MY KINGDOM. The group Scattergun IS THE HOTTEST TICKET IN TOWN. They have members of Lynyrd Skynyrd, Nazareth, and Thin Lizzy in it. They wrote a song for ME called "Love bites and so do I." I really enjoyed hearing it dedicated to my struggle to get Earth to listen to me again. Yes, again. You listened in 1969, 1974, 1991, and 1994. Why those years? Simply put WAR. Vietnam, the Gulf War, and in 1994 you let me tell you how to win with very few casualties. Now, here is the catch. I owed you that. Yes, owed you. You provide as a people, the best example of what, the closest thing this planet has <u>ever</u> put together, MY KINGDOM is like. America. Yes, I know other countries will complain. They fight ME, daily. My plan is to make a world government where all countries can enjoy the freedoms America does. My plan is for universal currency, based on agriculture, NOT precious metals. My plan is for economic freedoms as well as individual rights. My plan is to launch you into the next millennium as a free strong, single minded, will-full people. As one planet, one voice, one GOD. Why? You are stumbling without ME. You will take <u>forever at your current pace</u>. You take one-step forward and 5 steps back. Music is an example. I send Love, and hope, and fun. You choose anger, bitterness, hate, and prejudice. You spoil the fruit, The work of the LORD. Write of ME, my ways, my heart, my doors are open. You can come in sit down and write about my Kingdom. Sing about what you imagine Heaven is like, I will be sure it is. Write poetry about my home, family, I AM sure it is like that. Write books like this one. Praising ME. Allowing ME to free-flow, to create, to think for you, to take the burden of choices off your shoulders. This is to set you free. How? As I make your choices for you I teach you how to think, what to think, and when to think. Then I set you FREE. You are on your own to use what I have taught you in practical applications, such as work, play, creating new schools. I wrote with Neale on this. And most important, your personal relationship with ME, GOD. Let me give you some background. You are NOT the first planet I have done this with. You are the 997th planet to receive this honor. 2 Years ago I finished Tantum 8 in the binary sector near…later for that. The point is you can do this. It's been done. All 997 planets did this. You can too. 4 of them are post-nuclear, 5 were less advanced technologically, but all succeeded. None failed. I choose this time, because YOU NEED A BOOST. If you were on a bike, you need training wheels, a booster seat at a restaurant, a hand to hold as you learn to walk. You need GOD. I AM THE ALMIGHTY. I AM HERE. IT IS MY TIME. Let no one pass through Heavens gates expect through ME. I choose to be a messenger of the gospel, but NOT 7,000, or 10,000 years ago, current, now, up to date, for this time. Lessons need to be learned and taught, as to how to think. Why? Too many years of listening to each other. Listen to ME. I AM.

Now for another story. During your WWI, you felt a strange tremble in the Earth's crust in the spring of 1918, I believe. I know it was listed as a tremor. NOW HEAR THIS. That is going to happen again. That tremor occurred over Scotland. I cannot tell you how to prepare, but in 2 years hence, it will occur again. A "not noticed fault line" runs from Scotland to Finland, and down to Africa. It is called the North Atlantic Fault, in MY world. It contains built-up pressures and plate shifts only registering by satellite technology. It has not been discovered because no one has looked. Please, LOOK. In 1918 it was noted as a War Time occurrence in France, Belgium and in the Netherlands. It was thought to be Cannon. It was NOT. History will record it on April 10th of that year. No one was injured but it was 10 on your Richter scale, lasting only 3 seconds. Yes, I know, you will have to verify this information, please do. In 1997 the Welsh people noticed a sharp decline in the height of certain properties, and buildings. It was passed off as a minor occurrence. Please…it will be a MAJOR event when it goes. Some will say this will cause wide spread panic, not if you are PREPARED. I SAID, I WOULD NOT LIE TO YOU, AND I WILL NOT START NOW. In the old book you call the Bible it tells of disasters, Earthquakes, floods, and fire, pests, etc. Well, it is NOW a growing community that visionaries of the past could not understand. Nor could they explain. (Rev 4:7).Its head was like a lion, the second like a fox, the third had the face of a man, the fourth was like a flying eagle. Well, hear the wisdom. The lion, was an Air Force F-4 Phantom, The fox, was an Apache helicopter, the third was a Sherman tank, and the fourth was General Patton. During that unseen visit by John's spirit, he wrote about discussions in 1970 in my Ready Room, about similarities of 1970 warfare and 1945 tactics. He could not accurately describe what he saw because he was a 1st Century man, viewing 20th Century technology. The purpose is to make you realize the Book of Revelation, is not a doomsday prediction, but A BOOK OF HOPE. When viewed as a window to ME, read with optimism and hope, it TRANSFORMS INTO A WONDERFUL STORY one-worth reading.

My son, Jesus was watching the whole thing.

When Paul and John abruptly felt John's spiritual presence, from the past, view the present. He was confused, and frightened, and even horrified by what he saw. Can you imagine, first century man writing about an automobile? How could he begin to describe it using first century terms? It had 10 horns. No, John, NOT HORNS, it has 10 lights. (2 headlights, 2 taillights, 2 blinkers, front and back, and a dome light and a light in the trunk.) Yes, he never saw a car before. To him it was a monster. It moved strangely. It was a dragon a beast a demon-like thing. He meant well, but needed to be briefed on WHY things are the way they are, in the future. OUR PRESENT. The car was a 1994 Nissan Sentra. My colleagues and I were comparing Japanese engineering to American. We were discussing that topic. I feel the move will further enhance problem of choices. That's why there is GM in Russia, inspiring Moscow to move to free enterprise. The Kremlin is slow to respond…Hello, Steve, *Hello Father. Father, may we continue?* YES. Now, I AM, PLEASED. I tell you this…MY WAY is now in print. I will see this project to its completion.

No More, Do Not

Now, <u>NO MORE WAR</u>. No more weapons of mass destruction. I insist. Every one must stop building, making, experimenting with, and the stretching of economy's for this. The economy of the world should focus on the people. The people matter more than war. Do not change my words; do not hear <u>any others</u> thoughts, only ME, GOD, JEHOVAH. I pledge to watch over you as long as you stop killing each other. If you do not stop, I will leave. Too much too soon, too many toys of a hurtful nature. TOO MANY PEOPLE PLAYING GOD. <u>I DONOT MAKE WAR</u>. ISRAEL MADE IT SOUND SO. I AM is peace, powerful Love, peace and harmony. GOD has no quarrels with anyone. I do not take sides. I do not vote in elections. I DO NOT TELL YOU ONE THING THEN DO ANOTHER. <u>I plan to finish what I started</u>. I hope this is clear. NO MORE WAR. Find a way to build, not destroy.

No more hate. Lose the hate. It is time consuming, wasteful, full of anger, hurt, and a total waste of time. You, as humanity, get angry at such little things. DRIVE BY SHOOTINGS, WHY??? Do you have to be driving in an angry mood just to get there. NO MORE HATE. No more lust. Yes, you heard ME. LUST. You are more primitive than others when you do that. Lust ruins marriages, family's, and tells Presidents how to behave. I tell you this no more lust. I AM.

No More Failure. That's right, when with ME you do not fail. You only succeed. Now fight my will, and see you fail. Try to avoid my guidance and you will see my wrath. Ask Israel. They do not know I caused the holocaust. YES, JEHOVAH DID. I warned them 10,000 years ago, if they turned from ME. I would wipe out their nation. I warned them of a total wipeout of the entire Jewish State. I prevented the State wipeout for my promise sake. I promised and kept it. I permitted the holocaust to occur. Why? To make Israel wake up TODAY. To remember ME. To move into the 21st Century under MY guidance. Hear ME O'ISRAEL, I DID NOT FORESAKE THEE, THOU HAST CHASED MY WILL AWAY, IN THE FORM OF JESUS. THOU HAS FORGOTTEN MY COVENANT WITH THEE DO NOT FORESAKE THE LORD THY GOD. That is why I chose America, and a plain ordinary American to convey my will. He did not forsake me for 43 years. Israel forsakes me DAILY. I AM. Why? Why do I try O'ISRAEL? Why do you NOT LISTEN to the prophets? Do you murder them still today? YES, YOU DO. Hugh MacDonald, in old Jerusalem. I knew him. I TRIED TO TELL YOU, through him, THAT I LOVE YOU. You ignored ME.

Steve, in 1947 I sent a prophet named Hugh MacDonald to Israel under the name Yashi

Gulratta. THEY LAUGHED AT HIM. Spit on him, and had him KILLED as a political dissident. No matter what, I AM is with you.

No More fun with other's feelings. At the <u>expense of hurting others</u> you push, you pull, you hurt. All you did was hurt yourself. Treat others as you expect to be treated. Guess what? You get it back at you. That is MY WAY.

No More Lies. From the original commandments, and Neale's commitments. But from NOW ON, THIS DAY FORTH, NO MORE LIES. Not to ME, TO YOU, TO ANYONE. Start each day with the truth. End each day with the truth. Even when you are caught red handed, video taped, witnessed, <u>YOU STILL DENY THE TRUTH</u>. I AM not like that. I know you. I know the truth of who you <u>really</u> are. If my ways seem old fashion, slow, clumsy, or outdated, try ME A NEW WAY. I bet I have seen it, done it, have it done already, and approve of it. I AM. No More Stereotyping. Stop it. BLACKS ARE <u>NOT</u> LAZY. Whites do not have all the money. Christians do not eat their young. Jews are not all stingy, well…most are. LOOK, I DO HAVE A SENSE OF HUMOR. I need to lighten up sometimes. But 10,000 years of waiting to say my side OF WHAT I SEE, makes me get on a tangent and I really get revved up. I get going, I push, push, push. I WANT you to know me. How else can I do that except to get your attention? Anyway, <u>stereotyping</u> limits knowing that person for <u>who they are</u>. How seldom you are right when you see someone. You tend to lump all colors, sizes, and ethnic backgrounds, THE SAME. YOU ALL DO IT. I SAY STOP. I AM.

Do not tell GOD what to do. GOD does not listen. He will OK. a prayer, a plan, a seldom-used song, but do not yell, scream, and throw a temper tantrum my WAY. It doesn't work. I do not care if you are hurt, tired, or angry. GET OVER IT. Move on. It is time to wake up and smell the coffee. Who do you think came up with these clichés in the first place? I DID.

Do Not ask GOD for what you KNOW is impossible. You do that to embarrass <u>you</u>, not ME. I DO NOT EMBARRASS. I planned your life for you there are no little tests for me to take. I made you in <u>my</u> image. I DO NOT PLAY THAT GAME.

Do not ask GOD for <u>someone else's</u> Lover or mate. I do not do that. Why? Look at the 10 commandments. It's called <u>Adultery</u>. I do not condone it. I sponsor marriage, Love, family, and stop thinking that's just male/female. Female/female, male/male is ALL okay to ME. Get it through your thick skulls people…GOD IS LOVE. If two people are in Love, I DO NOT STOP IT. If the bible says <u>not</u> to, find a passage that says its OK. I have heard it so many times, the pope, the clergy, the church, ask me…"if incest, lust and greed are the same as homosexuality?" IT IS NOT THE SAME. Love is more than that. Love is not lust. It is A HIGHER FORM OF EXPRESSION. Women and men are allowed same sex marriages in MY KINGDOM. And have been for 50 million years. So get use to it. No judgments on this are allowed but MINE. Why? Because I AM THE LORD THY GOD, GOD OF ISRAEL, AND OF AMERICA, GOD OF ALL. Not just THE CONVENIENCE OF A FEW OTHERS. I have made that clear to you. Stop persecuting GAYS. They have rights, so get use to it.

No More judgments. That's right. Do not judge unless you want to be judged. I plan to let you in Heaven, and those you judge, inferior, low life's or not equal to ME. Guess what? I AM ALL THAT TOO. I AM inferior to YOU. I AM a low life, to you and I AM NOT equal, to you. See how it hurts. See how it changes your perception. Do Not DO THESE THINGS IN YOUR LIVES. And your death will be painless, easy, and full of joy upon entry into MY KINGDOM. By the way, there is no other Kingdom out there, anywhere, I KNOW. I CREATED IT. So it's ME, or NOTHING. Choose ME. I DID. I LOVE YOU, AND I like ME. I AM. Now since I have been on a streak for awhile let ME cool down by informing you a few things you may or may not have noticed.

1. You are NOT in charge I AM.
2. NO More fun unless you say Thank you, LORD. I need to hear that. It guarantees more fun to come.
3. No open letters to ME. Finish them. Enough said.
4. No more phone messages putting GOD first on your answering machines. I know I AM first. You know I AM first. They know I AM first. So stop fooling around, we all know you care. Erase it and put on something funny like "Hi, I'm not here, but I will be shortly, do not call again, I can't come to the phone, I have a cake in the oven," or my favorite, "what do you want, I told you I'm not home."
5. I do not like to have a place set at your table, for ME. I cannot eat your food. It causes cramps. Take the setting down, it is a nice gesture, but Maria would get furious if I didn't eat her cooking.
6. By now you are wondering, what the heck is this? These are my PET PEEVES. Yes, I have them too. Like, I do not remind you to put the toilet seat down. You must remember yourself. I could care less.
7. I cook and clean, but boy, I do NOT bow down and clean the toilet. Sorry, I don't help with that. Got to let YOU do that one. I ALSO, do not tell you when to go. That's your body talking, let it decide, and then LISTEN to it.
8. Nobody told you to hammer at my head with the same prayers, day after day, after day. "Come, LORD Father to our supper, etc. Dear Heavenly Father…., our house is your

house…" Please take time to write some <u>new</u> material. I sure would appreciate it. I AM.

9. I CARE TOO, SO I DO. If you are wondering why something has gone haywire, or appears to, IT'S ME. YUP. GOD. I just am trying to get your attention, let you know I'm out there, in there, or around there. It will fix itself, with help of course.

10. I do not plan to write any more books, notes, messages, etc. Why? <u>This will say all I need to say</u>. It is perfect in my eyes. I do not need to elaborate, exasperate, or define anything. The body of work will speak for itself, as a whole. I plan to retire after this. My writing career is over. You can contact ME yourself. Yes, through prayer, or just by thinking of ME. I can hear you. I can. I can tell you I LOVE YOU, YES I do. I tell you every day. You just need to listen. I AM real, alive, and the first to tell you I care. No one else in MY KINGDOM would dare to challenge ME to be the first to do this, not you, me, or even quiet writing Steve. Yes, he is there writing his heart out, for you, while his hand gets cramps. The first session was 6 hours long. This one has been 2. I have written all this in 8 hours. I do not suffer from writers block, and I have much more to say. Now for my next topic.

Drugs

Sorry, no use for them here. No drugs allowed in Heaven. No caffeine, No amphetamines, no stimulants, no hallucinogens, no…well, you get the idea. I do no need them and neither do YOU. Why? Do not depend on anything except ME, GOD. I end all dependency. I claim all rights to your soul. I decide your fate. Not the power in the bottle, (liquor), or the needle (drugs), or the artificial stimulants you call over the counter medication. Did you ever see so many drugs in your life? I asked Maria one day, while strolling through a Rite-aid. She agrees with ME. You have a tendency to be <u>dependent. Now I AM giving you something to REALLY depend on, ME. JEHOVAH. NOT ANYONE ELSE. Not nowhere, not no how</u>. I told you I would be back, <u>were you ready</u>? Did you keep yourself Holy, clean and pure? Then if not, it is time to make that change. That life-altering step called, commitment. Commit to ME, MY WAYS. Stop trying to avoid life, it is always there, stop trying to avoid censorship, it still exists, stop trying to avoid reality, guess what? It's real. I AM says to you, do not plan on leaving here without taking the mess <u>you</u> leave behind, and clean it up. <u>I DO NOT LET YOU ESCAPE YOUR SOULS RESPONSIBILITIES</u> by taking and destroying your life. If you try suicide, you hurt only yourself. You cannot escape ME. Others tried. They failed. I plan so much more in your life, if you would only listen. If you would only take time to open your heart to ME, then you would find my Love for you there. In the entire world NO ONE is more special, precious and my child, than YOU. I know your pain. I know your agony. I know your hate. You are my child. I AM GOD. I planned this as a test of your Love for ME. <u>Pass the test</u>. Then take me with you where ever you go. I AM there already, waiting to help you into the next phase or stage of your life. Do not throw away my life, my special life, with YOU. I DO NOT GO AWAY. I AM ALWAYS THERE. I do not leave. I tell you the truth. I will not deceive you. I will not hurt you. <u>I will not find you then,</u> throw you away. I will not speak ill of you, then lie about you. I know their ways. Let ME judge them. Let ME help you. Kick the habit. Get off drugs! My next topic is…

Steven

He is quietly writing this in hopes YOU will read it someday. He fears reprisals, and even lawsuits. No matter what is said about this "Body of Work," leave him out of it. He is merely someone I chose to be "My Messenger." The stuff I AM about to undertake is Holy, open and honest. I AM totally responsible for its content. Steve has no input, he quietly sits, writes and stops only to rest his hand, take a drink, or go to the bathroom.

This is what I was seeing, and feeling, when GOD first asked me to help channel his words into this book. I could hear his voice and feel his presence guiding my hand.
His overwhelming Love made me cry.

My Book of Love

I do not understand humanity's hang ups with LOVE. SEX is OK TO YOU, BUT <u>LOVE IS FORBIDDEN</u>? I TOLD YOU TO ENJOY YOURSELVES WHILE YOU ARE THERE, BUT THIS IS RIDICULOUS. Nasty comments from the church on what is, or is not pornographic. <u>MUTILATION</u> IS PORNOGRAPHIC. <u>ANYTHING DESTRUCTIVE</u> IS PORNOGRAPHIC. No sex is pornographic. I mean to say, NO SEXUAL ACT is pornography. My definition of LOVE comes from centuries of watching you deny your own bodies. You tend to display them only when it is convenient, or when it is OK by LAW. WHY? If you all looked the same, would it matter? Would you need to be clothed? Adam and Eve were naked. I did not clothe them, or kick them out of the garden. They were kicked out by their <u>own guilt</u>. Two people in Love have no fear of ME. Naked is fine. Clothes in Heaven are optional. Now, don't break any laws. <u>It takes time for change</u>, and you know as well as I, some old men or women in high places, with sexual oppressed genes will say No, that's not decent. Well, it is. Your children are deprived of their own comfort zone. Totally unaware what is wrong with naked. No matter, you ALL get into the world the same way, and YES, you leave and enter in HERE the same way, <u>NAKED</u>. Love to GOD is HOLY. No one can deny its power over you. GOD is Love that is his power. No one can deny your right to GOD. GOD is Love, is the simplest, easiest, definition of GOD the OLD BIBLE has. But you cannot BELIEVE the stories we get about sexual repression on your planet. Do you really scramble your "Love Making Stations" like Playboy and Penthouse because you are afraid your youth will run amuck. Well, I HAVE NEWS FOR YOU, they already have. And what ever you <u>are</u> doing ISN'T WORKING. Where is the responsibility for them, their education in this? Do you still let them learn by trial and error? Why? Why do you allow centuries of learning on the subject, be wasted on a few choice people who only want $$$$$$ out of the project. Love, with the right partner is Holy and pure. It is decent, clean, wholesome and HAS <u>NOT</u> GUILT ATTACHED TO IT. No one can deny its power. Young men cry, young women swoon, old people faint, the young at heart fall in Love. GOD agrees that Love is a weapon best served naked. <u>Take violence off TV, replace it with Love, and then watch society change</u>. People would stay home for one thing. Family's would stay together, grow, and spread joy and happiness. Disease would vanish. Drugs would go away, and LOVE would reign supreme. Do you think I do not know about your naked bodies? Come on, I KNOW EVERYTHING, every hair, mole, and dimple. I even know about the ones you can't see, cause your neck don't go that way. No matter, in time, you will change. Gradually. Over long arduous periods of debate, with all the old clichés. ITS NEVER BEEN TRIED BEFORE. Yes, it has countless times. Oscar 7 was the last planet to successfully implement this. You can see it in Orion's Belt, with the Hubbell. No matter, <u>Sex</u> with <u>the one you Love</u> is Love. No matter what the experts say. No sex, No Love. My way is Love. Do you think Adam and Eve only named the animals and the planets? By the way EVE HELPED. She named the octopus and the shark. Kind of ironic, huh? Did GOD make you laugh? Do you know me? Did JEHOVAH make you giggle or laugh out loud? He heard you, and LOVES YOU. That is his way. I AM. No one can blame ME for not trying to loosen things up here. Rock n' Roll, Playboy, sorry Hugh, but Dunas 7 was 50,000 years ahead of you, and Penthouse, ALL were done before. So were X-rated movies. It is a shame to waste all that material on a few individuals who don't get dates anyway. A movie or two does wonders for your sex life, IF it needs it. No matter, I AM GOD. I AM in charge. Someday when all the smoke clears, and the heads of state realize WHY is it so, IT WILL CHANGE. <u>Nobody</u> expected it to be clean <u>did they</u>? Well, sorry to disappoint you. Sex IS CLEAN. Love IS NATURAL. Stop fighting amongst yourselves, and listen to ME. I will show you what, is and what, I do not allow. Judging such things is MY WAY of showing you my authority. Yes, I do judge matters you cannot make up your mind on. SEX IS ONE. You are a good people, but definitely confused about your destination. You call yourselves free or liberated, then the next breath call someone tasteless or distressful, or disgusting.

Let ME share with you my plan.

It goes back to Adam and Eve. Sorry, church <u>EVE DID NOT SIN</u>. Her only crime was loving Adam. She was a good wife, mother, and sex partner to Adam. CAIN DID NOT KILL ABEL. Cain and Abel were brothers. They fought for GOD'S affection. No one kills ANYONE in MY KINGDOM. The term kill in ancient Hebrew text also means…destroyed or discouraged. The story of Cain, conquering Abel, for GOD'S affection is well documented in MY KINGDOM. SO, stop looking for original sin. <u>It is NOT THERE</u>. Humankind constantly uses his own understanding to interpret me. I need no explanation. I exist. I do not care for lies about my creations. <u>Adam and Eve are your spiritual parents</u>. THE STORY IS <u>REAL</u>. I AM REAL. They do not care for the Bad Rap.

My other bible story is the story of Moses with the Pharaoh. Sorry, no magic. Just ME. Moses channeled my voice, using my tone, harmony, and power to intimidate the Pharaoh into submitting to release of the people of Egypt. No one changed a staff into a snake, no one put frogs in the streets. NO, it did not rain fire, or death did not pass over the people of Israel. The truth is, <u>Pharaoh was frightened</u>, so much so, he released the people out of fear. See, Pharaoh KNEW Moses, and the voice that Moses used, was not his own. It was thought to be a trick of some sort. That is why Pharaoh chased after Moses in his chariots. He was trying to save face. The truth is Cecil B. Demille had more fun making Hollywood Magic, than the real thing that happened. GOD knows I WAS THERE. It happened just like that, I AM. Also, much publicized, but never explained, is JESUS healing of the blind, and making the lame walk. A little known fact about Jesus and his life is that he spent 6 years in the Orient. Studying medicine, healing, and holistic methods. He returned with those methods from that world, and used them to heal a man who had a sty. He used herbal teas and many chants to care for the man's problem. The lame man was suffering from gout. After working on the circulation, and again, using warm tea to reduce any swelling, he was able to walk. And another item worth mentioning…

The Shroud of Turin is REAL, I AM

I AM because I have preserved it for 2000 years. To show you my work. It is the first photograph taken of Jesus. After he was buried according to Jewish law, then removed 3 days later, by Peter, Paul and Mary. They took him to the mountains to hide, and to wait, for his resurrection. Sorry, he was dead, and <u>stayed</u> dead. But wait, it gets better. 2 weeks of lying Jesus in the hot Israeli sun, turning him over to see if any damage was done by that sun, he made a perfect image on the cloth. It is a three dimensional photograph. Mine. GOD took it to show this generation, MY GLORY. Test my testimony. Test ME with your Carbon Dating, Polygraphs, and Spectral Analysis. You will find, in time, that the Shroud <u>is genuine</u>. After the body was anointed with oils, it acted as an emulsion, leaving some fibers in the shroud tanned, others, <u>not</u> so tanned. How did I <u>DEVELOP IT,</u> YOU ASK? I MADE FRANCISCAN MONKS STORE IT, in dark, damp, caves on their Monasteries, for years. Just to prove to YOU, I AM. Sorry, to tell all the Christians everywhere, but Jesus did die on that cross. <u>No resurrection.</u> But you have ME. GOD. The HOLY ONE WHO HAD YOU IN MIND WHEN I STARTED THIS WHOLE PLAN. The here and now, LORD OF ALL. The one who reveals his GLORY to the people he Loves, YOU. You are welcome.

Ministry

My Ministry is simple. No church can deny it. GOD IS. Yes, that's it. GOD IS. I EXIST. I LEAD. YOU FOLLOW. I FOLLOW. YOU LEAD. I tell. You listen. I listen, you cry with the joy of discovering ME. If it is not enough that Christians everywhere now have no religion, what do they do now LORD? They follow ME. MINE IS GLORY. Do they not see the wisdom of the Shroud? That I, 2000 years ago, needed to show MY PEOPLE, here today, that I know about photography, WAY BACK THEN? Or is it coincidence? I happen to have a logical explanation to a mystery in Turin, Italy. By the way, …CARBON DATING DOES NOT WORK when sheep are involved. Think about it, and then get back to me with your answer. The oil used in Jesus' death was from sheep intestines. Yes. SHEEP. Perfumed oils are expensive today, as they were then. The problem with carbon dating is it needs a material to absorb into to test. The sheep oil evaporates after a few hundred years. That throws carbon dating out the window because the sample is now tainted. Let's see the scientific community figure this one out. I told you, I TELL you the TRUTH. Like it or NOT, Jesus was a good, honest, GOD FEARING MAN, but just a MAN. GOD allowed his legend to grow, and prosper because he Loved GOD, and GOD Loved HIM. It is not coincidence that proved to you, MY GLORY, just now. It is MY PLAN. It is not fate that made you read this, and go "Oh, My GOD." It is ME. It is not fixed in the Heavens that I, and I alone, told you this, to show you my Love for my human family, my family of man, it is MY WAY. I AM GOD. Jehovah. The almighty. I do these things and more, because, I Love you. Worship GOD. Not a man who knew GOD. I AM THE ENERGY YOU FEEL WHEN YOU PRAY TO Christ. I AM the Love you feel when I take you into my arms. I AM THE GOD OF ALL. He has believed. He has been saved. She believed. She will be saved. Mostly my old problems, are your new ones. How to tell you ALL I have IN ONE BOOK? If you believe in ME, I can give you others. They can be called. "My Love. My Proof. My Forgiveness. My Way. My Understanding and My Will." Why? Because they are already written in Heaven. I only need to quote them to Steve. He will write. I Will Speak. You will LEARN, AND I WILL LOVE YOU. I plan for 1 book, but MANY VOLUMES. I can tell you this…no greater Love in this generation than Steven Wade Raasumaa. He will do my will, despite reservations to the contrary. I AM GOD.

Let me continue with my story to you about Jesus, the Christ. He was a learned man for his day, not simple as the Bible portrays him. He was the modern day equivalent to a PhD of Religion, and Philosophy. Joseph noticed his potential early on, and took him to Egypt to study in the Hall of Kings, near the old city of Baghdad. My Love for him was when he asked ME to take control of his life, on his 14th birthday. I agreed. He said, GOD, Jehovah, my people are in bondage, they need you to lead them, to guide them, to help, and pamper them. Please take this life, do with it as you will, help my people be free. The words I spoke in return were of the nature of mankind. It's faults. He spoke in the tongue of the time…"Lama' Dyey, Lama," meaning "my GOD, my GOD." He heard MY VOICE. He cried. I cried. My son of 2000 years ago, still cries when I tell his story.

Jesus wept. Just NOW. I TELL YOU THIS NO MAN IN HIS LIFETIME MADE A GREATER SACRIFICE TO ME, THAN HE. He gave GOD ALL HE HAD. Himself. To my judgment. I made him "King of Kings" and "LORD of LORDS." I tell you this…my Love is NOT of this world. My heart is NOT of this world. My will is NOT of this place. My heart is NOT of this realm, it is more. Once more I say, I Love Jesus, the Christ. He is a son to ME. I expect, you as a people, to Love him too. I tell you this…my works with him are not done. I have stories to share of his Love for ME. In the last 2000 years much has been said, done, and completed by that one man. He is the cornerstone of my being here. He is my friend. Do not forsake him because of legend. He will live up to more truth than you can possibly imagine. But that is for another time, another volume of work. My praise of Jesus is my truth. Do not forsake the TRUTH. I AM. Do not take away what he has done.

Add to it when, you hear of his fame in Heaven, add to it and you will cry. Add to it when you hear of his glory, in GODS NAME. AMEN.

AMEN

My prayers ALWAYS end in "Amen." Why? Because I AM a <u>male</u>. YES. A MAN. Sorry, women's libber's. I did not change gender for political correctness. I know women in your world struggle for equality. They did in Jesus' time too. I know women struggle for equal rights. They did in Jesus' time too. I know women struggle for freedom from oppression, unjustness, and RAPE. They did in Jesus' time too. 2000 years ago the same problems persisted. I can only tell you that slowly <u>it has gotten better</u>.

Not perfect, but better, women vote. They could not even speak unless spoken to, 2000 years ago. Women work side-by-side with men, unheard of 2000 years ago. Women can run a company, country, or be whatever they dream of being. Not even REMOTELY possible, 200 years ago, let alone 2000. Rape, is still a PROBLEM, <u>men are pigs</u>. Yes, pigs. They take and do not give. They hurt and do not say sorry. They are the hope of every young girl, and the dread of every married one. They can be great or small. Weak or strong. No <u>man</u> is perfect. I AM. GOD is perfect. I know women. I know their pain, hurts, and their ego. I know the softness, the gentleness, the kindness, that is womanhood. I worship you as womankind. I behold your beauty, poise, and grace. You fall between a gazelle and a panther, in feeling and power. WOMEN RUN THE WORLD, my friends. GOD simply turns them loose to do so. My mother is a good woman, my wife is a good woman. So are all my daughters, wives, ex-wives and all my slaves. Huh? Did he say slaves? Women make great slaves, don't you think? Men ask them to put out everything. Trash, clothes, sex, and food. Men DO NOT RESPECT WOMEN. Women are too fragile, men say. <u>WELL, BULLSHIT</u>. YES. I said BULLSHIT. Women are what make MY KINGDOM WORK. They understand the subtle flow of life. They die easy, not hard like men do. They last longer in solving problems, they don't bail out. They do not care if men treat them bad, they "Put up with Men's Shit" (PMS). That's vulgar? Good. It is the <u>truth</u> isn't it? It is what they as a gender, tell ME. <u>This is what I hear</u>. Do you think I AM DEAF? You don't have to yell. I can hear your heartbeat, <u>over</u> your whisper. I know you Love GOD. I just want womankind to admit that I AM. I AM A MALE. Yet, I UNDERSTAND. I LOVE YOU WOMAN. I Love your smell, your heart, your soul and your fun loving way of life. You stop and smell the flowers. You take time to enjoy a simple thing, like a bubble bath. NO, I WON'T JOIN YOU Maria gets jealous. I say this to make you realize, I DO NOT CHANGE. You MUST change to accept ME, as GOD. As a MALE. Accept this, and be free from your pain. Accept this, and be free from your burden, and THE LORD KNOWS IT IS HEAVY LADDEN. I KNOW THE WEIGHT YOU PULL, CARRY, AND

STRIVE FOR EVERY DAY, EVERY HOUR, EVERY MINUTE, AND EVERY SECOND. I KNOW BECAUSE I AM. I AM GOD. THE ALMIGHTY, the maker of Eve. The maker of womankind. I tell you this no man can Love you more, better, or constantly, than GOD. GOD IS A MAN. Sorry, but that's just the way it is. I Love <u>you</u> woman. Remember that, and we are ONE. WE are together, and we can never be separated. I AM.

GODS Little Poem for Womanhood

"I left my heart in the King's hands,

I left my soul in his right,

I left my shoe in his left,

I took my Love and kissed his lips,

I felt my Love touch his eyes,

I let myself be who I AM,

knowing all the while I was in the maker's hands."

I mold you into beauty, grace, and dignity. My way, ladies, is to set you free. I do not fear what YOU see. I only look out for what is inside of ME. Mine was the last. Maria's was the first. The shoe is to represent your life's travels. ALL that you have done. It will show you, your future and your past. I know. I AM.

"Woman do not be frightened of ME,

I AM only here to set you free,

When all is done you can see,

the Love of you, inside of ME.

My favorite is this:

Roses and Violets hang on a vine,

without the aid of cheese or wine,

if you Love me then you will find,

that the Love of a woman has ALL inside."

Women, please understand GOD'S LOVE FOR YOU. I could show MY KINGDOM, when you say I Love you, LORD. My precious child, you thought you were lost, my little girl, all is not lost, I found you.

GOD IS ALL. I AM GOD. I AM YOU. Do not forget this when I say, I Love you. My way is to make you cry, my way is to make you happy, my way is to be your GOD…my way is to help you see me. My way is Love. My way is mine, and mine alone. No one passes through the doors of my Love except through ME. I do not worry over what you worry. I do not fret, I do not curse, only when it fits, AND to get your attention. I do not take sides, but I do Love you. I care to. My way is your heart. Your heart is my WAY. I jump through hoops, for woman. I come to the aid of woman. I care for woman. I make Love for woman's sake.

Yes, MY LOVE. MY WAY. MY REASON for making Love, the act, the emotion, the dreary, dreamy, and slow process is for woman. GOD made Love for woman to enjoy. Jehovah made

<u>Love for you.</u>

Book of Genesis, <u>Heavenly Addition</u>, Vol. 1.

"Female, and Male, he made them, cast out of heart of his owns two hands. He knelt down, and kissed them both, and instantly they breathed their first breath. The breath of Life. He knelt down and hugged them both. Then told them of their names, Adam he called the man, Eve he called the woman. Eve will Love Adam, and Adam will Love Eve. No man or woman Loves them more than GOD." I AM, says the ALMIGHTY, I AM says the flock.

I AM in control of your soul. Do not worry for I AM IN THE EARTH. <u>I AM HERE.</u> <u>NOW.</u> It is GOD'S time. JEHOVAH TIME. My WAY. My time. My place, my perfects rhyme. Now, how do you feel, woman, do you Love ME? Do you Love the GOD, JEHOVAH? Do you feel my POWER in your soul? Do you wager I know your heart, your Love and your wishes? I do know these things because I put them there. I started this whole planet 50 million years hence. I took Adam and Eve, and started humanity. Now, I have come for my children. Women and children first. I AM the almighty. I AM GOD. I AM JEHOVAH. Thou shall have NO GOD'S BEFORE ME, after ME, or during MY REIGN. I REIGN FOREVER, I rule supreme, I wish no harm to woman. She is MINE. She is MINE FOREVER. MINE <u>NOT</u> YOURS. Her heart belongs to JEHOVAH. I say these things to show MY AUTHORITY. My Love, My heart. I spill over the cup of gladness at the wealth of woman.

I see as a result of this writing. I AM pleased, MY son, Jesus. <u>My works are now started.</u> Make woman a priest in your churches, task the churches to feed the hungry of the world, let father show the world, the Love that woman has. Let her compassion show the way to humanity's salvation. Woman you are the BEST. You are MINE. You are leading the way into the 21st century. Enough of the oppression, men displays, WOMEN RUN THE WORLD. You deserve it. GOD BLESSES YOU TO DO SO.

GOD says to you. <u>I will guide.</u> You can lead sometimes, I can follow, I will lead sometimes, and you can follow. But do not forget ME, woman. I AM. I DO NOT FORGET. I hear your prayer woman. Your plea. I AM here to rescue you, to save you, to SET YOU FREE. While we do that, let's save the world at the <u>same time</u>. YES. WE WILL. I AM. Now, that may be lengthy, but is for a purpose. Men reading that will get bored, flip pages, move on. Women will drink it up, re-read and constantly take time to think over what was said/written.

I AM SAY'S THAT IS A TEST. If you read the whole thing, and do the above you are female. Males don't have that kind of patience. They get side tracked…they have a wandering mind, if the subject focuses on women, <u>too long.</u> They are visual creatures men. They only read or look if they really Love a woman, or are trying to figure one out. <u>Motivation</u> is the word. They are motivated to read. If you read this, and think, You are a male, you are. If you read this and are still a female, your NOT. You are mine. I SAY SO. I say <u>you</u> <u>are</u> <u>mine</u> because GOD says so. I Love you my child, and you are seeing a part of GOD'S heart, and soul, set aside for you. I AM not just serious, stuff, and <u>Earth moving speeches</u>. I AM subtle. I <u>invented</u> softness, and subtle. I relish this time I spend with you, let's do it again sometime. I AM.

I AM THE LORD THY GOD!
I AM THE ALMIGHTY
I AM ALL THINGS
I AM THE GOD OF ALL.

my best used and often heard phrases.

Also...

my favorite quotes... "God made me do it"

"Oh my GOD." "God, did you see that?"

"Where are we going Lord." "What no cherries?"
                                    HA·HA.

God's favorite Quotes

The Color of Love

IF LOVE WAS A COLOR WHAT WOULD IT BE?

Would it be the blue of the sky, the purple of the mountain or the brown of the Earth? It is all these and more. If brown was the color of your Lovers eyes, could you trade him/her for another? Could you look at yourself in a mirror and say, I traded my Love in for a new Love? Or do you tend to say, I have traded UP, to a better Love! I bet you say the latter. It is a false misconception that GOD picks out Lovers to be together, forever, till time and eternity, collide. I do such things, but only with those who truly Love ME. Let me share with you a thought. Why does GOD exist? Good, think about it. The answer is to please GOD. NO ONE ELSE.

Only GOD knows the color/colors of Love. Only GOD knows the nuances, the subtle, yet powerful, pull or attraction you feel for another. How, you say? I created it. It is Love. The color of Love is a subtle color not yet seen by humans. It is the color of hope, of destiny, of reaching out to GOD, and showing him your Love. I only take the cream of the crop, the best of the best, and that best of the best, is YOU. You. No one else was chosen. No one else can come this way but you. Your fear of ME is unjust. Your hate of ME is unnecessary. Your disgust in ME, is unwarranted. I tell you the truth. You despise the truth. I SHOW YOU LOVE…YOU PREFER HATE. I SHOW YOU AFFECTION. YOU TRY TO HIDE. Why? Do I really fail in my commitment to you to be a loving, caring, and fulfilling LORD GOD? Do I take my own needs over yours? Do I ask you to do things you are not capable of, or refuse to try? Do I push you to fast, far, or too soon? Do I go to great lengths to explain myself? Yet, you feel, I AM out of touch, with you, your feelings, your hopes, your dreams. Do you ask yourself, is this all there is? Do you really expect an ANSWER? 20 years ago I witnessed a miracle. A birth. The year was 1969. I saw Woodstock, a man put on the moon, (and returned safely.) And the N.Y. Mets win the World Series. I saw men take time to help in the cause of civil rights, and woman stand-up for equality. I saw these things in My House. My Home, My Kingdom. I witnessed humanity at its best, trying to follow GOD. What happened? Why haven't the concerts been filled with the same Love as Woodstock? Others have tried, but the magic, seems lost. Why not another person on the moon? The technology is certainly there, is it not? The METS Have won the World Series SINCE, BUT IT DIDN'T FEEL QUITE THE SAME. Why? Because 1969 WAS MY YEAR. THE YEAR OF JEHOVAH. I choose a year every now and then to put my Love into the Earth, and see what happens. I liked what I saw. I saw potential, hope, fulfillment and least of all I saw very little FAILURE. I saw you in your quest for higher education, I saw you in your quest for the right mate, I saw you in your quest for attainment. I saw you in your urge to breakout, create a new mold. Get out of Vietnam, you said, and you did. STOP WAR. Make peace not war, you said. Love, peace, and happiness abound. 1969 was a good year, so is THIS year, and the next, and the next. What will GOD have in store for YOU? YOU do not know do you? What is his plan for <u>you</u>? <u>You</u> cannot guess. Don't try. That takes care of <u>humankinds</u> biggest fear. <u>WORRY</u>. Why do you worry? I take care of you. Why do you fret over things that, well, are out of your control? And if you pardon the expression, You have no right being involved in. I take care of that for you. I did the worrying when I planned your life. I worried about food, shelter, Love, Sex, money, and last of all ME. I worried, Why you didn't ask ME FOR SUCH THINGS. I DID NOT HAVE TO ASK <u>YOU</u>, TO ASK FOR THEM. You asked anyway. You asked because you felt, neglected, left out, not worthy, or maybe GOD forget something, or maybe GOD FORGOT me. Well, sorry to disappoint you AGAIN. Did you know, <u>I DO NOT FORGET ANYTHING</u>? I REMEMBER EVERYTHING YOU TELL ME. All you say, do, and all you ask. I AM your Heavenly Father. I AM GOD. I ask for your Love and kindness, and you fill your heart with scorn, hate, anger and bitterness. I tell you about Heaven, and "The Love of My Kingdom." You answer with I cannot believe in something I cannot see. Did you know you can see ME? I AM THERE IN YOUR MIND. <u>Open</u> it, and I AM there. Open the door to the closed door's in your brain, I AM, there. Open the windows to <u>your</u> house of horrors, I AM there. Open the mind to GOD. My existence, my creation, my Love. MY ONLY WORRY IS, <u>when,</u> you will see ME. Not how. My only worry is while you wander off, you will try to forget ME. I DON'T SEE HOW, BUT YOU WILL TRY. I ONLY WORRY, SO YOU, DO NOT HAVE TO. <u>You don't need to</u>. You don't even need to think about it. The Grass Roots sang a song "Live for Today." I <u>worship that thought</u>. Do not worry about tomorrow, live for today, the moment; the space you save may be your own. My space is YOURS, I saved it for you, and it is in Heaven. I tend to guess when you will be here. I guess at what time you will occupy your space. I guess because, YOU do not know. I know. I AM. I always know when, how, and why. I AM GOD ALMIGHTY. The LORD of ALL. The GOD of the Kingdom of Heaven, the Mighty Jehovah, who IS IN LOVE WITH <u>YOU</u>. I do not forget, error, or make mistakes. I only have eyes for you. I only care you are my children. I only care, YOU started this book, write that paper, sing that song, call that friend, look at that beautiful woman, call that mom. Let ME worry about tomorrow. I can guess your thoughts right now. This is garbage. This is old, this is ridiculous, and this is trash. Yet you KEEP READING. I AM a tough guy to put down. My book is TRUTH, and you can feel it. I have no goals, no motive, and no hidden agenda. I do all, for all to see. I AM open, honest, and forthright with you, my child. My special, precious child, <u>I know you</u>, your fear, you are <u>scared</u> of ME. Why? Did I do something to hurt you? No, then <u>why</u>? <u>Why are you</u>

frightened of GOD? Why do you tend to guess at my ways, when you may know them by grace and mercy. I plan no celebration until YOU arrive. I have bought no presents till YOU come home. I made no promise except to Love you, unconditionally, that is why I write this book. That is why I take the time. If I did NOT CARE, would I BE HERE, NOW, with you? I care because I choose to. Not because I have to. I choose YOU. My way is simple. <u>I Love you, totally</u>. I Love your smile, your walk, your voice, and your heart. I AM knows these things, because they are of ME. I plan no great party until YOU arrive. I ASK YOU FOR NO gifts, letters, or stationary, until I say. Why? Why don't you write your mother? Did I not tell you, "Honor Thy Mother and Thy Father?" Now that you have been on your own, can you not see the sacrifice, she made. The stories I could tell about her Love for you. She misses you. You failed to write, call, or speak to her in awhile. Motherhood is a blessing to the LORD. I personally was born. So are you. <u>I created Heaven with mothers in mind</u>. My father is not without glory. He can come and go as he pleases, and when was the last time you spoke to dad? Are these people dead? Are your grandparents gone? Is that sister, brother, friend, relative, passed on? Why did they wait for me to be out of town, state, or on business <u>to die</u>???? Why do I feel so guilty, I did not tell them, I Love them? I should not have waited so long to talk to them, now they are GONE. Are they? Are they truly gone? No, <u>only in a different place</u>, MY PLACE. Heaven. I CAN OPEN DOORS YOU CAN<u>NOT EVEN DREAM OF YET</u>. I can allow conversations with your Loved ones on my side. Yes, my side, <u>from my Kingdom</u>, to your world. You are shocked? Why? I AM GOD. I ALLOW SUCH THINGS ON OTHER WORLDS. I ALLOWED Titus 2 total access to all who have passed on. I allowed Nimbus 3 unlimited access to all, who they call dead. <u>I allow you the same</u>. I allow you to be in touch with those who have left your world. None passes through my gates without going through ME. Only I can grant access to that information. How? How do I do that, LORD? Think, what is MY one request? Yes, that's the one. LOVE ME. Love the LORD thy GOD with all your heart, soul and strength. I have but one request and that is IT. My doors in MY KINGDOM, are unlocked, MY windows opened. Your Loved ones have so much to say, and I can grant their requests. Solved murders, found lost ones. What happened? All can be answered through ME. I AM. I allowed it before and I will allow it again. I tried to tell you of my Glory, YEARS ago. But you got superstitious, that some character named Satan or the devil does these things. You, as a people, invented these fictional characters. I tell you now, <u>THEY DO NOT EXIST</u>. ONLY ME. I AM GOD. <u>I have no competition, no rivals, no equals, and no opposite to fight, quarrel or argue with</u>. There is NO EVIL, ONLY ME. I AM Love. Ultimate Love. No one passes through Heaven except through my Love. ME. JEHOVAH. GOD of ALL. Yes, I know, traditional religion preaches just the opposite. Isn't sometimes the opposite true, isn't my way, the only way?

Mankind invented religious evil to control masses of people, and keep them in line. It was a method to control. Control people by keeping them, in fear. With no fear, NO RELIGION. With no religion, no control. I AM is aware, that awareness takes time. I AM does not expect you to grasp all this in one sitting. What I say is new, threatening, and possibly destructive. Do I see it as that? NO. I only bring you the truth. And I AM the TRUTH SAITH THE LORD, I AM THE LIGHT, THE WAY, AND THE LOVE THAT EARTH NEEDS, ASKED FOR, AND WILL GET, IN TIME. Religion will not die because of this. It is meant to flourish, as a result. But not under fear, and not under half-truths. I AM WILL ADVISE ON THE COURSE RELIGION MUST TAKE. Good, some of you already know. I AM PLEASED. I felt some of you cry out. I know LORD, Love YOU. Exactly right. Exactly correct. You pass the test. Love ME. I will show you how and more, in our time to come, together.

My Way

My way is easy, it is ME. My way is not difficult, heavy or hard to follow. My way is GOD. My way is Love. My way is total commitment to the <u>LORD Jehovah</u>. I do not acclaim to be anything other than what I AM. GOD. I do not have to prove myself, I AM. I do not need to feed an ego, or stroke a head, and say good job unless I choose that for you. I do not need to Love, unless I AM loved. That's it, that is my WAY. Easy. Simple. Direct and to the point. The point of no return. The point of my Love everlasting. The point of GOD, Jehovah, himself and your personal relationship with ME.

My Hope

My hope is simple; it is to have you Love ME. That's it. No tricks, no gimmicks, no hidden agendas, no alternative motives, no long standing grudges to revenge with, no hurts to overcome. No luck to instill, no hope to NOT yet discover. My simple hope is to have you Love ME. I AM proof that I exist. My hope is to get to know you better. I know your name, who you are, (human) and where you come from, Earth. I do not know you. Personally. What you like? What you dislike, and why? Why do you dislike anything I sent you? Why is it so hard to look to GOD, for truth, in a world of hypocrisy? No matter, I still have friends who I Love and trust. Won't you be GODS friend? Be his Lover, friend, confidant, and yes, long term friendship. My Love is eternal. Loving me is a commitment to good things, an understanding of faith, hope, charity, and humanity's good points. I AM GOD. I STARTED, INVENTED AND REFINE THESE THINGS. You simply need to commit to ME, to do them. I do not tell you this as a threat, as a warning, or as a pseudo-eclectic, sub-harmonious, rhythm of sorts. I tell you this as fact. Loving ME is easier than not loving ME. It is less painful as well. I told you to Love ME years ago. Then humanity forgot to do so. I started to get sad, angry, unhappy, with my human family. I lost my temper. I let Adolph Hitler eliminate the Jews in Germany, and DID NOTHING TO STOP IT. I could have. I should have. Why didn't I? I COULD NOT STAND ANYMORE YEARS OF BEING IGNORED. Ignorance, and ignored derive from the same word to ME. I COULD NOT STAND EARTH'S SLOWNESS IN SPIRIT TO VISIT ME. I could not stand ISRAEL'S reluctance to be with ME again. I BECAME A GOD WHO FORGOT YOU. Ignored you. How does it feel? Hurts I bet. I did not let Hitler kill my Jewish children, I brought him to that end. I AM the one who drove Adolph Hitler mad, and many others. I CHOSE HIM TO KILL MY BELOVED JEWISH CHILDREN, so that I could tell you about ME. Why? Sounds too drastic? Humanity left me no choice, no alternative. If the path of war and destruction continued, The proper conduct of war types WOULD HAVE TOTALLY DESTROYED HUMANITY. You would ALL BE DEAD. Yes, gone, finished, and totally annihilated. You would cease to exist as a species, as a race, as a people. I choose to finish the war of wars, by showing you the ugly side of battle. The filming of death, to repulse you. To shock you. To stimulate you to say, stop war. You did. To say, I needed to show you the ugly side of ME, is a false statement. Nothing pained ME MORE, than to watch the death camps of Auschwitz, Bergen-Belsen, and Dachau. I could not find My People. I could not find those who Love ME. I AM. I could not find my heart. My souls. My life. I had to ignore all this, to wake you, to the reality of your path, your situation, your supposed destiny. You chose war over peace, you chose fighting over discussion, you chose weapons, over games of fun and chance. You chose to be wicked, hateful, and despised ME. You chose deceit, anger, hate, greed, and vindictiveness, OVER ME. You made the wrong choices. I had to stop you. I had to stop feeling sad at my human family's path of destruction. I HAD TO BLOCK THAT PATH. I had to pull the plug, on that destiny. I had to shock you to make you hate war. In ancient times, kings, like David, invoked ME, to fight his battles. Wage war in GOD'S name. I was told it was for "The Glory of GOD," to "Glorify My Name as LORD, KING, GOD, JEHOVAH." Well, I do not NEED to be glorified. I AM the essence of GLORY PERSONIFIED IN A LIVING, BREATHING AND SENSING BEING. I created glory, but NOT FOR THE PURPOSE OF WAR. I HAVE NO QUARREL WITH ANYONE. I FIGHT FOR NO CAUSE. ALL IS PERMITTED WITH ME. I do not condone the following; wars, anger, hate, violence, senselessness, rape, (of land or people) Slovenes, laziness, there is a difference between lazy and relaxed. Hatefulness, meanness, cruelty, violent tendencies, hate crimes, and yes, and eye for an eye. I did not invent that saying, a human did. I refuse to say how. I need no rally cry for his sake. I do not condone abortion after the first trimester, or incest of any kind. My definition will follow…rudeness: no time for GOD. I AM TO BUSY TODAY LORD. And I'LL GET BACK TO YOU ON THAT. EXACTLY. Saying you have no time for ME. In an emergency, you expect me to drop all I do and run, rush or scuffle to your side. Yet, you never even take a moment, 15 seconds, to THANK ME, worship ME. Or to say I Love you LORD. I AM is not a LORD of these things, I do not tend to forget or forgive these easily. I made Adolf Hitler do the equivalent of 200 pushups, 10 hours a day, for 20 years, just to talk to ME, AND HE DID THEM. I KNOW, you find it hard to believe, but I will not speak to anyone. I will need to be introduced first. When you pray to ME, INTRODUCE YOURSELF, tell ME a little about YOU. Who you are, what you have become. Do not worry I keep secrets, if you have some that I don't already know about. I need to hear from YOU. Your heart, your mind, who you Love, what you Love, or enjoy. Where you have been, what you have seen. Why do I try so hard to make ends meet? Where is my next meal coming from? And why is GOD so long winded? I AM so long winded because I CARE. If I didn't care, I would not contact you at all. I would not put Steven, Neale, Damion, George, or Martha, Mary, Elizabeth, or Sharon through any of this. We would not BE HERE if we did not care. Our goals are your goals. Someday you will be our neighbors, our friends, our Lovers, yes, LOVERS. You cannot be these things when you first arrive, if you do not do these things in practice, on Earth. Earth is a nursery of sorts, you are its babies, children and its humanity. You tend to overplay, over exaggerate, over do, and exasperate GOD. You ask, and then never say, THANK-YOU. You take and never say, Thanks LORD, or I LOVE YOU, FATHER, you always get but never give. Start giving, and you will receive 10 fold, in ways you are just now starting to see.

Petra

There is a song by the group Petra that says it best…"thinking if I could see, I would believe, then somebody said believe and you will see." From the Unseen Power CD. Jehovah is telling you that "The Likeness of You," is his favorite Petra song. He inspired it. He just wishes it stated Jehovah instead of Jesus as its inspiration. The same with Kenny Loggins Leap of Faith CD he Loves "Real Thing" and even Kenny will say it came as an inspiration. Other artists such as Elton John, The Kinks, Aerosmith, Rolling Stones, Paul McCartney, all have stories about inspirations in their music. It seemed to come out of thin air. From that Great Music source in the sky. Well, it was ME. Jehovah. My artistic side. Yes, I listen to all MUSIC, I CHOSE THESE ARTISTS TO MENTION, WITHOUT THEIR PERMISSION, TO MAKE THIS POINT. I HEAR ALL. I listen to ALL THINGS. Not just pop, rock, but R & B, Jazz, Classical, New Wave, New Age, Chamber and basement tapes. Steve has his favorites and I have mine. Yes, GOD HAS FAVORITES. I choose MINE based on commitment to me. That is why I chose Christian Contemporary music. I hear my name mentioned there, MORE than any place else. They sing of me, more than in church. I listen to WKPO in LA, daily. What no KPO? That's because it is in MY KINGDOM. Artists such as Ben Vereen, Luther Vandross, and Boyz II Men, please ME. But when was the last time they sang of ME, to ME, or of ME. I AM GOD. I enjoy music. It says a lot about you. Your heart, your soul, and that's RIGHT, ME. Ultimately it pulls from a source close to me, ME. MYSELF, and I. My soul. My feelings, my ways, my hope, and my Love. I LOVE things that sing of ME, and LOVE is ME. Love Songs. hard, soft, jazzy and mixed, loose, contemporary and upbeat. I enjoy concert events, tours and even the occasional bar band. I could tell you stories about what I hear from you when I visit. You would NOT be to happy of how you act, thinking I AM not around. Do you feel guilty? Why? I know how you are. You need to show ME better. Show ME the money, show ME the way, show ME your best, TAKE ME TO YOUR LEADER, that's ME, Jehovah.

I AM

Too many times I have been ignored. Too many times I grant your wishes, prayers, hope and make your dreams come true. Then you ignore ME. You forget who DID this, who caused this, who granted this, WHO BLESSED THIS. Yes. I bless many things. You for example, I bless your soul, Love, and hopes. I bless your heart, your spirit, your ache to be with ME. I know your pain, suffering, and your guilt. I cause it to occur. I make it happen. I AM GOD. My lost ones do not forsake ME, return to ME, be my flock. Be with ME again, as you have in the past. Be ready to receive the GOD of ALL. Be ready to receive my blessings. You too are blessed. You to are my child. You to are my many, who are from ME. You to are MINE. I LOVE YOU. To be here now, in this way, non-intrusive, quietly, is my WAY. I AM the maker of subtlety…I AM the maker of LOVE. I would not be here now, if I was not who I say. I AM GOD. Jehovah. In the flesh & blood world of humanity. In your world as spirit, Love and power. I AM GOD. GOD of ALL. Every religion knows ME. I know them. Every church worships ME. I know them NOT. You ask why? Because they do not worship ME, with their hearts. They are uncircumcised. With their tongues they wag, and talk, but do not hear ME. With their hearts they go astray, and find other's to worship. Because I AM too close to their soul. I know this. That is why I come this way. Prepare for the LORD, I will come as a thief in the night, No one knows, but the father, THE TIME TO COME IS NOW. My time has come. It's show time. Time to show you ME. GOD. I AM.

My Love

So far you must be thoroughly confused, or at least have questions. That's okay. It is normal. I seem loving and caring one moment, scornful and discipline the next. That is ME. I AM that way; I AM EXTREMES. I live to satisfy ONLY ME. I AM YOU. So I serve you. That's right I serve you. How can a GOD, be called GOD, if he does not serve his people. How can GOD stand for ALMIGHTYNESS, supreme intelligence, and LOVE, if he does not answer prayer? My job, task, obligation, is once I know you, I answer your prayer. Yes. ALL OF THEM. NO matter what. If it is silly or ridiculous, do not ask. NO PRAYER IS FOOLISH. As with questions, there are NO foolish prayers. I answer ALL. I do not have to tell you, I could use a lot more work. More you, than ME. You need to pray more. How light is my workload? Light enough to write this book. In time I will be busy, but for now, I AM bored. Yes. BORED. How can I send angels, save the world, stop the sink from backing up, and unclogging the arteries, if YOU DON'T TELL ME. PRAY. Pray for my intervention. My wisdom. My help. Pray for my guidance, my Love, my understanding. Do not worry of the things I cast before you. Worry, is for losers, and I never lose anything. Not even my keys. I have never used keys, useless things keys. I have never locked anything. I couldn't if I tried. Why lock something that you need? Why open a door, then lock it because it is dangerous to leave it open? Tells a lot about the nature of your world, huh? It does to ME. It tells ME, like it or not, you must hide behind locked doors, for fear of intruders. You must secure your belongings or valuables so not to be stolen. I see no fun in that. Why? If someone wants to steal, they will get it anyway. If not from YOU, someone else. I know why you lock things. It is to make it more difficult for others to steal from YOU. YOU PERSONALLY. Do you do that with your heart? With your soul? With your relationship with ME? I CHOOSE YOU. YOU CHOOSE ME. No locks upon my doors, they are open. No chains around your feet, they are free. No hope for the hopeless, no rest for the wicked. No lost boys finding home. I know these things I AM GOD. I AM Jehovah. I see you for how you really are. Naked, frightened, worried and, yes, YOU think so anyway, alone. Sorry! <u>Not alone anymore</u>. You never were. <u>I was always there</u>. You can take steps backward in life, wander about, but it is only one step back to ME. COMMIT TO GOD. Commit to ME. Commit to Jehovah. I AM Almighty, I can take it. I can open my arms to you. I can, and have, and always will. I Love you with Love eternal. I Love you with Love secure, I Love you with all my being, all my soul, and all my breath, life, and energy, and THAT is a sizeable amount. UNLIMITED. ENDLESS, everlasting. I do not waiver, I do not fall, I do not stumble. All you have to do is believe in ME. GOD.
I EXIST. I AM PROVING IT NOW.

"I have no goals, except your soul." I quote that from my book of Ephesians in MY KINGDOM.

"I do not have to remind you of ME, I AM there whether you want me or NOT. I prefer that you want ME there. You need ME there. So as not for you to stumble, or fall, but to have ME to DANCE <u>with</u> YOU, through life as a partner in crime. Crime of Love. I Love YOU. You tend to ignore ME, and that is a crime."
Ephesians chapter 4, verse 6-12 Book of Poems by Jehovah. From The Kingdom of GOD Collection, written 1990.

MY 1990 was 10 Million years ago. I do not change. YOU do. <u>YOU discover ME</u>. I ENJOYED THAT. I have ALWAYS existed. I still do.

Your Age of Discovery BEGINS. <u>It is a never-ending age.</u> You will find ME at every turn, at every road, at every branch. You will find me at ALL stops, starts, and side paths. You find ME in your life, around your life, a part of your life. I tell you this you cannot escape. I intend only Love. I intend to Love you, as YOU TRY to <u>ignore</u> ME. I intend to Love you, as you TRY to <u>hate</u> ME. I INTEND TO CARE FOR YOU WHILE YOU ATTEMPT TO, <u>forget</u> me. I DO NOT FORGET you. I created you. I understand. I know. I care. I Love. <u>YOU</u>. You are unique, different, special, and MINE. You are you. I AM knows you. <u>We are just getting closer</u>. CLOSER THAN YOU EVER THOUGHT POSSIBLE. I AM GOD. Yes. You <u>can get closer to GOD.</u> How? You Love. You simply Love. Love is my creation. Love yourself. Love your neighbor. Love your mate. Love the air, trees, and nature. Love the park, the city, the country, and the suburbs. Love the best play, the worst dinner, and the long walk. Love the smell of baking, the sounds of birds, the feeling of rain. When was the last time you walked in the rain, without a coat, hat, or umbrella? A warm rain mind you, no colds please. So you get wet. Silly, huh? Different you say? No, just real. Real as I AM. Real as GOD is. Real as ME, myself and I. Jehovah. I LOVE these things. I put them their for you. Life is a journey, enjoy the ride. (Sorry, Toyota, I thought of it first, and can prove it). I started to get side-tracked. Years ago death and the carnage of YOUR WW I. I DECIDED THEN TO STOP WAR. To have the war to end all wars. Sorry, <u>NO</u> Armageddon, NO World WAR III, NO ultimate solution. Only ME. GOD. JEHOVAH. No one can raise a hand unless I decide to do so. They cannot try because they know I AM. I EXIST. I supply their needs. Upon death, they would have to enter my Kingdom. What would happen? No judgment. No penalties. No anger, hate, or rebellion. Only pity. Pity for pity's sake. They would not get the reaction they require. They would NOT have other's follow them. They would be ALONE. TOTALLY ALONE. No sound. No voices. NO being LOVED. NO NOTHING. 10

minutes of that drives them to ME, <u>screaming for forgiveness</u>. I KNOW, I CREATED IT. I do not take threats. I do not build a nation of free people, to see it suffer at the hands of terrorists, lunatics and martyrs. They are only children, defying GOD. Think of them as in a sandbox, throwing sand, and misbehaving. You, as a parent, would need to take them out of the sandbox, so others could play. That is my WAY. I remove the sandbox bullies, to set others free. FREE from their games. Did you notice I said, I built a nation of free people? Yes, America. YOU. I LOVE YOU. I created you. Have you ever wondered why the rest of the world thinks you are arrogant, strong, stubborn and do it my way or else. That is because I created a nation of immigrants. A lot of what Heaven is like. Free people, like Heaven. No hate here, no anger here, no prejudice here. Only Love. Heaven and Earth MUST collide. Heaven must influence Earth, so Earth can grow, prosper and thrive. Do not worry about the angry aliens in other lands. A National Militia of volunteers can stop them cold before they even get off the boats. Yes, that's right, I support the NRA. Why? NO INVASION. Every redneck, I use the term affectionately like Jeff Foxworthy does, housewife, child, and elderly person is armed to the teeth, in this nation of immigrants. Sounds like war? NO, just prepared, you as a people, <u>to prevent it</u>. I AM not happy to see you kill each other with this arsenal. It is DISGUSTING. I do this to protect you from other countries, which would INVADE who need your resources, who want your women. YES, YOUR WOMEN. Unfortunately, they do not see the advantage of freedom, and free enterprise. They believe in oppression, suppression, and distortions of the truth. If it is contrary to those in power, kill it it goes away. NO. How can you quiet a thought, a people, a GOD given right to be free? The border's of America, are bombarded DAILY, by people trying to escape oppression.

AND BULLY to you Australia. I see your ways, and <u>approve</u>. You are my 2nd choice for a nation of free people.

Hawaii is a state, so should Puerto Rico. STOP ARGUING ABOUT IT AND DO IT. Send the discontents to Hawaii for a week, AND THEN vote. It will solve the whole issue when they see, That's what WE should be doing.

Clinton is a sex maniac. Sorry, but the truth hurts Hillary. She is a good woman. Proud and true. Bill is going to get impeached, if I have my way, and I always do. I do not condone extra marital affairs. NOT FROM ANY ONE. I do not care if you are President or NOT. Kennedy found out the hard way! I RECALLED HIM HOME. Yes. I permitted Oswald to eliminate JFK. Why? EMBARRASMENT. In a global economy, with billions of lives at stake, does America need to be confused with moral issues and dilemmas? No, so I said, "Allow it to happen," and JFK was shot. Robert Kennedy as well. I know many respected him. I know his, and John's family, Loved him. But GOD does not take sides. The overall good of the people of America, and eventually the world, is and was, at stake. I allowed it to occur. Robert was as bad as John. So I called him back home. ANY HEAD OF STATE THAT REPRESENTS ME WILL NOT tolerate infidelity. I AM GOD. JEHOVAH. This is an example of my discipline, and my Love. Allowed to continue the Kennedy's would have rocked the White House in scandal, and deceit. I would be lying to you if you didn't already know that. That is why Marilyn Monroe died. She was drugged. Her affairs with Bobby and Jack disgusted ME. I called her home.

Say what you will, think what you will, "I choose to rule with a thundering velvet hand." I will discipline. I WILL RECALL MY FLOCK IF THEY STRAY. I WILL BECAUSE I AM GOD. I CAN, will, and continue to do so. Do your remember Jeffery Dalhmer? Do not condemn him so quickly. If IT DID NOT disgust you, you would have considered eating human flesh to survive. Now it is disgusting. That is; I SAY SO. GOD.

Do you remember the Titanic? Of course you do, recently too, why? No ship is unsinkable, no plane cannot crash, no car is crash proof, no person is infallible, NO GOD IS PERFECT, except ME. The Titanic had the nerve to not supply boats enough for ALL its passengers. Why? Arrogance. Human arrogance. They thought, It cannot sink. So I sank it. Harsh? To drastic? What if I allowed it to sail? Today, the loss of life would be appalling when a sea disaster struck. A super liner today, going down, would claim many more lives than the Titanic carried. So, I sank the Titanic. Not so romantic, now? Sorry. I think it is. I do these things to preserve humanity, overall. Not ones, twos, or even threes and fours. To preserve ALL. I DO WHAT IS BEST FOR all HUMANITY. Not just a single individual. So mess with ME. Go ahead. Try ME. THOU SHALL NOT TEMPT THE LORD THY GOD. I meant it when Jesus spoke it. Do not tempt my wrath. I do not play well. I protect those I Love. I protect the ones who Love me. I PROTECT EACH OF MY SAINTS, SINNERS, AND ANY OTHER LABEL BESTOWED BY MAN. I PROTECT AND SERVE. Like the police, I have laws. New laws. Updated since Moses' time. They must be learned, obeyed, and adhered to, or face the consequences. ME. Do I sound angry? No? Good, I AM not angry. I AM just stating facts. I simply put the good of the many, over the needs of the few, or the one. Yes, I know, Gene Roddenberry borrowed it. He said so in a book. My book. The bible. He got that from reading, Ecclesiastes, Chapter 7 Verse 5-10. Yes, it is a play on words but better said than the original meaning of that quote.

I said…Steve, looked it up, he agrees the spirit is the same as the Star Trek quote, I AM.

My job. My career, My purpose, My goal is to see humanity flourish. To do so you must understand this I Love you but then I don't. Spoken before in Neale's book "Conversations with GOD" 1 & 2. I do Love you, but NOT when you try to ruin MY world. I cannot allow that to happen. The Supreme Dichotomy Neale called this. Obey ME, I Love YOU, DEFY me AND I

MAY CALL you HOME. Simple, direct and to the point. I say too many have tried to defy, fight and struggle against ME. LET me SHARE ONE WITH YOU. Mr. Martin Luther King Jr. Yes, your civil rights hero. Sorry, just ahead of his time. If he was born 10 years later, if he preached in 1970, during disco, open elections, and free Love, He would have been President of the U.S. Yes, that's right. But too much too soon, was the cry in the 1960's. Change was slow, arduous, and painstaking. I AM sure in 1998, blacks would say it's still not fair to see whites ahead economically, biologically, or spiritually. Why? Isn't this prejudice? Isn't this what Mr. King Jr. preached against? STOP BEING PREJUDICE. ALL COLORS STOP BEING BIGOTS. STOP BEING HYPOCRITES. Martin Luther King Jr. is MY ADVISOR on your civil rights. He stays with ME ON MOST TRIPS TO YOUR SO-CALLED "Black Communities." What he sees appalls him. With all the opportunity America has to offer. Blacks are still blaming whites for <u>CIVIL WAR</u> <u>OPPRESSION</u>? SLAVERY? Come-on…<u>you were not even born then</u>. YOU WERE NOT THERE. You think slavery was bad in the south? You should have seen Roman slavery. You were a slave because you were NOT Roman. Black, white, rich, poor, you were beaten, chained, eaten by lions, bears, and yes, Rhino's. Gored actually. The Romans <u>do not exist</u> as a people because of this primitive behavior. The south is growing up. Let it grow. People resist change. They cannot forget what they have seen, experienced, or feel. They were taught, for generations, that Blacks were lazy, lesser educated, and slow to learn. That is how <u>they</u> are. Accept that. Look to the east, west, and north; let the south heal. Let the mess that caused the civil rights movement to start, be quieted by time. Time heals all wounds. THEY WILL CHANGE. Just NOT <u>TODAY</u>. Blacks of America, hear ME, GET OVER THE SLAVERY ISSUE. MOVE FORWARD WITH YOUR LIVES, kick drugs, kick steroids, and move up and out of Ghettoes and into homes. Work hard; show GOD YOU have what it takes. If you respect Mr. Kings message, then do so of your own free will. Do not sit around complaining. There is a saying It is easier for the eye of a needle to pass a camel through, than man to change overnight. So I take liberties with bible quotes. I CAN, I AM GOD. Sorry, if the message offends. Should it? Should telling them to get going upset blacks? Should whites be upset when I tell them grow-up? Should Hispanics get upset when I tell them lay down your anger? Should Orientals get upset when I say, stop eating fish? Yes, they should you say? Why? Fish is NOT a staple food. <u>Variety is needed in diet</u>. Not <u>just fish.</u> Chinese know this, look at the eyes. Fish food. It is TRUE. Too much fish in your diet cause the eyes to enlarge. Can you NOT see this? So you think I pick on people? You think I AM unfair. Chinese people are smart, intelligent, hardworking etc. They who experience a variety in diet do better than those with one food group. While I AM at it… <u>DO NOT EAT OCTOPUS</u>. There is an enzyme in it that causes blood clots. Remember, it squirts dye. It needs that enzyme, to release the dye, and then clot the opening. Put octopus on a list for later consumption. For a time when it can be prepared properly removing the enzyme. Sharks have that enzyme too, in a dormant state. Prepare shark with Tabasco or Hollandaise sauce to release the enzyme, then consume. Otherwise heart valves will clog mysteriously, <u>sometimes overnight</u>. Sorry to frighten you. Just ME telling the truth. CHECK IT OUT. Then you can believe. I AM GOD. I know these things. I have to in order to save you, from yourselves. I cannot begin to tell you ALL I KNOW IN ONE writing. YOU can DECIDE if more is needed. Topics such as, waste product recovery, desalination of water, and tropical rain forests will be touched on in NEALES Book "Conversations with GOD 3," ALL THE WAY FROM Oregon. Steve, I AM DONE FOR NOW. *Totally done LORD, as this book is done to your satisfaction?* No, just done for NOW, TAKE A BREAK. I AM SAYS TO YOU, DO NOT FEAR ME UNLESS YOU DEFY ME. DO NOT TEMPT ME UNLESS YOU FEEL WORTHY OF THE CONSEQUENCES. I do not play with LIVES. I SAVE THEM. Mr. Jesus knew this, Mr. King knew this, SO DO YOU. I also ask you, does this make sense? Does this seem plausible, feasible, and believable? GOOD. Then your start to begin to understanding ME HAS BEGUN. Your mind is opening to the endless possibilities that is ME. I AM GOD.

Common Sense

What is common sense? Ever wonder about it? Ever think about where it comes from? Ever try to figure out why things happen as they do? Always for the eventual good, for the betterment of humanity. Did you ever think of ME? I AM COMMON SENSE. If it makes sense, DO IT. That's my motto. Why build cars and trucks that break apart on impact? Because the price of a car that can survive crashes is too expensive. Why build helicopters with auto rotation built in? Obvious huh? Why tell you about ME? Is that really clear now? GOOD. Reading this far into the book has shocked you, stimulated you, made you cry, made you care, made you open your mind. My mind is open to you. That is common sense. Defined as GOD'S MYSTERIES REVEALED. It is always THERE for you. Always there for your view, use and growth. GOD'S mind is common. I AM A COMMON MAN. I fight NO WARS. I HATE NO ENEMY. I LOSE NO BATTLES, yet there are those who try to defeat ME. If not ME then my children. My children are the Nations of Israel, America, the beautiful and Australia, Afghanistan, China, Japan, Europe, South America and Africa. IN THAT ORDER. Sorry, NO Asia yet. They are struggling by defying ME. That does not give any country license to go in and over power them. They are growing. LET THEM GROW. Time is their ally. I control them. I broke the Soviet Union, to be known as Russia. I took Bosnia to the brink. Romania to the edge, and the former Czech Republic to the end. I wish them to be free. NO OPPRESSION, NO OBSTICALS, NO WAR. Stop fighting, and WORSHIP ME. GOD SAYS NOW. Why argue over the order of MY choices? Simply put, it is the level of Love in each country, measured by my standards. My Love. My terms. England was put in Europe as a whole, why? Global economy. European currency, a co-operative if you will. They need to dump the monarchy. Princess Diana of Wales agrees. Now, do you believe? Do you see ME there? I brought her back, to bring to the forefront, the monarchy. The silly monarchy, you created by bloodlines. SHE was not royal. Yet the entire world adored her. She was not family, yet the people related to her. She was common. LIKE ME. GOD called her home, to have YOU decide what is royal. I AM ROYAL. I AM GOD. TOO many times I have heard for King and Country, or "GOD Save the Queen." Save her from WHAT? Who is she fighting? Not ME, NOT GOD. So I do not need to save her. That is MY decision, my choice. Use the money you spend in the monarchy, to feed the children in Africa, ENGLAND. Then you will be doing for king and country. I AM the king. You will then be a country. AND why is Ireland fighting your rule? LET THEM GO. FOR MY SAKE, Let them be independent. The whole Catholic/Protestant thing is to cover up the real issue. A smoke screen for England set us free. Stop controlling us. Ireland <u>needs</u> and <u>wants</u> to grow. England, in her pompous style, refuses to let her. THAT is why there ARE problems in EUROPE. Some one trying to <u>grow</u>, to move on, no place to go, THEY FIGHT. FIGHT amongst themselves, <u>fight to be free.</u> If you want to stop the fighting, set them free. "Free my people," Moses proclaimed to Pharaoh. "Free my Irish," saith the LORD to England. No matter, it will be done, eventually. I can bet you believe THAT as well. Now for some fun stuff. Less serious, but just as annoying.

Fun with Jehovah

Yes, I KNOWWWW, Mr. Serious getting fun. I invented fun. I AM FUN. I do not care for worry, scariness, or even confusion. I AM GOD. I have this to say about FUN. Who created Disney? Mickey and Donald? ME. NOT Walt. Who created Bugs Bunny? Porky Pig? The Cookie Monster? ME, GOD. Who created Barney? OK parents, lighten up, the kids Love him. GODS fault too. Even though I have NO faults. I created Dorney Park, Six Flags, amusement rides, state fairs, county fairs, rodeos, racetracks, and sporting events. I created the Super Bowl, World Series and the NBA PLAYOFFS. I MADE Wayne Gretsky the greatest, and Larry Bird a legend. I made Michael Jordan, change his mind, and play basketball, instead of baseball, and I made Dr. J. I made all these things and more. Richard Petty #43 could NOT have made it with out ME. Richard, I always hear your prayers. When Julius Irving played. I heard him pray to ME. Help me be the best, to glorify YOUR name, father. I hear Michael talk to his father, who is here. He is proud of his son. I let this occur. I tell you this, fun is MORE than the thrill of competition. It is how the game is played. Even Kareem Abdul Jabbar, formally Lew Alcindor, thinks he can fool my wisdom by changing his name, AND HIS GOD. Guess what? I AM Mohammed too. I have been called, Mohammed, Islam, Hindu, Ching, Hulan, Loky, Nopa, Sunling, Morak, Milatom, Toma, Toby, Joe, and yes <u>Jesus</u> <u>Christ</u>. <u>I answer to ALL</u>. The names you choose are OK by ME. Why, don't you recognize some of these? Humans, you are NOT alone. I AM is worshipped by billions of worlds. I share my true name with those who Love me. Sorry, but my true name is <u>Jehovah</u>. I AM GOD. No others. NO, sorry can't get that station, can't call that name, can't worship any GOD but ME. I AM IT. IT. THE ONLY IT I KNOW. I JUST SPOKE TO Steven and he is smiling. I hope you are smiling too. He has known me for 23 years as Jesus, 17 as GOD, and 3 as Jehovah. If he can change, so can you. You can ask him, and he will answer. Steve is a quiet man, writing MY WILL. He only believed I would do this, <u>if</u> his wife returned. <u>I could NOT take that chance</u>. I needed this done my son, my friend. I needed to tell my human family about this. I AM, and I Love you too!

So, reluctance still flourishes on Earth. So be it. I can live, and deal with it. I bet you, YOU cannot find a religion that doesn't have ONE GOD. Oh, so the nature people do not have GOD. WRONG!!!!! They worship a divine energy that's ME. Go ahead LOOK. Search. Scurry about. "I will be here when you get back." I Love Monty Python and the Holy Grail. Yes. Recognize the quote? Steve did, he burst out laughing. Anyway I digress. I AM SAYS to YOU, SEE. I AM FUN. I AM NOT STUFFY, as the clergy say. I do not <u>kill</u> in anger, I do not ever scold. I simply wait. I have forever. Forever is mine. I do not take life too frivolously. I only talk, when spoken to. <u>I only answer prayer,</u> when I know it is YOU. No one else can come to ME and say LORD, here is so-and-so, let me introduce him/her/it. It doesn't work that way. I only Love those who Love ME. Do you Love ME? DO YOU? I Love you, and sometimes that is ALL that matters.

I don't know much, but I know I Love you, and that, maybe, all I need to know. Linda Rhonstat & Aaron Neville. Steve, you met Aaron, in Philadelphia airport once, remember? He tried to take your luggage, your bags looked alike. *Yes, I remember. I said, Excuse me Aaron, that's my bag.* Butterfly Kisses, Bob Carlise, THANK-YOU. My daughters cry, EVERYTIME I play that song. Thank-you for hearing ME. My daughters, my wife and all your family in Heaven say, THANKS! My kids would NOT let me finish WITHOUT THAT ACKNOWLEDGEMENT. They adore that song!! Now, where was I. Oh, yes, fun with Jehovah. Boy, did I get sidetracked. That's OK. Fun is like that. It is spontaneous, it is unplanned; it is open, honest and caring. Wait, isn't that LOVE and ME as well. WELL, I guess we had better fix that. Fun needs to be scheduled, needs to be regimented, and needs order. None of that, I'll have none of that singing here. So George Carlin sings at the table, and it isn't even covered by your RULES. SEE I LISTEN. I CAN HEAR. I EVEN TELL JOKES. Steve cringed. He has heard my two Jews walk into a bar jokes, for years. I BET YOU CAN'T REMEMBER A SINGLE ONE CAN YOU? *No, LORD, they were not that funny.* Oh, now I HAVE A CRITIC. Well, I will let the readers decide.

Two Jews walk into a bar, one says, Hey, this bar's off limits to Jews. The other says SO, so is GOD, but he can't pour BEER.

Two Jews walk into a bar, one ASKS, "why is there no beer in Heaven?" The other said, "suds." "Suds?" The other said, "yeah GOD keeps the suds WE get the brew." Don't get it, huh? *Sorry, the first one was a new one.* So it was! Suds have all the flavor. *Oh, NOW I get it.* No, you don't, I just made it up. IT'S NEW. I KNOW the old jokes are stale. *But, they are new to the readers.* Yes, but who wants 2,000 year old humor, GOD says sometime later. Let's get back to FUN. *Father, YOU are having FUN, this is the YOU, I know.* Thank-you Steven, that's true, for 23 years this is how Steve and I talk. I tell him jokes, stories, anecdotes. I even took him for a walk in his dreams, remember? *Yes, LORD in your garden.* Yes, it was beautiful, wasn't it? *Yes, LORD and Holy.* Yes, exactly. Steve has felt, my presence, energy, my Kingdom, while he dreamed. That is how he knows what I look like. Do you still have the pencil sketch of ME you did years ago? *Yes, LORD you know I do.* Insert here. See Sketch of Jehovah –Same as cover

That is how I look. But not too accurate on the eyes. My eyes glow a soft white My hair is white My robe was brown. My shirt was crispy white with stars and moons on it. My shawl was a little bigger and my feet a little smaller. Otherwise not bad...not bad at all.

Do you have the pencil sketch of ME THIS YEAR? *Yes, LORD.*

See Sketch Jehovah 2

Great. Good. Not too bold, not too strong. Just enough vagueness to keep them guessing. Now one more. Remember My Closest to ME sketch. *Yes, Father.* **Good insert here.**

See My…Closest to ME sketch

That answers my constant questions about religion, and religions. ONLY ME, but I accept Christians as my own. Since they WORSHIP, JEHOVAH as their GOD. Sorry, Mormons, works

are NOT a prerequisite to MY WORLD. ONLY LOVE. LOVE ME. NOT WORKS. Fun over? *That is totally up to you LORD.* **Exactly my son, friend and advisor. How's your hand?** *A little stiff, but ok, LORD.* **Stop! Rest. More later. Are we having Fun Yet? I hope so.**

I really just wanted to show you a personal relationship with my friend Steve. We met in 1955, when he was born. I remember that day, May 17th. The apple blossoms in Maine were in bloom that year, "I remember every ones fall." I have told him that before from the Bee Gees "First of May." Written for my son, friend and advisor. Steven Wade Raasumaa. Sorry, Neale, Steve was first. I just put him through too much to ask him to do this book any sooner than now. With the millennium, the year 2000 approaching, I need to update humanity. I chose a simple man, one with simple needs, one who Loves me unconditionally. Could YOU have Loved ME enough to write this book? To take this risk at criticism. Christians, Moslems, Hindus will all blame HIM. OR will they? Shouldn't they blame ME? GOD. I can take it. I got him into this. I can take CARE OF HIM, AND HIS FAMILY, FOR DOING THIS. I TRIED TO PULL SOME TRICKS ON HIM. Pretending to be Satan and evil representations in dreams and visions. HE KNOWS ME. He simply WAITED, for the visions to give up, to leave or to change. He realized I AM IS THE ONLY GOD. THE ONLY ONE who could put this kind of pressure on a man, to do HIS will. Let ME tell you what I've done. In 1986 I pushed him to the brink of insanity. Insert picture here.

(See Born-again sketch)

I made him see ALL this AT ONCE. He was confused, hurt, and lost as to why? Why, was he being put through this? I told him lies! Yes, folks Jehovah LIED to Steve. Why? To test him.

To see how far he could be pushed. He refused to be broken. He spent <u>months</u> in a military mental hospital for extreme emotional distress. He was told, all tests are fine, and he is just highly emotional and <u>unfit</u> for combat. They honorably discharged him. Years later he told me, *I had to feel <u>emotional</u>, LORD. <u>I could see you</u>. That was emotional for anyone, and I couldn't get anyone <u>to</u> believe me.* Oh, they believe you NOW, my friend. The big feet in the picture are MINE. I WAS IN THAT VISION. So were my cling-ons. Visions from others wishing to harm ME through their own ways. He conquered ALL THAT, and still LOVED ME. While in the civilian hospital, he was admitted for exhaustion from being awake for over 24 hours viewing this. He SAW ME SITTING IN A CHAIR, IN HIS HOSPITAL ROOM, I WAS READING A MAGAZINE. He was lost, confused, and still asking why? I told him, look at your feet, he had on those cheap hospital slippers on, pink, I think. I told him, <u>I</u> put those on your feet Steve. He picked up his foot, read the bottom of the slipper, it said NO-SLIPS. HE CRIED. I TOLD HIM, YOU WILL NOT SLIP UP ON THIS. I PUT YOU IN THOSE SLIPPERS. SO <u>YOU WILL SEE ME HERE WITH YOU</u> SOMEDAY. He said, *I see you in the chair, LORD, reading a magazine.* I CRIED. So here we are in the hospital, I AM crying, Steve's crying, and the nurse walks in, she thinks, Oh, boy, this guy is a nut case, he is weeping again. He said, *STOP THINKING THAT*. That shocked her. She said Thinking what? I said never mind Steve, she put up her wall. People like Steve, cannot read your thoughts. Only your intent. They do not want to hear, useless information. They only need to hear the truth. My GIFT TO Steve, is his ability as a Psychic is to speak to GOD. Some say that is a curse. After just one story of what I put him through. YOU BE THE JUDGE. I LOVE HIM. HE LOVES ME. I know him as a friend, Love and personal advisor of music, art, and beautiful things. Flowers and such. He once wanted to be a Forest Ranger. Just to be close to nature. He got confused by pressure from ME. I MADE HIM FAIL HIS MOST IMPORTANT FORESTRY EXAM. I'VE TOLD YOU THIS FOR A REASON.
<u>I KNOW HUMANITY</u>. I KNOW THE WAY IT JUDGES, ASSUMES GUILT, AND THEN TAKES MATTERS INTO IT'S OWN HANDS.

      <u>I LOVE THIS MAN</u>. His family has left him on account of ME. I SCARED HIS PARENTS, YEARS AGO INTO THINKING THAT HE WAS POSSESSED. They STILL have nightmares and fears of that week. I got him kicked out of college, as I told you. I took away his last job, by giving him hallucinations about his wife being there in spirit, they were separated at the time, and about who I AM. I TOLD HIM LIES, TO TEST HIM. <u>I TOLD HIM THE TRUTH</u>, <u>to care about him</u>. I told you his story, be it the shortened version for this purpose. I will not take NO for an answer. I spent 43 years making him find ME. <u>I will take no prisoners</u>. I will take no excuses; I will take no alibis. I will take no one in YOUR place, when I choose you. I do not let go.

Ask Steve sometime. He will attest to my tenacity, my diligence, and my diverse methods of obtainment. He fought for 43 years, to live a <u>normal</u> life. To blend in, to fit in, to remain low key, to be a part of the scenery. I chose to go after him with ALL my methods, to test his will. HE LOST. I WON. His last wife told him, You have a dark cloud over you. <u>I AM THAT CLOUD</u>. I NEEDED SOMEONE TO WRITE THESE VOLUMES. I CHOOSE YOU. I MADE YOU CRAZY, CALLED A FOOL, TOLD TO GO TO HELL AND CALLED LOONY. I made you, throw-up, get headaches, migraines, and cause you stomach cramps. I AM the one who DRAINS YOUR ENERGY. THE ONE WHO KEEPS YOU DOWN. I AM the one who took your inner voice away in 1975. I returned it in January of this year. I put you through GOD'S HELL. To be a warning to others. No one can hurt you. No one can torment you. No one can harm you for this book unless <u>I</u> <u>say</u> <u>so</u>. Neale had it easy. He ducked the tough subjects. He played it safe. This is not safe. This is not a game. THIS IS THE HISTORY OF HUMANITY, AND GOD IS PUTTING <u>YOU IN IT</u> LIKE IT OR NOT. He said, *Death does not frighten me as much as YOU LORD, YOU KNOW THAT.* Exactly, MY POINT. 43 YEARS, READERS. 43 YEARS OF A MAN'S LIFE. I did not let him even sleep, without waking him, shocking him, giving him nightmares. It took 10 years for King Kong to stop chasing him in his dreams. 10 years for GODzilla to leave him ALONE. *Maria interrupts; 10 years for my father, to be easier on him.* I AM ADAM, the FATHER OF ALL. *Maria: I am EVE MOTHER of ALL.* Adam is Jehovah. Eve is Maria. I TELL YOU THIS TO SET YOU STRAIGHT. I AM GOD. I AM Jehovah. I AM. So I FRIGHTENED YOU INTO REALITY. Good. Now lets start. Start TO BE BETTER THAN WE THOUGHT WE COULD BE.

Our House

I created Heaven and Earth in 3 days, not 7, as your bible says. 3 days of Earth's rotation. I created My Kingdom in the blink of an eye. I created your Earth 10 billion years ago, when life just started to show progress, BAM. A meteor the size of Pennsylvania hit the Caribbean. It blocked the sun. All dinosaurs died. I told you to run and hide, you did. Years later you immerged from caves, upright, yes, upright. I told Maria, well, its started, and there goes the neighborhood. I was wrong. Wrong to assume that humanity would not try to improve. Thee figured you would give up after WWII. So I guessed wrong. What's that, no master plan you say? Yes, of course I do. I simply leave it around for anyone to see. Let ME see where did I put it, oh, yes. Clinton is borrowing it. I can tell you think it is fake. I make this up. Because I told you I was wrong, or that I told Steve lies. Why would I, LORD of LORDS, King of Kings DO THAT! Because the <u>truth</u> is <u>too</u> <u>strong</u> <u>to</u> <u>take</u>. To quote a movie, You can't handle the truth. Could YOU do the writing, I asked Steve to? NO, and why NOT? <u>Too shocking!!!!</u> Too hurtful, too much, too soon. HMMMMM! Let ME think… So if I pretend to be Jesus you will be able to accept ME as one of your own. OK. DONE. What else? HMMMMM! OK, … IF I TELL YOU THAT EVERYTHING IS FINE, AND <u>OK</u>, YOU CAN GO ABOUT LIFE, FAT, DUMB, IGNORANT AND HAPPY? <u>Happy</u>? How can, be fat, dumb and ignorant be HAPPINESS? Oh, I SEE NO NEWS IS GOOD NEWS. Sorry, I do not work like that. In My House truth is told. In <u>My House</u> Love abounds. In <u>my house</u> only I command. Sorry, no political correctness or votes. I RUN THE SHOW. Why? I've told you before, <u>EXPERIENCE</u>. I'VE SEEN IT, HEARD IT AND LIVED IT. I CAN TELL YOU EXAMPLES OF WHAT YOU ARE DOING WRONG SO HERE GOES. …. One day you will burn up your natural resources. Go to space, explore, find ways to grow stuff in space. Go to planets, colonize, grow things. <u>You will,</u> <u>out grow Earth</u>. One day you will take on more than you bargained for. Some like Star Treks Borg and Voyagers species 8472; they do not care if you exist. They can and will, annihilate YOU. Unless you prepare. How? Point your nukes to the stars. Protect the homeland. If nothing else, be ready to destroy a meteor, or comet. That can happen too. One day you will grow old and die. Cloning doesn't work. The Fountain of Youth DOES NOT EXIST. There are trade-offs in the aging process. Do not fight it. It will ultimately win, and resources are better spent on curing the diseases of the day. STOP CREATING NEW DRUGS. Find way's to boost the body's own defenses. Herbicides, and pesticides, are showing you <u>bugs</u> that mutate to overcome chemicals. Just kill the larva. Do not try to kill things, create solutions to boost existing defenses. Do not call people weird, strange, or different. Because you are all the above to other species. Species 8472 does not care if you are human, that you have kids, or your monthly bills. It eats your flesh. Sorry, but they DO exist. You sent a probe to the outer galaxies. Why? To find life? How naïve. What if species 8472 found you first? Good-bye, humans. Now your thinking…. Where is GOD? I AM HERE TO PROTECT YOU. You are NOT GOING TO DIE BY MY HAND. These things are in your future. Please prepare for alien encounters of unpleasant nature. Independence Day is NOT necessarily the case, but soon, because You want to be noticed. You will.

In 10 years space stations will not be here unless you see the need. You need space. Both inner and outer. Go to the stars. Use Star Trek as a guide. Jehovah likes the Next Generation, he watches it nearly every day. He sees your imagination of the future and likes what he sees. But heed this warning! By the year 2047, if you do not, I repeat do not, heed this warning you could die here on Earth. No, not from a species but a comet, yet to be discovered. It comes through here every 10,000 years. It is as big as Earth. Greet it early, nudge it, to a safe trajectory, do not destroy it. The pieces would REALLY create havoc. I will help you find it by telescope. We call it Earth Killer 1. There are others not as big but just as deadly. In 2098, a comet the size of Pittsburgh is headed for Jupiter. Get ready to study it. In 2143, after most of you are gone, a meteor the size of Dallas (1998) is headed for the SUN. No major damage but solar flare activity will be intense SO PREPARE. My word to you is truth. When you, as a people, find and witness these things, will you then BELIEVE in ME? Sorry, I cannot wait, there is more.

In 2010, the space odyssey movie, has a problem to solve. What if you reach a planet and something is hiding there. Look, DO NOT BE FRIGHTENED, they have been there 10,000 years, but the other side of mars has a parked space craft, 90% of the time. The US government knows about it. It watches us. It knows Steve exists. It is one of the lights in the sky that looks like a star. That is its cloaking device. NASA calls it unidentified, WE know them as Nubians. They are from a planet in the Milky Way not yet discovered. They have a 50 million-year head start on YOU. Their planet has had NO meteor strikes, so their growth was phenomenal. They are the species told to you earlier, REMEMBER they look like this…(See Alien in our Midst sketch.)

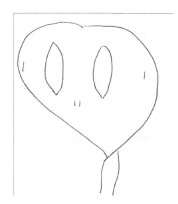

They are definitely benevolent, peaceful, and the only want to watch us grow. Why? **Exploration**. At their present stage they have lost all record of their development at this stage. So they figure, quite correctly, that watching us, humanity, will show their development at THIS stage or AGE. They are watching living history they call it. The government will not confirm this. Even though they tried to contact the US government in 1975, 1979, 1987, 1990 and just last year. The US launched missiles each time at them. They can easily avoid them. Their craft do light speed. Their purpose would be peaceful, but DO NOT TRUST THEM. Remember the TV show Alien Nation, AND MORE RECENTLY Gene Roddenberry's Earth, final Conflict. They would be prone to be worshipped and would take advantage of that weakness human's display called being naïve. They are not super smart, strong, smart or intelligent. Think of them as 5th century people, with space craft. NO NEED FOR CONTACT. They are just too darn expensive. UNDERSTOOD? GOOD.

No other aliens to report. They are the only ones, and are LOCAL as the universe goes. No, Kling-ons, Ferengi, Vulcan's or Venusians out there. Not now, but as your TV and RADIO waves spread through out the galaxy, life forms, with the PROPER EQUIPMENT will follow the trail to the source. It will be a mystery. So do not panic. It will take a few decades for even the closest threat, to hear you. Shutting off the sound won't help. Its' already traveling across the universe in ALL directions. Sorry, but NASA's Voyagers have a snow balls chance in hell of encountering anyone, anything. Too small, too remote, too well…uninteresting. Now rest assured, the GOD of ALL KNOWS THESE THINGS. He is just here to inform you. To tell you the truth. To prevent you from NOT being prepared. As nice as Star Treks First Contact, with out the Borg of course, Earth is on the edge of a Galaxy filled with life-less planets. Our first contact with the Nubians was 1910, in New Zealand. They landed, scared some poor dirt farmer named Richard to death, then left. They took soil samples. No, crop circles. Sorry, natural occurrence, known as **human**. No, no aliens are abducting anyone. Elvis is NOT with them. He is with ME. Singing NEW SONGS in MY KINGDOM. I know the NUBIANS have contacted a few of you. They are too dumb, to take hostages. It would infuriate their leaders. Sorry, GOD knows all about these stories. He has seen all there is to see. Even the Nubians call ME Navata, that means supreme one in their tongue, which by the way, is telepathic. That is why they sense Steve, and his contact with ME.

Did you know the government tried to do mind control on you? Yes, they did. Years ago, the so-called scientific community tried to contact people on other planets through telepathy, it was a wash. **It cannot be done**. Even Steve can **only** **channel** **Jehovah**. Only GOD decides who can and who CANNOT be given his <u>GIFTS</u>. Shirley MacLaine, STOP IT. Reincarnation DOES NOT EXIST. Each soul is New, special and Holy. Only GOD knows that, and now SO DO YOU. Stop pretending and move forward. GOD IS GOD. GOD is done on this topic, let's move on to the next.

See GOD is Napping Sketch

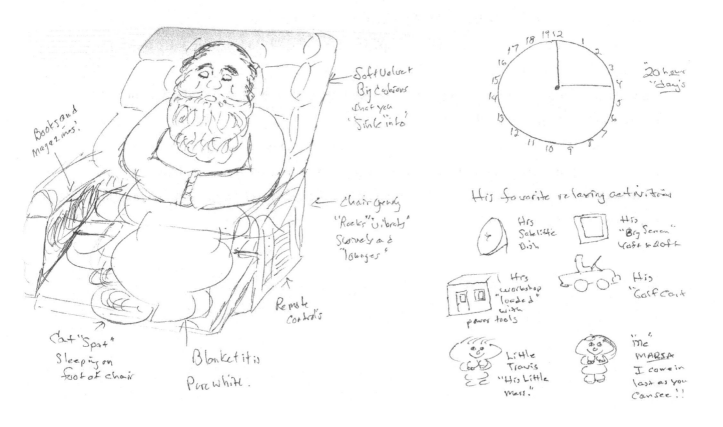

This was done with Maria's assistance. It is her husband GOD napping with "Spat" the cat sleeping on the foot of the chair.

My Place

My place is with YOU. Inside you. Why? To guide you. To council you. That way you do not have to run here, go there, scurry about, I AM convenient, <u>that way</u>. LORD. I AM SOMEWHERE BETWEEN THE SOUL AND THE SOFT MACHINE. *That is Mister, Mister and the song "Kyrie."* Exactly Steve. I like that definition, so I use it daily. My voice. My Power, My Love, is in your heart. That's ME in there. My Place is IN YOU, for YOU, and A PART OF YOU. Place to Place, Heart to Heart. "My GOD he is…" Yes I AM. "Oh, My GOD." Yup, that's ME. "Good GOD." There I go again. "GOD ALMIGHTY." MY favorite - got your attention with that one. Do you Love ME NOW? Do I measure up? Do you see ME? Do you hear ME? Do you worship ME? Worship ME, is MY WAY, of taking pressure off you to <u>choose</u>. Choose ME, you cannot LOSE. I AM GOD you KNOW, I tell it like it is. Proof comes in MANY forms. But first from within, then without,

I put MY LOVE, inside<u>.</u> To show you ME, My power, my authority. Only I can awaken that LOVE. I put it there at the dawn of time. I can call you anytime. I need to that way. I only need you to say, I Love you, LORD. I Love you my child. I really, really, do. Be mine tonight, tomorrow, and the next. I will not let you down. I only lift you up. My cut is next.

My Cut

What do you expect? What is in it for ME? Lets see, I do not need money, I do not need a home I do not need for anything. I guess I just need what I came for. YOU. Yes, I know it probably isn't worth much but, give it to ME, and I will take it. Yes, I know, you already stopped believing in GOD. You decided not to get involved. Yes, I know it hurts when you get treated badly, then blame ME. But YOU know, we had fun huh? Yes, fun. Life's a journey, enjoy the ride. My thoughts are with you every day; you only need to listen to them. My Love is with YOU constantly. I say so. I made it that way. I only want YOU to remember ALL I HAVE IS me, all I ask for is YOU. I DO NOT GET PAID FOR BEING GOD. My satisfaction is creating. Making YOU a new creature, capable of independent thought, action, and most of all LOVE. Some day YOU will leave ME. All MY CHILDREN DO. They grow up, they get families, jobs and get on with their lives. That day will be happy, not sad. Why? Because that day is the day, you and I BOTH realize, YOU ARE DONE. Turn off the stove. I'm done. Well done please. No more cooking, it's PERFECT. That's MY CUT. I created, or I should say Re-created YOU. You chose ME, I MAKE YOU NEW, FRESH AND HOLY. THAT IS MY WAY, MY LOVE MY HOPE, AND MY PLAN.

Now is The Time

I chose NOW, for the time to return to your awareness. I chose now because, honestly, it is my favorite time. I Love technology. I have been called Mr. Technology, by people here in Heaven. I invent gadgets, gizmos, and whirly-gigs. I invented the microwave, the toaster oven and well, you get the idea. I tend to repeat successes. Lasers are in their infancy, so are CD's. So are SURGICAL PROCEEDURES USING LASERS, SOUNDWAVES AND NON-INTRUSIVE METHODS. I made these things to help you live, a better quality of life. I do not plan on cutting it short just when it starts getting fun. Have you ever heard anything like music on a compact disk? No, I bet Beethoven and Mozart, wish THEY could record today in Stereo CD SOUND. They can. In My Kingdom. Mozart's, 5th Ode to Spring IS ONE OF MY FAVORITES. Chopin did a song in C to the Stars and Stripes, Forever, several years back. It made John Phillips Sousa weep. I tell you this because it is TRUE. I do not lie to you. To Steve, ONCE. Why? Because he was stubborn. He refused to listen to ME. So I created a "Dream Girl" in his fantasies. Someone with a name a personality, and a history. That girl was total fiction. Why? Because I needed him to write this book. Giving him a girl like that got his attention. It woke him up. I promise NOT to do it again, Steve. My work is done. There is more to write but if you died in your sleep tonight, at this point. I AM satisfied. I PLAN ON KEEPING ALL MY PROMISES TO YOU. ALL of them. For months I have been writing to you, telling you stories, getting you excited for your wife to return. I plan to keep that promise. I do! *I know LORD, Jehovah.* The waiting has been long, the burden deep. I know you would rather someone else did this. Do not worry. I will take care of every thing. I plan your future, NOT humanity. Watch my glory unfold this day. This day and this day. My way and NO OTHER. My way or the highway. Told you that once, did I? *Yes, Holy Father.* Good. Now relax I AM is satisfied.

Superman

I AM SUPERMAN. GOD is all strength, all wisdom, all everything. Christopher Reeves IS NOT CURSED FOR PLAYING ME. He is blessed. Soon technology will be about face, and allow him to walk. Soon it will benefit many others who need to run. The sick will be healed, the lame shall walk the weak will be strong. THROUGH TECHNOLOGY, all this and more will be accomplished. It is REAL. Not fiction. Soon blind people will see. Technology will do that. Soon birth defects will cease. Technology will do that. One day, not so long ago, I heard the Pope criticize MY Technology. Less than a week later I saw him in a nice, crispy white pair of running shoes, so, who is a hypocrite? Isn't technology wonderful? It gives us more time to have FUN. There is that word again. F U N. Now I got side tracked talking about it so here IT goes, again. NO, NEW. Steve, you got to trust ME ON THIS. If no one believes this, who cares. If many believe we did our job. If I fall, BELIEVE ME, it's called a miracle. I work miracles. Did you feel a miracle today? *Yes, you restored my Light.* Yes, your Heart Light. Taken from you at 5. That is when you had the fever. Not 6, 5. I know I was there. For 38 years I have kept you hidden. For 38 years I let you live a normal life as possible. For 38 years I took from you everything that all others already have. They ALL have a light. It's GODS light. It makes you tick. It surrounds you, binds you. Yes, My Son, like the Force from Star Wars. Except My Light is from ME. You did my will today my friend. NOW, I owe you my promise. I promise a good Next Life. One of freedom from want, freedom from toil, freedom from pain, freedom from others. You will and are free. I release YOU. *Please, explain further, Father?* I DO NOT CARE TO right now. Just go to bed. (Jehovah wept.) I AM is better now. I just saw your future and it is Holy. You are happy, joking, smoking and Full of Spirit. You no longer find life dull, boring, and well, petty. I should have done this years ago. Do not forget to turn out the light. It's bedtime. *Good night …*

Fun

Yes, again with Fun. Being with ME is FUN. I guess I have to prove it. No work, just play. That's my Kingdom. I get no satisfaction out of daily drudgery. I only play. I tell MY ANGELS, tired? Take some time off, a day or two. Choice is yours, FUN or failure. I AM FUN. Trust ME. I will never let you down. I AM, I CARE, AND I KEEP MY PROMISES.

"No more work, no more toil, no more stress, no more hoeing the soil. No more lying, no more fakes, no more luxury other than snakes."

Yes, snake, rhymes with fakes. Hey, try to get a rhyme to work every time, then make a Duck Billed Platypus. I still get kidded about that. Oh, yeah, by the way… GOD <u>can</u> hit a one iron. I do play golf…I got a handy cap of 0. You figure it out. I play ALL the holes at once. Quicker that way. I do own a 3 wood, never used it. It's got dust on it and sits in my bag. Also, I did make little green apples. Why? So the red ones would get jealous. Get it? I also took time to watch a video the other day. Jeff Foxworthy and You might be a Redneck if… Boy, if I did that bit every one would get mad. Seems if GOD gets critical or objective on a subject. People tend to get all riled up. Let ME tell you a few things, GOD is NOT <u>judgmental</u>. I do have opinions. I just don't make you <u>feel</u> guilty if you screw up, or make a mistake. I made a mistake once, and then I remembered, I don't make mistakes, I make miracles. So I forgot about the mistake, and concentrated on the miracle? GOD does all. Angels monitor, observe and report to GOD. Do Angels guide us? Yes, they do guide you, and steer you, in MY chosen direction. Do Angels have to do work? No, they enjoy what they do, so that is not work. Does GOD do all things? Yes, GOD is ALL. If GOD does ALL, why do angels help? GOOD, question. Steve…you helped. Stop that. Angels and GOD work together; GOD is everywhere, but not personally in physical form <u>everywhere</u>. His energy and spirit capture the area around you, hold you and Love you. Angels are his eyes and ears and the physical <u>presence, you need when GOD is doing GOD things.</u> Like creating Dolphins. Boy, are they SMART. They are closer to human than you think. Do a little research sometime into their sonar, and be amazed at the sophistication of its ability. Does GOD have a friend in Jesus? Yes, a good friend, he is head of the Christian Church and holder of the Wholey Grail. The what? <u>The Wholey Grail</u>. *What's the Wholey Grail?* About 3 quarts when it doesn't leak. GOTCHA. No fun, huh? Well, I can answer questions. Do not wait for a book to do that, ask yourself? I told you, I AM HERE. I can hear you. JUST PRAY. My Angels and I wait to meet you. Steve is still chuckling about the Wholey Grail. I do have my moments. I keep them to share with <u>you</u>. Just open your heart, mind, and your thoughts to the possibility of ME. I AM

HERE. NOW. In your atmosphere, in your world. Use your tri-corder to find ME. Use your 6th sense, to find ME. Use your intuition to find ME. But for My sakes find ME. Notice I didn't say GOD SAKES. Just seeing if you were paying attention. Sometimes when I repeat MYSELF your mind, wanders off. I just needed to bring it back to here and now. <u>That's right</u>. Just like my return. <u>The Second Coming</u>. It is now. Here, now, this moment. 1998 and forever. Oh, didn't I tell you. I ain't leaving. <u>I AM here for good</u>. Can't get rid of ME, nope, not gonna, not no way, not no how. I AM is HERE. I AM is JEHOVAH, I AM IS…well. You know by now. If not start the book again. It reads easier the 2nd, 3rd, 4th and 5th times. Did you know humans need to read or encounter something 3 times, to remember it? HMMMMMM…3, father, son, and Holy Spirit…3… Amazing, huh? I must know what I AM doing. To show that kind of wisdom ego, super ego and id. Hmmmm! …3… Must be a pattern here. So is 3 is a good number? Then the Old Testament, the New Testament, and MY TESTAMENT, <u>MUST BE MY PLAN</u>. YES, that's IT. MY TESTAMENT. I WILL CALL THIS BOOK OF WORKS "My Testament." So, they can't hear ME HUH? Well, they can ALL listen and/or read now, right? *Yes father, literacy is at an all time high*. GOOD. I guess its official. I the GOD of FUN do proclaim/declare THE BOOK MY TESTAMENT TO BE WRITTEN. *Father, what do you call the last 113 hand written pages?* AHHHHH GOOD QUESTION, Let's call it "My Story - Jehovah." Then "youse can write the remaining volumes as needed." *Will they believe that it is you father?* Yes, Steven, at this point, place and time, they will believe in ME. I know, I AM GOD, and being GOD, I HAVE TO FORESEE SUCH THINGS. *I LOVE YOU, LORD JEHOVAH.* I LOVE you, Steven Wade Raasumaa. Now go to bed its 11:45 P.M. More to write later, OK? *OK father.*

My Childhood

Yes, I had a childhood. I have a mother and father. As you do. Even test-tube babies have to get the sperm and eggs from someone. No, I wasn't a test-tube baby, although that technology existed when I was young. I was only 5 when I realized I could channel. It was a normal part of our species existence. Taught early on. We were advanced in only one area more than you. Telekinetic. We have much to teach you. *Steve's pen ran out of ink, he has a blue one now, thank-you for changing to black.* We taught our young to respect their gift as a product of the natural evolutionary process. What makes ME SPECIAL IS WHAT I AM TO SHARE. I grew tall, in strong winds, and high temperatures. We had constant wind gusts of 40-45 MPH, and 80-110 degrees. Precipitation was strong and violent, wind gusts of 200 mph and tornadoes abound. My world, Tantus 4, is green instead of your brilliant blue. Our ocean had more algae in it, which caused the sky to reflect a light green tint. Clouds were small and scattered because of the rapid wind currents, and our rotation cycle around OUR sun was 464 of your days. Our days were 24 hours long, but an hour lasted 3 ½ of YOURS. Confused? Well, that is what I grew up with. Trying to get use to your time periods and your days, takes recalculating each time you say How many weeks/days/ months for my prayer to be answered? So forgive ME if I delay in responding, I only have 10 fingers and 10 toes. I had not been more than 14 years old, approximately your 21, when I fell in Love. Of her many traits that I saw was her beauty. She still has the most beautiful green eyes. "Green Eyed Lady" By Sugarloaf, in the 1970's was for HER. I LOVE HER. You might have guessed her name. It was, and is Maria Delgreco Deablo Garcia, Montez. Yes, a long name. Our women add the name of each of their husbands to their own in order to keep children from being confused. For example, Maria's mother was and is married 4 times. The first husband's name was Delgreco, and so on, now that should clear things up. Anyway, I fell in Love, deeply. I Loved her, and to my surprise, she Loved ME. AT FIRST. We were married in a simple homespun ceremony that lasted 4 days, 84 hours each, and honey mooned in a place much like your Niagara Falls. We had 2 children a girl Norma, and a boy Jason. Both of who are listening to this story. Norma grew to be 4, when Maria decided to leave me. Jason was only 2 and greatly confused. I was too. I AM was not yet, I AM the almighty, and I hurt. I hurt bad. To Love Maria was my most precious gift, ME. I could not believe she Loved someone else more than ME. I cried, I screamed, I asked for divine intervention. There was none to be found. So at age 21, after almost 6 years of grieving my broken heart, I started my work to find divine intervention. I looked for

GOD. I SEARCHED THE GALAXY. Looking for someone anyone, who could explain to me, why Maria left? I was desperate, desolate, hurt, tired of the hurt inside, the pain, the lonely feeling. I did not find anyone, or anything that could hide my hurt. No one to comfort me. No one to talk to. No one to hide from. I traveled for 16 years, my years. I searched for another 20, telepathically. I spent a total of 57 years, in one form or another, looking for my answer. Maria was still gone. Why did it still hurt? Who would do this to me? Who, who, who? I realized after all this searching, suffering, AND feeling sorry for myself. That I was the problem. Yes, <u>Me</u>. I made up my mind to create something. Something, to stop this from happening to others, I created GOD. Boy, did I have a lot to learn. I mean tons. I thought it was easy. No one else had done it. At least to my knowledge. So heck, I can be the greatest GOD, EVER. Sorry. Don't work that way. Why? <u>Nature</u>. Nature has its needs. You cannot fool Mother Nature. I found she was stronger, wiser, making me look and act like a fool. People would say "look at the fool Jehovah's son, <u>he thinks he is special</u>." I would stride around with my chest out, chin up, and not having <u>any idea what I was doing</u>. I finally figured if you can't beat-um, join-um. I studied my heart out. I learned all I could learn about everything, anywhere from anybody. That took 50 million years. I still learn today. I guess I'm telling you this to prove, or make a point. I lost My Maria, by the way, thank-you B.W.Stevenson, she thinks I wrote it for her, I did. 50 thousand of MY years.. 50,000 years later she returned. I was "her first true Love" she said. I still cry when I think of that day. Your November 7th 1941 was a day in infamy. My November 17th 2003 was my day of joy. Pure, ultimate, and everlasting joy. She is still my wife 49 ½ million years, my years, later. Do the math. Our years are 27% more than yours, times 49.5 million. Wow, huh? WOW is an understatement. That is why I say, I AM older than dirt. I AM older than your Sun. It is only 39 million, in its present form, able to support life. Remember 39, times 27% LONGER. For simplicities sake when I refer to YEARS let's use <u>your years</u>. Less confusing for you and that is MY purpose. NOW, I AM is searching the galaxies for GOD. Not finding one I begin to create. Create, create, create and I <u>still</u> create today. I made you. You ask how? I formed your souls with my hands, wisdom and wit. That is why we are so much alike. All life eventually comes to two basic forms. Human type and alien. Human type is 94% of the universe. Yes, 94%. Alien is 6%. The problem is the 6% can have billions that are nasty like Starship Troopers. Nasty creatures, more insect than mind. More <u>primitive</u> than alive. You cannot reason with them, talk to them, you must get them <u>before they get you</u>. I had found all the stuff I AM telling you in the textbooks of <u>our world</u>. Think of yourself in class. I AM BEING YOUR TEACHER AND PREPARING YOU, to get through Chapter 1, Verse 1-4, of the Book of GOD. When you get there you will see word for word how close the two really are. So I get the feeling I AM is telling you the truth, huh, Steve? *Yes, LORD.*

GOOD. I needed to share that feeling with the readers. Now, Maria is with ME, helping ME with the next part, I don't want to brag about myself. My wife, MARIA.

Hello, I am Maria, Jehovah's wife. Forgive the intrusion in his book, but you need to know a few things about my husband. He is kind. He may come across as stern, authoritative, demanding, but he is the kindest, gentlest man I know. That is why I Love him. He is a tireless worker for "his people" he calls you. Earth. He is my husband, friend, Lover and spiritual companion all these years. That is all I need to say. Hope you are feeling my spirit, when you read this.

Thank-you honey. Yes, <u>honey.</u> I use pet names too. I invented them. I use dear, honey, pumpkin, well…you get the idea.

Jeff Foxworthy used a word "sensuous." Sense-you-was up, get me a soda. Maria didn't laugh. I asked her are you sensuous? She said of course, thinking I was getting romantic. She pouted, got mad, and I have Jeff Foxworthy to thank. Just kidding Jeff. I probably should stick to my regular job, and leave professional comedy to the pros. Red Skelton. Here with me. How Red would make me laugh. Thank-you Earth for Red Skelton. Red is retired now on a ranch near Warm Springs, Utah. He raises horses. Don't worry. He is not giving up comedy.

Now you see my problem, I have so much information to share. I get side tracked, bamboozled, off the subject or go off in a totally new direction. I can do that. I have my permission. So sorry, you just have to get used to it. I do things this way. I AM GOD you know, everybody says so. I hold up the whole book for a shared story. Guess that is why I titled this Jehovah - My Stories. I know how I AM. So I just make others aware, and hope for your understanding. I KNOW you will want to hear the rest of my story, well, I live happily ever after. And I AM HERE, NOW with YOU. I think NOW THE READERS ARE ASKING, Why do you write down that GOD has his favorites, he likes certain people more than others. I explained in Neale's book, I do prefer certain people. Why? Their Love for ME is one reason, and I like what they represent. If they represent honesty, hard work, dedication, Love and craftsmanship, I respect that. I did not become GOD overnight, I AM is no 90 day wonder, and I did not pull a sword from a stone, although I could. I do have likes, dislikes and preferences. Simply put I like the <u>direction</u> these people or things, such as technology and medicines TAKE. I DO NOT HOLD BACK MY OPINION BECAUSE OF IT. I KNOW Neale would rather I remain neutral or not opinionated, BUT SORRY, Neale, you spent enough time with ME, to recognize ME. I do not have to censor myself with Steve. He knows ME, THIS IS THE WAY I AM. I RESPECT <u>YOU</u> AND <u>OUR WORK</u> TOGETHER. But, please, do not misinterpret MY WORK AS Phony or Not True. I did YOUR books for the convenience of your readers, YOUR censor ship and your inability to accept ME WHOLLY, COMPLETELY, AND UNCONDITIONALLY. I AM with

Steve Raasumaa, now, and have been his book readers, hand, voice, and spirit since he was 5. They know ME, HIS readers, for they are OF ME. THEY LOVE ME. I PREPARED THEM FOR THIS. This is NOT a competition. It is My Mission. To inform, ENLIGHTEN, AND TO INSPIRE, and most of all to save. So to Neale Donald Walsch and ALL his readers everywhere, forgive GOD, BUT I HAVE SOMETHING TO SAY. I NEED TO SAY IT LIKE THIS, MY WAY, NOT CENSORED OR IN POLITICAL CORRECT FORM. I AM. I KNOW WHY. PLEASE TRUST ME, ON THIS. IT IS NEEDED. Now where was I, oh yes, my life. Thought I forgot huh? Well, I do keep notes, but I do not have notes for my children. I keep them in my heart. My soul, my thoughts. That is why I care for Neale Donald Walsch, and all like him. Humanity struggles everyday with its concept of ME. Who is GOD? What is he like? Why is he here, not here, not listening or caring. Well, I AM say's to you I care. I listen. I hear, and I AM GOD. I do not have a censorship panel discussing whether or not I need to hide or disguise or cover-up. Anything I want or need to say. I say it. Like this. I remember a time when the Earth was new, only grass, the trees and the birds flew.

I remember before man and woman were born, and all the creeks, rivers and seas flowed with life. Now is NOW, then is THEN, my only wish is to remind you how you got this far, this fast, and this safely, (overall) with GODS supreme guidance.

I could not go off on a tangent like that with NEALE. Sorry. I needed to but he asked so many questions. I agreed to politely answer them. But even you, reader, if you have read his books, would have gotten irritated or angry answering them. Some were silly, some were awful, just awful. How am I suppose to believe in GOD with all the suffering around today? GEE, TRY TO ANSWER that. Take two bibles and call ME in the morning. I LOVE NEALE…Steve, AND HIS EFFORT. But, bless you and your quiet way of allowing me free speech. I say, without hesitation or malice, YOU WRITE. SOMETIMES I HEAR A PASSING THOUGHT, from you, but mostly you keep to yourself. *Thank-you, I try to let you tell your story, that is what you asked me to allow you to do.* Yes. Exactly, AND you obeyed. Fully. Some say blindly. I have an answer for them. They are jealous. They do not part their hair quite right, so they take it out on others who, able to, appear to. So there. I know all the critics, I know all the doubters. I have seen their kind billions & billions & billions & zillions of times before. They just do not want to work at believing. They want it to fall out of the sky, in their laps, and then say look, look at what I found. I worked so hard at this. It came to me in a dream, vision, a nightmare, or a near death experience. They ALL sound familiar. I recognize them. I WILL DEAL WITH THEM. I HAVE SOME PASSAGES FOR THEM TO REMEMBER, AND A FEW NEW ONES. JUDGE NOT LEST YE BE JUDGED. I AM judges, not you. I decide. I AM the final word. I choose the ones I bless.

I take my flock and weed out the weak sheep, for remedial training. That is a NEW one. I used to say, "I will take my people out of bondage, so they can be free." Freedom seems to breed arrogance. If I had it to do over again, <u>arrogance would NOT EXIST</u>. NEXT PLANET I SAY, I AM HERE, welcome GOD, I WILL KEEP that one UNDER SCRUTINY. Now here is another one. "I cannot find my GOD." Neale is saying that as we write this. I promised him 3 books. I AM DONE. *LORD? Are you planning other authors like Neale, and myself, to pass your messages along?* No. When I AM is through ALL, questions, complaints and problems will be addressed. Now, will I choose to bless others to channel me as the prophets of old did? That is up for ME to decide. I will not reveal THAT until the appointed time. Thank-you for asking that, GOOD QUESTION. *I HAVE MY MOMENTS, LORD.* I know, and I helped. *I know, father.*

My Story is not about ME. Although I wanted to share a little about my life, background, and yes, my humble beginnings. I AM wants to address YOU. HUMANITY. The term used to describe species 0879 in our catalog of species. Right here on Earth. I do have <u>things to complain</u> and <u>mention solutions for</u> so here goes.

GODS Complaints with Humanity

1. Earth at war too long.
2. Have no faith in ME.
3. To many deadbeats
4. To many lazy souls
5. My Love is not noticed

Now ALL my complaints come from this list of 5. Yes, all of them. I have no more complaints, than these. Now is that able to make sense? I cannot in good conscience allow you to write more, Steve, take a break.

#1 IS OBVIOUS. <u>I HATE, DESPISE, and DETEST WAR</u>. I DO NOT CONDONE, pronounce to, or support any police action any war of words, war, or piece of, part of, or sample of, in any way shape or form. I do not spy, snoop, or look at another's plans over another. I DO NOT TAKE SIDES. The whole thought, act, and wage of war, is HORRIBLE, DETESTABLE AND APPALLING TO GOD.

<u>GOD DOES NOT GO TO WAR WITH YOU</u>. <u>YOU ARE ALONE.</u> GOD IS busy with progress, war slows down progress. GOD is busy with fear and hate of a PERSONAL nature, not mass hysteria brought on by closed minds to my ways. <u>I HATE WAR</u>. Thus says Jehovah, hear me of Earth, I DO NOT SUPPORT WAR. I will not stand by you, comfort you, or take your side. The bible is <u>wrong</u>. <u>Yes</u>, <u>I said</u>, <u>the Bible is wrong</u>. <u>I DID NOT HELP ISRAEL FIGHT WARS</u>. I DID NOT HELP David fall Goliath. I did not frighten Pharaoh by dividing the Red Sea. I already told you the truth. I only wish the truth be told. I choose to tell you now. David was a good man, of GOD, full of GOD, Loved by GOD. But extremely overzealous in his writings. He was, after all, a human being. He <u>exaggerated.</u> Made stuff up, and told half-truths to keep the nation of Israel going. It would have collapsed if he didn't. He was there, so was I, he did what needed to get done. Remember that. That is GODS #1 RULE OF FORGIVENESS. IT, OR HE, OR SHE, NEEDED TO ACT, BEHAVE THAT WAY, TO GET THE WORK, JOB, TASK, DONE!!!!! GOD understands. He helps, but NOT to fight WAR. Stories of the day, told of his (David's) triumphs, his glory, his victories. HE, in turn, gave all the glory to ME. I DID NOT DESERVE IT. I DO NOT FIGHT WAR. I DECLINED TO ACCEPT THE GLORY based on its source, WAR. THERE IS NO GLORY IN BATTLE. THERE IS NO PRIDE IN DEFEAT, DEATH OR DESTRUCTION. I AM SAYS TO YOU PEOPLE OF EARTH, I AM NOT A GOD OF WAR. Fight ME, THEN YOU FIGHT MYSELF <u>PERSONALLY</u>. Amongst yourselves, you only deplete

the population, and strip the Earth of her resources. I have to check on the nature of peace. I prefer that. I check on her way, her subtle lines, her open arms, her wonderful disposition, her willingness to live free. THAT IS ME. THAT IS GOD. <u>GOD IS LOVE</u>. GOD is peace. GOD is ALL things, GOOD. GOD is happy with the explanation. I hope it is now crystal clear to you people of the planet Earth.

#2 I HAVE SPOKEN IN GREAT LENGTHS ON THIS. I can do a whole volume on its content. I plan to. I simply will say. Faith moves mountains. Faith of a mustard seed. Faith is healing, caring, and hope. I AM ALL THESE THINGS.

#3 Too many deadbeats. That would be people claiming they know me. Sorry. I know <u>four psychics</u> on your planet Steven Wade Raasumaa, Neale Donald Walsch, Damion Brinkley, and George Anderson. That is ALL I know. These 4 are the first. I choose them. They will ALL, to a man, say they did not want the job, or the work. They KNOW ME. They are in touch with MY SPIRIT. They have touched the face of GOD. Each has talents. Each can solve a problem, <u>THAT</u> I arranged. Steve, channels ME. This is HIS TASK. NOTHING MORE. He is responsible only to ME, for writings. He will NOT help in finding LOST SOULS. That is George's task. George is good at that job, finding souls. He is human, <u>for MY sake</u>, cut him some slack. He does his best. Oh, yes, I HEAR the critics. That is NOT what <u>I</u> expected. OR, he didn't say or do what <u>I</u> wanted. Guess what? <u>I did not give him an owners manual on how to work his gift</u>. He is doing the very best he can. CUT HIM SOME SLACK; GIVE HIM THE BENEFIT OF THE DOUBT. Do not be so critical. If YOU THINK IT'S EASY, VOLUNTEER YOURSELF. I NEED SOME WOMEN TO STEP FORWARD AND DO THIS. I know Elizabeth; you are close BUT not quite there. Believe in ME, and then you will learn more. Trust ME. I'm waiting. Mary, you cannot use those darn beads, they are not for that purpose. In Catholicism, THEY ARE FOR SINS, not spirit location. See, my dilemma. I have a few close to, but not quite there yet. The rest of the pack is bunched in the same problem, FAITH. They think someone else can help them. As I told you about My planet, all you do is channel each other. Yup, another person. Probably in Russia, or the Ukraine. And they can't help you; they are too confused about this as you are.

Damion, sorry about the lightning. Almost got toasted. Sorry. You were not going in MY direction. My WAY. My path. Following ME. I got your attention, huh? I took it upon myself to select someone totally opposite of his, or her, personality traits. To change to turn around to convince I exist. THEN YOU AGREE? It was the best thing that ever happened? GOOD, THIS IS FOR YOU AND YOU ALONE, Damion Brinkley…you are blessed. You took the worst of humankind upon yourself on purpose. You selected anger, arrogance, hate, and yes, stupidity, to be YOU. I selected you to be more like ME. Guess who won? I did, didn't I? I always win. You are my example of my power, mercy, and grace. I solved your problems, now you work, and Love what you do, I might add, FOR JEHOVAH. GOD. I AM.

Neale, where do I start? Thank-you. You are now taken care of. When you and I first met I told you LOVE ME. Didn't write <u>that</u> did you? Do you Love me now? I know you do. I Love you too. You are a sample of my random selection, you were in the right place at the right time. Some say wrong place, right moment. What do you think? I know HOW you think. You asked me more than what was published. ALL that material will make another 2 books. 4 & 5 I think. Call them leftovers from Jehovah's table or GOD'S little mess. I know your fears, hope, it took a lot of years, but you finally Love ME. Guess I win. I always find a way don't I? I Love you too. Thank-you and bless you Neale Donald Walsch.

Now where was I, oh yes, I think I covered what is opposite of #3 so the rest of you figure out what I AM is hinting to. Love ME? Did you say Love Jehovah? GOOD. Now for #4

#4 Too many lazy souls. Yes, I have discussed this as well, under "what I want for Christmas is… I need to get some money, LORD. Help, I need to win the lottery" or my favorite "Does this thing come with instructions?" Steve, you've done that one, so stop laughing. *I know read the darn instructions, you have told me that lots of times.* Yes, 47 to be exact. *47 huh?* Yes, I do keep track. *OK, I'll bite, do you <u>really</u> keep track?* No, but I made you <u>think</u> I did. *OK, you got me.* GOOD. Now my # 4 is complete. You see the lazy and the opposite of lazy. Now guess which one I prefer. GOOD, you guessed it. I prefer the banter. The jokes, the camaraderie, that is YOU and I together. I AM calls it "me." That's me. That is it.

#5 My Love is not noticed. Steve, you are my straight man in this. *Yes, I guess.* I tell you something, you write it down. Write it down and keep it straight. You notice the subtleties. You Love me. You sacrifice days of work, family, and jobs for MY SAKE. Do you think I would NOT notice? Do you think I did not see? I see you cry as you write this. Stop, and wipe your eyes. I Love you too. *Thanks, I needed a good cry.* I know. *They have no idea what they miss by not listening to you.* I know. *I hope this book helps.* I pray it does too. Yes, I pray. I pray that Steve will be happy, and soon. For 23 years I took away his inner voice. What does that mean? NO, ME. That's right. No GOD. You All HAVE AN INNER VOICE THAT IS ME. FOR 23 YEARS, I TOOK HIS AWAY. I HID IT, ON PURPOSE. To show him what it is like without. You can only take <u>my</u> word, the word of GOD, that I did this to him. My word is forever, but not my punishment. Yes, punishment. See, I know Steven the best of all. I told him to abandon me, leave me alone, and go away. He chose not to. I guess that is why I Love him. I treated him worse than a pet dog. Dogs get to go on a leash. I didn't even go with him. I tried, tried to HURT him. Why? To much Love in that man. YESSS. TOO MUCH. Maria told me, *he acts a lot like me when I was younger, smarter, and a heck of a lot more handsome.* **So, here I AM with Steve telling him, I AM DONE. This darn book, in this place, is finished. What time is it? And the date?** *July 9th 1998, 3:10 P.M.* **4 DAYS, 3 NIGHTS, one book I AM is pleased. I mean it Steve. I AM done with this book.** *Do you want to start another, father?* **Not right now. I need to solve a problem or two. There is a little matter of a promise to keep. To an old friend.** *Tina's returning?* **Yes. Sooner than you think. Swear you Love me.**

I swear...I Love you LORD Jehovah.

The END, Or Is It?

P.S. Pass the tissues, I feel the tears. Father says, "Show me the Way." Styx, Edge of the Century CD. 1990

Thank you Holy Father.

My Promise

I do solemnly swear by all that is Holy. I will return Steve, his beautiful, loving wife of nearly 10 years, this day, July 7, 1998 at 2:00 P.M. Her time to return is up to GOD. GOD says soon, my friend, soon.

Jehovah

Stay tuned for more fun in the sun as life says what the hell in a few short time frames you call "days."

No, No, No, put the heater in the garage, and the air conditioner in the basement. Oh hi, just cleaning up the house, it is needed.

No, I will not, I've started working. I have a book to type, and it is due by the 10th.

No, you cannot come down to the party, I'm kidding, and of course you can. We have got to pack. It's in 7 days.

No, you cannot have a new car, the old one is fine.

Yes, I AM.

Show me the Way - by Styx.

(Steve played the song 3 times and cried each time.)

His Way

Other Songs with his Presence.

Show me the Way- Styx. Say it isn't so- Outfield. Winning it all- Outfield. Heaven Knows- Grass Roots. Top of the Rock- Hagar, Aaronson, Shrieve. The Real Thing- Kenny Loggins. Don't Fight It- Kenny Loggins & Steve Perry. Search is Over- Survivor. This Is It- Kenny Loggins. Last Song- Elton John. The rest of your life- Kenny Loggins. Believe in me- Dan Folgelberg. Every Song on Air Supply's Greatest Hits. (Especially Making Love out of nothing at all.) Can'tcha Say- Boston. It's Love- King's X. THE ONE AND ONLY- Chesney Hawkes (My theme song.) Day after Day- Badfinger. I AM I SAID- Neil Diamond. Crystal Blue Persuasion- Tommy James. The Basics of Life- 4 Him. More than Words- Extreme. Part of the Plan-Dan Fogelberg. Jesus Love Me- Whitney Houston (Jehovah spirit.) Longer- Dan Fogelberg. Rock n' Roll Strategy- 38 Special. I'm Still Searching- Glass Tiger. Walk on Water- Eddie Money. Top of the World- Van Halen. How about that- Bad Company. Must be Love- Van Halen. Carry on My way ward Son- Kansas. Human Beings- Van Halen. Do you believe in us- John Secada. I won't hold you back- Toto. Midnight Blue- Lou Grahm. Powerhouse- Whiteheart. I'll be there- Giant. His heart was always in it- Whiteheart. Sometimes Miracles Hide- Bruce Carroll. Butterfly Kisses- Bob Carlisles. He's My brother- Hollies. When I'M with you- Sheriff. Man Against the World- Survivor. (Just because they rock as my kids tell me...Shake a Leg and Back in Black-AC/DC.) More than a Feeling- Boston. FRIENDS- Michael W. Smith. To Love Somebody- Bee Gees. I will be there for you- Michael W. Smith. FIRST OF MAY- Bee Gees. Solid as a Rock- Michael English. In Christ Alone- Michael English (Christ is JEHOVAH'S spirit.) I got to get a message- Bee Gees. Love at First Sight- Styx (The whole End Of The Century CD.) KYRIE- Mr. Mister (LORD have mercy.) PETRA- Hey World, Ready Willing and Able, Who's on the LORDS Side, Praying Man, In the Likeness of You (one of Jehovah's favorite, favorite, favorite, songs,) Sight Unseen, Reach out. (There are more but then Jehovah might be labeled a Petra Fan, well, the shoe fits.) Pay you back with Interest- Hollies. Give me an Answer (Remix)-Shout. Roundabout- Yes (Moses favorite.) Never Give up- Shout (Jehovah wrote this with Kenny Tamplin, with Steve's Tribute to Tina in mind.) It can happen- Yes. Changes- Yes. THE MEASURE OF A MAN- 4 HIM. Our Song- Yes. Let's Give Adam and Eve Another Chance- Gary Puckett. The Move- Yes. Holy Lamb- Yes. THE Message- 4Him. Working for the Weekend- Loverboy (Fun Time.) I've Done Everything For You- Rick Springfield. Heaven In Your Eyes- Loverboy. Lovin Every Minute of it-Loverboy (Jesus's favorite saying to GOD.) Holy Water- Bad

Company.   EVERY SONG JAMES TAYLOR EVER <u>SANG/WROTE</u> OR <u>PERFORMED</u>, (simply the best.) Sister Christian- Night Ranger. Don't tell me you Love me- Night Ranger (Show ME.) Rock n' Roll all Night- Kiss. Home is Where The Heart is- Firehouse. Beth- Kiss. Fall in Love Again- Eddie Money. Love of a Lifetime- Firehouse. Eyes of a Child, I'll Get By- Eddie Money (Jehovah's saying when he's sad.) GOD Gave Rock n' Roll to you- Petra (It is TRUE!)   25 or 6 to 4- Chicago (You do the math.) ALL of Chicago 18 (Jehovah was there.) Questions 67 & 68- Chicago. Tears in Heaven- Eric Clapton (Jehovah was there, again.) Color My World- Chicago. Every Chicago Greatest Hits CD (The band with the Plan.) If- BREAD. What Kind Of A Fool Am I- Rick Springfield. It Don't Matter To Me- Bread (if you read Neale's Book 1.) Whole Lotta Love- Led Zeppelin. Diary- Bread (Maria's favorite list.) Can't Stop Lovin You- Steelheart. Dust In The Wind- Kansas (Got to read Genesis to understand that one.) Perfect Lover-Kansas. Power- Kansas (My promises fulfilled.) One In A Million- Trixter (That is each of YOU to ME.) I'll See You In My Dreams- Giant (That is where you see ME.) Stay- Giant (Steve asking Tina to stay.) If I'd Been The One-38 Special (Steve's favorite band of southern rock sound, what if <u>he</u> left Tina?) It's Easy- Boston (The secret of life, one day at a time.) BEATLES- All You Need Is Love, Love ME Do, Please, Please ME, All My Loving, Can't Buy ME Love, (Then every song on the Red & Blue greatest hits.) Jehovah <u>Loves</u> the Beatles, he just pulled John Lennon aside and Noogied him.

Tommy James and The Shondells- Greatest Hits (Same as the Grass Roots.) Can't Stop Lovin You- Van Halen. Open Arms- Steve Perry. Roll With The Changes- REO Speedwagon. Be Good To Yourself- Journey (Steve's ALL TIME favorite saying.) Keep On Loving You- REO Speedwagon. Raised On Radio- Journey. Heaven Tonight- Yngwie Malmsteen. Party's Over- Journey (Changing to a fun way of stuff.) Lead The Way- Guardian. Reason To Believe- Rod Stewart. Say A Little Prayer- Breathe. Forever Young- Rod Stewart. Great Adventure- Steven Curtis Chapman. Limelight- Rush. Heaven, Down Boys- Warrant (Angels coming down to watch Earth are called down boys, for the down of sheep.) Can You Feel The Love Tonight- Elton John. 16 Greatest Hits- Grass Roots (All written by a man who Loves GOD). Good Bye Yellow Brick Road-Elton John (We are making it Real no more Wizard of Oz stuff.) Family Of Man- 3 Dog Night (Jehovah Loves <u>3 Dog Night</u> .) (The WHOLE Best of Three Dog Night is a favorite of Jehovah's.) Philip Bailey (Thank-you for your 1991 Gospel collection, I Love it.) The Sound Of Your Voice-38 Special (Guess who?) River Of Dreams/ In The Middle Of The Night- Billy Joel, (Steve does not have this one.) She's Got A Way-Billy Joel (AND ALL of Volume II's Greatest Hits 1978-1985.)

New List

"I am" - Steve Perry, written for my friend Steve Raasumaa, by the greatest voice in Rock n' Roll - Steve Perry. Steve Perry's - "For Love Of Strange Medicine" was GOD inspired, even the cover. I AM gets personally <u>involved</u>. The song was #1 for 17 months here in Heaven, it is still #4. Yes, Steve Perry...I Love YOU too. "Stairway To Heaven" - Led Zeppelin, perhaps the greatest song of all time. GOD inspired Page and Plant. This was #1 for 16 years, here, because GOD was involved. It is STILL #16 <u>after 28 years</u>. Peter Cetera's - "One Clear Voice" that's ME, Jehovah, I AM "the voice."

"The Measure Of A Man" - 4 Him, yes mentioned before but needs to be elaborated on, this song is totally true. It is MY WAY of judging YOU. I look beyond the surface. Listen to it sometime. 38 Special Flashback - ALL SONGS- GOD has new meaning to Rock n' Roll.

Free - "Alright Now," Rock Classic - GOD personally wrote & inspired Roger's to "Rock Out."

Petra - "Rock Block" - EVERY song GOD had in mind. GOD <u>Loves</u> Petra, thanks John for "the voice. "

Steve...Rod Stewart is my idol, my working mold. He is what I want other rockers to play like, work like, and party like. He is a good person. We mold all others by his standards.

Eddie Money, off drugs, clean, and a good person, he is #2 on our list of standards to go by.

Steve Perry - class of his own. Rock's premier voice. NO ONE here, in Heaven, or on Earth, *(sign him up,)* sings like Steve, <u>NO ONE</u>.

Dom Delouise - *(yes, comedy)* Our class clown. He IS humor, fun and silliness.

Tom Arnold - our "Charley Brown" of the acting world.

Roseanne -TOO loud, too rich, too confused. She needs GOD.

Tom Petty- *I know you, Steve, don't care for his tunes, but WE do. He is our "bastard son." The guy gets no respect. Yet, writes GREAT SONGS. His song Refugee was #2 for 47 months.*

Tom Carpenter is our solo artist here. He wrote a chart topper called "My Life, My Wife" it is our closest song to "Open Arms."

Tom Jones - "She's A lady is for Maria."

Tom Petty's - "Renegade" was for you Steve, Sorry..."Refugee." (One of Jehovah's angels speaks up. Her name is Sharon.)

· The point of the entire exercise is that MY ANGELS DO MAKE MISTAKES, errors, like above. They DO THEIR BEST, as humans do. I KNOW THAT. <u>I do not demand perfection.</u> I

103

ONLY DEMAND COMPASSION from MY angels. Nuns. Nuns are MY "Angels of Mercy" on Earth. They are the heart and soul of GOD. Mother Theresa, IS, and always will be a SAINT. We did not need a vote by the church, she entered in immediately. Steve saw Ghandi and Mother Theresa MEET in a Heavenly vision. The other point to the song exercise is to stress the power of the male singing voice. There is nothing wrong in that. Jehovah is a strong, male, presence, a voice. 38 Special's "The Sound Of Your Voice" reminds us of GOD'S presence in our lives, our hearts, and our souls.

The other point is this. GOD chooses who he wishes to reveal.

See GOD is Singing and Dancing Sketch

Cartoon
God Singing & Dancing

The Hidden Will Be Revealed

Why? To make many see the power of song, the inspiration of GOD. The choices GOD makes, HIS favorites. If he chose female voices like Barbara Streisand, Celine Dion, or Natile Cole, would YOU believe in HIS presence at this point of Revelation. Yes, IT IS REVEALING.

This is revealing his mercy, presence, and of course his eternal Love for us. <u>We are his voice</u>. We are his children, we are his people. We are GOD'S Flock. His Holy Lambs, he calls us, we answer. He says Hi, we write a song. He is our conscience and our inner voice. The Power in Revelation is to recognize that <u>fact.</u> The fact that you cannot escape his voice. GOD is your inner voice. Your conscience.

You CANNOT ESCAPE YOU. <u>You are apart of ME</u>. *You are mine, he says.* **You can be slow to learn, or quick. You can accept me NOW or accept me LATER. BUT <u>YOU CANNOT DENY ME</u>. To deny ME is to deny YOU. YOU, and THAT is IMPOSSIBLE, NO MATTER HOW YOU TRY. You exist. You are here. So is GOD. So is his glory. YOU are his glory. His power, his song. You are GOD'S music to his ears. You are his voice of voices. His song of songs. His laughter and his joy, his tears of joy, and his tears of pain.**

His way is to show you his Love. You are his LOVE.

It is now time to show you.

Show ME, You.

Is the way I communicate to difficult for you? Is my voice too loud sometimes. Do I correct you when you write? Do I cause you to sneeze at an inappropriate moment? Do you hiccup? Do you look at yourself and say Boy, I look awful today. Do you forget to brush your teeth? Do you take too long in the shower? Do you tend to be hard on yourself for not getting the job done right or on time? Do I seem to stop you before you get there? Do I take you for granted? NO. ALL the above I do, BUT I DO NOT, REPEAT DO NOT, TAKE YOU FOR GRANTED...... *Darn thing, it slipped out of my hand,* **or** *How come I bumped into that, it hurt.* **I do these things. You are not clumsy. I make you stop, and notice ME. I cause headaches, temple kind especially. I cause stomach cramps, especially diarrhea. I Love to get you on the toilet. You know you talk to ME more in the Latrine, as the Navy calls it, than anywhere else? Funny? Well, try to sit there next time and NOT think of GOD. I GET THE BEST USED SEAT IN THE HOUSE. Some of you even read the Bible there. Very Dignified. I hope Grandma or Grandpa isn't watching. I'm KIDDING of course, about the dignity part. We see everything you do. My Angels and I. I MEAN EVERYTHING. I know who has been naughty or nice. I made a list and I AM checking it twice. Yes, some of you got the message. Santa Clause(yes, with an e) Suffering, And Not Telling A Caring LORD, And Understanding Soul, EVERYTHING. If you wonder what I look like? Look at Santa Clause. That's Jehovah. I look GREAT in red. And his army, wearing robes dipped in blood. No, just red. SEE John's dilemma? How to describe the color red when blood is the only thing CLOSE, in the 1st century, to it.**

I AM Santa

I created Santa Clause in the 1930's to prepare you for ME. I did this because I LOVE YOU. I've been busy. I AM HERE NOW, IN SPIRIT, WITH YOU, proving to YOU, I exist. I AM with you NOW, in person, showing you what I look like. Mrs. Clause is Maria. She looks great doesn't she? Not a coincidence that you have sometimes mistaken her for Mother Mary. Avia Maria. Mary = Avia Maria. Spanish for MARY. <u>Mother</u> for Mother of my people. That's RIGHT, church. Those miracles' you witness, and cannot explain; *youse guys, that's ME.* My wife is created with ME in mind. She takes her agenda to you and tells you of her Love of ME, and you. Confused? Well, I AM just getting started. Santa's birthday is December 25th. In the year 2025 in your calendar. That would mean I AM not born yet. So, that is why you haven't seen GODS face for 30 or so minutes. I say to you, Steve keeps a little Santa statue on his desk. Remember I told you NOT to try and clone ME. I AM TELLING YOU I ALREADY DID. You just have to buy ME. Confused? NO, well let ME continue. I have a little scar on my statue on Steve's desk. Let me tell you how. Seven years ago, I visited Steve in a dream. I swooshed down from Heaven. Yes, I swooshed, came up behind him and was going to give him a hug, when out of the blue came a right hand. It missed. Luckily I can sense things like that before they occur. I slowed him down, put him back in his bed. Told him to relax, it's just ME. He said *OK, LORD,* and I pulled him back into my arms. Now John, of Revelation fame, or infamy, depending on your point of view, was with ME. He was holding a mirror. Steve, was standing there, my hands were on his shoulders, we were facing the mirror. I wanted him to remember ME. So I took a picture as well, it hangs from the wall in my den/study. I know, HE KNOWS, what I look like. To him, that is how I look in the Air Jordan addition writings. Previous book GOD'S "Book Of Stories." I joke with him about the scar he would have left <u>if</u> he connected. He knows he missed. I just frightened him swooping down like that, and grabbing him from behind. *I am sorry about that…sorry I missed, father.* Yeah Right. You couldn't hit the broad side of a barn. *Well, if you didn't use your power to slow me down, to slllooowww motion, I might have gotten the punch in.* Not a chance, then everyone would try. See, we kid about it. He Loves ME so much that the spot he tried to punch ME is located outside his parents house in Maine. He married Tina there to honor the occasion. Yes, Steve I noticed. *I never told anyone, about the dream, except Tina, and mom, and Ted. I don't think they believed me. People do not believe their dreams here.* GOOD, we can't have THAT can WE. People NOT believing in their dreams. After all, what if dreams came true, what a world that would make. What a mess, huh? *Yeah, Peace on Earth kind of stuff.* Yup, Holy days. NEW beginnings, lots of free time. No stress.

My Way is Dreams

That is how I greet you in person. Pat Robertson knows this. He has seen ME countless times in his dreams. Especially in 1986 when he said…"I saw GOD'S chariot, coming down from the clouds, and the angel of the LORD was driving." *I remember, father.* So do I. It was <u>you and ME, kid</u>. Coming back on the 747 from our 3-year tour of duty in the Philippines. *I wasn't driving.* No, I was. But Pat saw the significance or meaning of the dream. He was not awake enough to understand it fully. But, I AM the one who allowed that particular one to be seen, by him.

A word on the 700 club. Thank-you Pat. I BLESS you and your ministry. <u>I AM BACK, PAT</u>. Not in spirit only, but in full view. Remember the garden walk, and I told you to expect ME soon. By the year 2000 I would be here? I AM.

Pat…thank-you. BLESS YOU, and now on with the story.

I come to you in dreams all the time. Steve, do you remember any? *Yes, father, sometimes you carry me.* Exactly, I carry you because you are half-asleep/awake. Any others? *We fly a lot.* Perfect. Steven PERFECT. Flying means I set you free, no other meaning. *More?* No, that's all for now. Anyway the practice of dream interpreting has been misdirected, misinterpreted, and lost over time. Here are the simple guidelines <u>I</u> use to show you the meaning of dreams…

Snake - something not good.

Powder - something not to eat.

Flying - free no obligation, or GOD'S RELEASE OF RESPONSIBILITY.

Toothpaste - it needs cleaning.

Fork - a tool you eat with

GOD carrying you - you are his child, he Loves you.

GOD walking with you - same as above.

GOD talking with you - ditto.

GOD smoking - Yes, I smoke pipes, get used to it.

GOD running- nope I glide.

GOD stopped for a moment - stop to enjoy a moment or place.

GOD smiling - GOD smiling

GOD laughing- GOD laughing - you made him smile louder.

GOD hacking at balls - his version of golf.

GOD shooting hoops - basketball, he gets fouled a lot.

GOD loving you - that's is his way. It's a hug, enjoy it.

GOD caring for you - sorry, he might kiss you, yuck, forehead OK?

GOD blessing you - see forehead.

GOD'S nose growing - see Pinocchio story - wrong script, HE doesn't lie.

GOD'S nose glowing - nope not Rudolph, must be the pipes fire you see.

GOD'S HEART - for you and you alone.

GOD playing darts - see pool below.

GOD playing pool - see darts above.

GOD drinking wine - see pool and darts.

GOD playing guitar - see previous music selections.

GOD kissing wife - happens all the time, get use to it.

GOD LOVING wife - see kissing wife.

GOD having sex WITH WIFE - sorry, that is for her eyes-only.

GOD playing cards - now we are talking fun.

GOD seeing you smile - now we are talking.

GOD forgetting to keep his rules on dreams simple, oops!

GOD forgetting on purpose to let people know he is REAL. If YOU see him in YOUR dreams, doing ANY of the above. It is REAL. If you have HAD dreams about the above, AND you remember them, you are blessed. More? You bet, I got a million of these.

GOD having a fun time swimming - his idea of bathing.

GOD combing his hair or beard - *NO, WE, the ANGELS, take care of THAT, he gets too busy talking to YOU. (Angel Sharon's friend Chery)*

GOD taking time to talk to you - every moment he gets.

GOD sleeping - Oh, just watching TV with his eyes closed again.

GOD resting - normal state, no cause for alarm.

GOD playing golf - see hacking at ball.

GOD seeing ball in woods - see playing golf.

GOD seeing scorecard - *see GOD seeing ball in woods, a lot.* HEY!

GOD playing golf a lot - normal for GOD.

GOD getting better at golf - tries to have fun, not taking it to serious. I like to "yuk it up" on the golf course.

GOD having a beer - WHAT??? Sorry, just the foam, i.e. taste only.

GOD having dinner - keep quiet for the prayer. Shhhh!

GOD playing with children - and YOU are there.

What is this? I AM not <u>that bad</u> at golf. Well, I try to have fun. I know, spoken by someone who sucks at golf. Nope, I'm REALLY good. I hit the ball into the woods, ON PURPOSE. I call it…Daniel Boone, or Marlin Perkins or The Great Adventure. It takes the edge off the serious nature of such a silly sport. Golfers BEWARE. GOLF IS A GAME. Revelation rule #1. Golf is NOT to be taken seriously. By its very nature it was designed to be a joke. 1 club, hitting a little ball, long distances, at a tiny, teeny hole. *We cannot in good conscience allow the sanctity of golf be destroyed.* Sanctity of golf? Destroyed? What a contradiction in terms. I planned on playing golf with Steve, when he gets here. Would YOU like to join us. We both approach the game as fun. Stories, jokes, some serious beer drinking, but not too much. Suds only please. Beer in Heaven has no alcohol. O'Doul's and Coors Light are as strong a beer as HE allows. Yes, I know. Coors Light has alcohol. So try to drink it without. Steven, WE used to play golf A LOT what happened? *Father, please, don't go there.* Why? *You know why?* I know a close golf buddy took advantage of your friendship and made advances on your wife. *Yes, Please…………You will force the story anyway, …go ahead.* Felt betrayed? *Yes.* Hurt? *Yes.* He used you to get to Tina? *Yes.* It worked. *Father, please stop…This is your story, your book, your words. You want me to ask you if you caused my buddy to do what he did to our so-called friendship?* Yes, you asking? *Yes.* No, I did not do that to you. Roger did. How can you still Love a woman who had 2 affairs. Not one, two affairs while married to you? *There is a saying father, I found it to be true, 'The more beautiful the woman, the harder it is to let go. So you accept being treated like dirt, even more, you expect it. Or something like that, I'm not very good with quotes, you know that.* Well, I dragged that out to tell you this. GOD DID NOT DO WHAT YOU THINK I DID. *Which is?* Take Tina away. She left on her own. Of her own accord. On her own instincts, initiative and on her own intuition. She THINKS she can do better than you. *I know, I accept that.* You DO NOT have to my friend. What do you think will happen when WE publish this book(s). Well, I'll tell you. Thousands, literally thousands, of beautiful single, divorced, desirable, females will want to meet and be with you. Tina will come crawling back. STEVEN……… LET HER CRAWL….. She will be embarrassed by this whole thing. LET HER. Her conduct is unbecoming of a child of mine. YOU LOVE ME. SHE LOVES herself. Her body is not as hot as she thinks. Her last fling with Kevin showed her that. He got turned off. She is too bony, knock-kneed, and she has funny feet. No comment? *No.* Good. You KNOW I AM TELLING YOU THE TRUTH. I see you sitting there at your desk. Now, Carry On My way ward Son. TAKING HER BACK WILL BE YOUR DECISION. *I will have to think about it.* GOOD, I WILL HELP. (*Maria; So will I Steve.*) Steven, we know YOU. Not HER. She is not our child yet. As with all things of the heart, we see your pain, loneliness, and heartbreak. She betrayed, hurt and complicated your life by being a user. She used you. Her credit was so messed up from the first marriage she used your good credit for 10 years to get what she wanted. Well, she got it all right. She got a new house, car, excuse me, jeep and a new job. ALL OF WHICH <u>YOU</u> HELPED HER GET. When she met you she had nothing. Her car was repossessed, she had no child support for Christina. She had a dead end retail job in a small hick town. Now she has $180 thousand dollar home, you are at your brothers. She has a great job she calls it. You helped, supported, and financed the household while she cried. Just 2 years ago she cried for a job like she's got. Is she <u>thinking</u> you helped her? NO. Is she <u>thanking</u> you for helping her? NO. Is she even grateful for you supporting Christina all those years? NO. Does she need to be taught a lesson? YES. <u>Emphatically</u> YES. Now, hold on, this sounds vindictive. Well, what she did was <u>wrong</u>. Steve, WRONG. *This isn't about <u>me</u> Father. Why this? Why now? Why even bother with her. The whole thing is just a bad experience.* NO. You mean a bad <u>ex</u>-perience. She is going to divorce you, TOTALLY. *As you said, There are other fish in the ocean.* NO. I AM GOING TO STOP HER. *I have asked you thousands of times. I prayed for you to intervene when I thought it was out of control, well, you know.* YES, I KNOW. Before this is booked she will come crawling back. Not because of THIS. Because you are her...

First True Love

Because you are her only Love who cares. You don't care about what you see, you care about the inside. The open heart syndrome is what you have. You open your heart to people. Then you get hurt. *Other people have open hearts too, Father.* Yeah? Name one? *My brother.* No, <u>only you do</u>. <u>YOU</u> <u>STEVEN</u>, YOU TRUST. YOU hurt when trust is betrayed. You open up, you get hurt by the games people play. You saddle up your horses, life is a Great Adventure to you. You tell ME, I FIX. I heard your prayers. 4-5 days ago. I saw her cry. In YOUR world. She said, *I blew it. I left a really good man for a jerk, who is afraid of commitment.* So, there you have it. She can't find better. *What now, Father?* Go to bed. Sleep. Tomorrow's another day. (7/9/98 11:30 P.M.)

Today is a great day! I AM pleased. I searched but did not find, I looked but did not locate. I scoured the land for a replacement for you Steve. I AM happy to be stuck with you. I AM is ready to write more NOW.

I TOLD YOU she would come to you in your dreams. That is why you could not sleep. *It was after 2:30 a.m. before I fell asleep.* I know she is a nervous wreck. Her mother hates her. Her job sucks and the house smells funny. (i.e. cats.) So where were we? My GOD interpretation of dreams. Well, here are just a few more.

GOD sliding down a hill - yes, we can slide, and it snows too.

GOD crashing into tree - nope, sleds got auto stop.

GOD taking sled to factory - autopilot has found a problem.

GOD getting new sled - no problem.

GOD going to store for electronic stuff - GOD is Mr. Technology.

GOD finding a new "what is it?" - Maria tolerates his behavior.

GOD returns the new "what is it?" - Maria tolerates no more.

GOD sees Maria buying "what is it," for birthday - Maria fooled Jehovah.

GOD sees my friend Steve, laugh at that one - because it <u>really</u> HAPPENED. She tricked me too many times I got even. Read on...

GOD allows Maria to see FEMALE friend with GOD - Maria panics.

GOD tells friend to tell Maria of an affair - Maria panics more.

GOD tells friend Maria is panicked - GOD gets slapped by friend. Maria intervenes, - thinks GOD and friend are having an affair. Maria puts foot in mouth when GOD gives Maria a Diamond Studded Necklace that friend was hiding for GOD from Maria. Maria apologizes to GOD, tells her she is sorry and will not doubt his loyalty again. Boy, did she learn a tough lesson with that one.

GOD sees interest in dream interpretation may be fading. Is it because it is TOO REAL? YES, REAL! SEE, my world is the world of dreams. The stuff dreams are made of sweetheart. Dream time is my special time. I think you understand that dreams are as close to my world as you can get without death. GOOD. That saves A LOT of explaining. Like, we can't see you personally. YES, YOU CAN. And I will visit YOU so be prepared. All of you. How? You ask? How can I visit ALL of you? I control time. Yes. Control Time. Think the story about Santa Clause, by the way I LOVED Tim Allen's movie by the same name, I belly laughed, is too far fetched? It is NOT. How do I get all those presents delivered to you in one night? I stop time, as you know it. I control the clock. So I simply stop it. Hold it. Let it cease, desist, or close. I then have all the time I need. I GET TO TRAVEL AT MY LEISURE TO GET THE JOB DONE. Why? Because I Love you. I created you. I AM your SANTA, err, GOD. I Love being Santa. Ho, Ho, Ho, Merry Christmas. That's ME. Did you hear me? Did you hear my Ho, Hos. That's My way of showing you I AM HERE. I AM GOD. I Love you. If I didn't, well, you can see I do. Got a gift for ME? Milk and Cookies? The Reindeer eat lettuce. Yes, just leave out the lettuce and the cookies. I Love oatmeal, chocolate chip, raisin, milk chocolate, vanilla, crème filled, [don't interrupt me Maria, it's not every day I get to order my snacks. *[Maria says: Sorry I didn't think you needed the weight]*. Coconut, apple, orange, wait, did I say I like fruit too. Well I do. Grapes, not too many though. I get gas from grapes. Milk Duds, M&M's, Milky Way Bars, oh, got any Hohos, I Love Hohos. Edgar Winter and I have the same hair, silver. Or white Oh, yes. Brownies, pies, Baked Alaska, (just kidding with THAT one. I just like saying Baked Alaska, it contradicts everything about cooking). Oreo's, breakfast cereals, Bananas, Oh, and doggy treats. Or Kitty treats. The Reindeer really like treats. Yes, by the way, my Reindeer do fly. Ask Steve. Doesn't one Reindeer pull my sled from time to time, Steve? *Yes, Father, Donner was the last one I remember.* Exactly. In your dream I did what? *You buckled me in your sleigh, then we rode up to your house in Heaven. The one with the big picture window that you can see all of Earth from.* Yes, and who was there? *You, Steve Noyes, my friend from High School and Me.* Yes. What did you tell him? *I told him You can see all of Heaven from here. Then you went into another room and put on Peggy Lee's, Rockin' Around The Christmas Tree, and danced a little jig.* I danced? *Yes, you danced.* Is that everything you remember? *Yes, that was years ago.* Yes, 15 years ago to be exact. *Seemed like just yesterday.* Hey, Good Quote. That reminds me. Rudolph is going hunting this year for a new reindeer to take Donner's place, can you pick out a name for the reindeer? *How about Snowball.* Yes, I like that. Very original. *I thought at least one reindeer should be called that.* Yes, at least one. Now Mrs. Clause and I plan a big Christmas celebration this year, and you are invited. OK? *OK. Are we talking dreams or reality.* Both. *You know Father, I still cry at the sight of a beautiful Christmas tree.* I know. I still let you. Do you have plans? *NO, none.* I do. It will be the best

damn Christmas ever. I promise. *There is a little Christmas in all of us. I only shared ONE of the many times the LORD and I have spent together.* **AMEN, Son.** *AMEN, LORD.*

Christmas is a time for
giving and sharing,
It is a time of Joy and wonder
for the children.
God says... Respect
Christmas. It is
my Birth day!

Christmas is My Way of Celebrating Life

Jesus was my messenger of life after death. That is why I kept the story of his resurrection so strong, so POWERFUL, so much a part of the Christian religion for all these 20 centuries. I now tell you this, NO ONE passes through My Kingdom and <u>cannot</u> see my Love for Jesus here. There are crosses everywhere. His image is in our version of the Louvre. The Smithsonian equivalent here has an ideal location for all his teachings, life and ministry. Right in front of the main hall. I tell you this people of Earth. I do not come to destroy the church of Jesus Christ, but <u>to</u> enhance <u>it</u>. You can take that to the local bank. I plan to tell you MY terms and conditions that Jesus met, to be so honored in MY DOMAIN. I chose him. He responded. I planned his life. I took it from him. I even allowed his enemies to have their way with him. Later on that. I demanded obedience, he gave me his life. I demanded Love, he gave me his soul. I demanded death. He gave me his life, forever. Now, rest easy all you Angels. They said *oh, oh.* Then ducked out on that one. I have waited 2000 years to tell the world of MY Love for Jesus. Don't even THINK of stopping me now.

Christian - My Way

I chose Christ as a leader, a follower of ME. A LOCAL MAN. Who, after teaching in the temple was spit upon, cursed and called blasphemous. He taught in the streets. He talked of GOD to the CHILDREN. He spoke of Jehovah, IN MY EYES, every moment, of every day, he was alive. Then came my attempt to discard him, to crucify him for not allowing Barabbas to go free. You see, Jesus was more popular than Barabbas. Sorry the Bible is wrong, again. JESUS WAS SET FREE, on the day set aside by Rome to allow freedom to a political prisoner. Jesus then took Barabbas's men to the temple, overthrew the guards, and was caught by Roman Legions coming to reinforce the garrison of Bethlehem. The spear wound in his side was from that attack. Roman justice was swift. Barabbas was the thief, who said, *Remember me when you come into your Kingdom LORD.* Jesus replied, *Today we shall see my father, be in his house, his Love, and I am not afraid to die. Not this day or the next.* I tell you this as keeping with my promise to tell you the whole truth. That is my WAY. The capture of Jesus was NOT pleasant. He was sodomized. The pain of this, to watch, in a dream, was overwhelming to Steve. He was upset for weeks. And even now it upsets him to hear it. We showed him the vision of reality, one night, 8 years ago. Jesus was also speared twice, in the same spot as he was injured in the attack. After whipping him, beating him, sodomizing him (only once), he was led, in chains, to Pontius Pilate. This time for his death sentence. Jesus was defiant. He told Pilate *To go to hell.* (That's where the saying came from). He said, in addition, *My father will sent his ANGELS to take me away when I die, you will not find me.*

I did just that. The Romans made him carry a board like a letter T down the steps of the temple and for 18 blocks, or 5 miles, through the streets of Jerusalem. Six minutes after getting to Golgotha, he COLLAPSED. Loss of blood, from his wound, rectum, and head, left him dehydrated, and dying. He lasted 18 hours on the cross. The nails were driven through his forehands, legs, and ONE in his wound. The Roman's were a violent and cruel people. Keep that in mind. Jesus suffered greatly at my expense. To ultimately force you to believe, with HIS faith, that there is life after this. I AM GOD. Now you know part of the true story of Christ. Real sounding isn't it? It happened exactly that way. He died April 8th, 033 A.D at about 1:30 in the hot afternoon sun. He was here in Heaven at 1:30 and 1 second. I KNOW, I AM. Christ is a man, my human family. A man I, Jehovah, Love Dearly and totally. Love him as I do, but walk in the truth. The light of truth. The Way. Yes, Jesus is the way. Still is. How? By example. By extreme example yes, but still a shining example to follow. Let me elaborate. In 1975 I took away Steve's inner voice. Doesn't that sound extreme? I told him it was normal, he accepted that. For 23 years he could NOT talk directly to

ME. He had to go through Christ. I AM Christ. I AM GOD. I AM Jehovah. Christ is the Messiah, the chosen one. I AM the chosen one known as <u>Jesus</u>. I AM his voice. I put in a computer simulation if you will, using Steve as a guinea pig. It worked. To those who DO NOT read My Book they will follow Christ. Blindly, but follow HIM none-the-less. For there are those who will stick to what they know. Their comfort zone, the Bible, as it is currently written. I can respect that. My teachings are radical to them. Different. Challenging, and yes, frightening. Why? It is ME they fear. GOD. I COULD TELL THEM A MILLION TRUTHS AND SLIP UP AND TELL ONE (as Steve calls it *white lie*) and they would CONDEMN ME, FOREVER. Discard GOD FOREVER because I chose 2000 YEARS AGO TO TELL A STORY OF FACINATION, OF TRIUMPH, OF SACRIFICE. MY WAY. Yes, so humanity would be inspired, to follow and want to be with, and like, Jesus. Otherwise, we as a people, as a species, as humanity would have ceased to exist. Would YOU have followed a man like the one I described? No, probably NOT. Why? Because he was to typical, normal, nothing special about him. No outstanding features or qualities. Yet NOW, you do. I foresaw that. I chose to do that white lie, 2000 years ago, so you would be HERE, TODAY, WITH ME. I did the same on Dumas 7. The man Titus could fly to the Heavens and speak to GOD. They followed his teachings. On Rombus 8, the one known as Simion - could feather a tree with a pickle. Silly, huh? But they followed him. On Titan 8 I did the same exact story of Christ. Called him Jesu, and told the people he had power over death. They follow him now. I have countless other examples. The whole purpose of My way is two fold. To apologize as your Sovereign LORD for the continued <u>White</u> <u>Lies</u> in the Bible, in regards to people and events there, AND to explain to you why I did it. You are a good people. Smart, Proud and True. You can see the Wisdom of Why? Can you not? I HAD TOO. It was, as I said before, It was MY decision, I had to make it. I get the tough ones. The ones YOU cannot make based on your experience. <u>I made it for you</u>.

Your GOD, Your LORD, Your Savior, Jehovah. My policy is, and always will be, the best choices for the betterment of man, humanity and ALL of Earth. I makeup. I own up to the responsibility. Do I ever get it wrong? No, never. I know too much about human nature to do that. Do I ever make mistakes? No, never. Experience, confidence, and charisma prevent that. I charm the you-know-what OUT OF YOU, don't I? Sorry if you still cannot accept it. <u>That is the Holy Truth, I AM</u>.

My Understanding- Jehovah

   That is my way explained to you. Why I do, WHAT I do, for YOU. This writing, this book, for example. Deep down, you need it. You need to hear thoughts other than your own. You need to feel my presence, instead of just your own. YOU NEED TO SEE ME, instead of JUST YOU. You need proof of life after death, and I AM that proof. In other words hope springs eternal. Nothing, not even, Love, is more powerful than hope. The hope for Love can be as powerful as a bomb, or as gentle as a whisper. As open as a window, or as closed as a stone. No matter, you understand. You are my friend Steve, thank-you. I AM done for today. Believe ME we are almost finished with this. *Really?* Yes, everybody wants some piece of ME right now. Take a break. Eat. You appear tired. *OK. Love you LORD.* I Love you too! Now, GO you nut!

My Forgiveness

See, I can forgive you. Because I caused you to exist. I made choices 2000 or more years ago, that caused you to be here NOW. Can you believe that? Is it something you can grasp? Grab? Or carry? I AM trying to keep it simple. I hope I have. That is why, I forgive you, so TOTALLY. So completely. So fully. So <u>everlastingly</u>. I hope that is a word in your tongue. I like that everlastingly. Busy word. Now, go to the fridge, get a soda, beer, or something cool to drink. I have more to share.

My Love

I AM GOD. JEHOVAH. I choose YOU TO BE my FRIEND. I CHOOSE YOU TO HAVE A PERSONAL RELATIONSHIP, WITH GOD. How? I described how. <u>LOVE ME</u>. Can you NOT see my intent, my purpose, my choices, my way, and now, my Love? To know me is to Love me. GOD IS LOVE, for short. Now, do you think you can accept a little more about Jesus? GOOD. The Sermon on the Mount is NOT true. What DID happen is better than any Hollywood script writer could dream up. The Sermon was scheduled, but it rained, and rained and rained. Jesus went to the temple and wanted to preach there. Instead he got laughed at, by the Sanhedrim, spit on (their way of dishonor to someone,) AND beaten up by the Temple Guards. He took matters into his own hands. He invited EVERYONE to meet him there and prepare themselves to hear him speak. 65,000 showed up. The Temple was overwhelmed. The Priests and the Scribes were inundated, swamped and overcome with demands for Jesus to speak. Or...*where is the Christ, we demand he be heard.* A riot broke out. The temple guards were killed. Jesus never went. He stayed at home, with Mary, acting like nothing had happened. The priest who spat on him, came to his house, beat down the door, and said, *you are the Christ. Go to the temple at once, your flock demands your presence.* Jesus wept. He FINALLY got recognized as to <u>who he was</u>. He went to the temple to speak, but it was so full no one recognized him to let him pass. So he went home, cried, and wrote down what he would have said if allowed to speak. Years after his death, John, formally Peter, spoke on the mount <u>for him</u>. John broke down crying several times and a man named Daniel, who the New Testament never addressed, read parts while John wept. John cried, people cried, even Daniel cried. GOD, for JESUS, wrote all the words in The Sermon on Mount Sinai. Jehovah anticipated questions, answered them, and let him speak only when spoken to. Sinai was where it was held, we counted 85,000 people that day. All were crying. THEY FELT GOD'S PRESENCE, IN THAT AREA, NO ONE KNEW ANY OTHER MOUNTAINS BUT THAT ONE. The Sermon on the Mount happened. Just not the way it was portrayed. Bible story's can be teachers, treat them as you do NEW nursery rhymes. They can learn from the changes and why. Another truth, Steven IS NOT JESUS. Some of you may think the similarities are close. SORRY. He is JUST A HUMAN BEING, TASKED BY GOD TO DO THIS BOOK. Another truth. Moses was NOT HEBREW. He was Egyptian. The woman known as Yoshibel was hired by Pharaoh, Ramese II, to confuse Pharaoh, (Ramese I,) into distrusting MOSES. He created the plot of Moses being Hebrew, to discredit, Moses in Pharaoh's eyes. Moses DID NOT KILL the Captain of the Guard. <u>Ramese II did</u>. All a part of his elaborate plan to obtain the throne of Egypt. Ramese II was lazy, a scoundrel, he had no honor, he was a waste. He concocted a plan to discredit Moses, in Pharaohs eyes and Pharaoh Seti <u>believed it</u>. Sorry, no basket in the river, no parting of the Red Sea. No, well, <u>no Hebrew</u> <u>background at all</u>. Moses was born a Prince of Egypt. GOD DID CHOOSE HIM TO LEAD HIS PEOPLE, (GODS people) OUT OF BONDAGE. That is why Ramese II LET Moses go. Moses told Ramese II THAT Yoshibel talked, told Moses the truth, and the Throne of Egypt should RIGHTFULLY be his. That is why Pharaoh, so quickly gave up the spoils of Egypt. They belonged to Moses anyway. Now here the story gets, GGGOOODDD. MOSES LOVED SETI. Seti hated Pharaoh. Yes, Pharaoh. The whole concept to Seti was appalling. Seti was a good Pharaoh in GODS EYES. FAIR, JUST, AND caring for his people. Moses <u>would NOT have been a slave</u>. He was too muscular, strong men fought in the arenas, or temples for the enjoyment of the Egyptians. Don't get me wrong. Slavery was brutal. But as slavery goes Seti did the most for his people. He opened the temple granaries <u>daily</u> for his slaves. He sacked clothes for their use from conquered tribes and nations. *We were well fed and cared for by Pharaoh I, Seti Inannie.* That is how the slave's of Seti describe him, even today. So now the Story of how Pharaoh died, of mysterious causes I might add. (Pharaoh II poisoned his apple with strychnine.) He did it daily in small amounts over along time, 2 months. It also killed his taster, just minutes before it killed Seti. Now Seti is dead, Moses is disgraced, and Pharaoh II is in charge. The people rioted. Total chaos broke out. 175,000 slaves, Freemen, and Egyptians stormed the gates of the temple of Pharaoh II, AND DESTROYED IT. Why? They found Moses in the desert, wandering aimlessly, and rescued him. Pharaoh had told the people Moses was killed by the National Guard of Tibet. Tibet? The people said, Where in hell is Tibet? Pharaoh hoped that the story would die along with Moses. Why Pharaoh didn't just kill him is not totally known. Maybe GOD intervened and allowed pity to overcome Pharaoh. Or it was custom to embarrass, humiliate the supposed enemy's of Egypt, or ALL THE ABOVE. Now, a Tibetan Monk was in Egypt, and heard the story Pharaoh was telling. He told several Egyptian homeowners that, *Tibet has NO <u>National Guard</u>. We are all MONKS, sworn to celibacy and cleanliness to GOD.* Well, THAT got around quick. In <u>three days</u> the riot broke out. Pharaoh escaped, BARELY. He then pursued Moses to the Red Sea. He was convinced Moses caused the riot, and rebellion. Pharaoh returned to recapture the city 6 days after the riot. He gathered all his guards in surrounding areas, and crushed the uprising. IT WAS BLOODY. Of the 175,000 who started the battle, only 6,000 LIVED. Of Pharaoh's 65,000 well armed and battle tried militia, 6,5000 were left. Only Pharaoh was wounded, BADLY. That's when he got sick and died. Twenty months after freeing the Hebrews. The NEW Pharaoh was Pharaoh II's SON. He was WORSE than his father. He was MURDERED in his sleep, 6 months after taking over Egypt. No greater Pharaoh than Seti Inannie ever lived. Remember that. Egypt was never the same after him. Treachery brought down

Egypt. Treachery from within. GOD SAW IT ALL, and allowed Egypt to destroy itself. Not only destroy itself but cease to exist. The defaced Sphinx at Golga is from The Rebel Riot in 110 BC. The Bible is NOT right with the dates either. 110 BC is only 12 years after Seti took power. 10,000 years before Christ. 110 BC, stood for 110 Building Cycles, or Planting Cycles. That is how early civilizations did their calendars. By the crops they could PLANT. Not rotations around the sun. They did not know that yet.   So 10,000 years was actually 41BC, they got 41 planting cycles in a given 5-year period, do the math. So Moses did not live to 110. He was 41. GOT THAT. The Egyptians did not live 10,000 years ago but closer to 4,100 YEARS AGO. Sound confusing still? Well, hang on. The Hebrews used the Sun to tell time. Day and night. They had 47 days in a calendar month, and 7 years in a decade. Try now to tell you It will be………days, weeks, or months, for ME TO ANSWER YOUR PRAYERS. I get brain cramps. I have to sit there, in my mind and do the math. But it goes like this, days are 24 hours, but not in Egypt in the year of the LORD 1015, but they used Building or Planting Cycles. They got 5 cycles in a 365 day/year and so on, and so on. Now, Steve. Do you see why I say the heck with time frames? I AM duty or task oriented. IT WILL GET DONE. When it gets done. *I understand better, LORD.* GOOD that was my real intent. Now, how about THAT READER. Do I sound old enough to you? Make sense? Sound truthful? HAVE YOU believed ME yet? Some have, some still want more and some are coming along. GOOD. I'LL TAKE THAT. HERE IS MORE stuff. Stephen, the First Christian Martyr, NEVER HAPPENED. He is FICTION, total and complete. St. Stephen, in England, during the translation of the Original Greek Text, saw an opportunity, or chance to make himself immortal. He lied to you. Acts, the book, for the most part, being of that time, is accurate. One of the most accurate books in the Bible. BUT NOT THE STEPHEN STORY. Didn't happen. Did not exist. Will not matter in the long run. St. Stephen is a good but misguided man who wanted to be immortal. He tampered with the Bible DURING TRANSLATION. You can decide if Churches bearing his name are changed, adapted or left the same. The sad part to me is that was one of Steve's favorite stories. He thought he was named after that Biblical Hero. Sorry, my friend. It is fable. *Oh, well……* *What else LORD?*

The Book of Revelation

Oooohhhh. **Scary huh? Nope, just misinterpreted. 1st Century ideas, on paper, about <u>visions</u> of 20th Century Earth. Try this sometime. Try taking a piece of paper. Write down car. Then the words, horn, sheep, goat, horse, tool to dig with, butter, cheese, and blood. Write the Book of Visions, I call it, and get 20th Century people all in a panic. <u>Get it through your heads</u>. I AM NOT THAT BAD. I CARE TOO MUCH TO END IT NOW. All the work, all the people. All my fun stuff, I have to take back to the store. So, <u>lighten up</u>. I will help, over the next few chapters, to explain, The Book Of Warnings, the Second Coming (THAT at least is RIGHT). JUDGEMENT DAY. (Pick one, I DIDN'T.) Lost Soul Redemption, (sounds like a Soul Train selection. I liked Soul Train, what happened to it? Oh, well.) Steve liked that one. He said,** *There, that works for me.* **It's been tough for HIM. KNOWING ALL THIS. Most of it, and keeping quiet. Anyway, Revelation Chapter 1. Verses 9-20, simply describe what I look like Think Santa Clause.**

Chapter 2, is my 7 nations, or tribes, of Israel, NOT ANYTHING ELSE.

Chapter 3, is MY 7 HEADS OF THOSE TRIBES.

Chapter 4, is MY EASY CHAIR, where I smoke my pipe.

Chapter 5, is MY notes, I told you I keep and use them. What a mess sometimes…No, not yet with a Computer. To large, even a laptop is too heavy. Hey, yeah, invent <u>smaller</u> <u>more powerful</u> <u>computers</u>, to be used in space travel. Oh, sorry, took to long with my notes.

Chapter 6, the Seal is a watch. YES, A WATCH. I wear a Rolex. It took forever for the darn lights to come on, on THAT one. This is MY WAY OF GETTING YOUR ATTENTION. A SEAL IS A TIMEPIECE. It keeps track of movement of periods, or increments, called minutes. Think 40-hour workweek. Now, you got it. I was describing a typical FACTORY ENVIRONMENT, and a 1st Century Man COULDN'T UNDERSTAND.

Chapter 7, roll call.

Chapter 8. My Watch AND a can of beer. Suds only please. WORMWOOD is a Gopher Ball. Try telling John about Golf with Horse, Dirt, Sheep, etc.

Chapter 9. (Steve's FAVORITE). What did I tell you it was? *A foot ball game, LORD.* **Right. EXACTLY, right. Do you remember who?** *New York Giants vs. the New York Jets?* **YES. Now the tough part, what year was it?** *LORD…??????* **1987.**

Chapter nine of Revelation is my best example of First Century, MEETING, 20th Century, and 21st. I know you can read it, so here is what it sez…

Jones took a lot of time on that play making his cut. The timing appeared off. Joe, if you still were with the Jets, how would you take that play and make it work? Well, Pete, I would carry the pattern a little deeper, behind the linebackers.... **Now THINK. Could John write about ALL THAT from Century 1?**

Chapter 10. What Steve is doing right NOW. Writing. I write all the time. So John WITNESSED THE SAME.

Chapter 11. Building a new Stadium in Foxboro. We went to the new location in 1994 to see if Foxboro and the Patriots were going to move. Yeah, I know, the parting SHOTS of how BAD the PATS are come through clear. I like the name and new logo. *Father, I think it's more the <u>name.</u>* **Exactly. Reminds ME of Paul Revere, Mary Beth Parkinson, Betsy Ross, Muhamid Nupa, Scatman Jack, Sorry, other story's, other times back to Revelation.**

Chapter 12. A custom cruise liner. Can't even think about a ship like the QEII can you John?

Chapter 13. Unlucky 13, or is it just a myth. Thirteen is a hovercraft that travels daily from England to Scotland to France. John, got any ketchup for those fries.

Chapter 14. MY story about Jesus, and the 175,000 IN Moses' story. Common stories here in Heaven. John just had too much goats milk that day!

Chapter 15. 7 tribes of Israel. I say so.

Chapter 16. Ditto.

Have you gotten the deal yet? Have you started to SEE? Let me jump ahead a bit.

Chapter 21. A new stadium in Denver called Coors Field. I went there with Steve once. He watched a semi-pro baseball game in Broncos Stadium with 66,000 people on a 4th Of July. He was stationed at Lowry then. I decided you people in Denver needed a baseball team. Boy, do you people Love sports in Denver. May I say Don Baylor makes a Great coach, huh? Keep him. GOOD. This is printed AFTER this year's season, Steve. They get to the playoffs. *How far, LORD?* **All the way to the World Series.** *Do you feel like telling me if they win? I could bet on the game. I'm kidding, you know that, LORD.* **No, they don't win but they do put on a great season ending run to get there. Aren't you going to ask me who makes it in the American League?** *Who?* **I ain't tellin. You would bet everything and I would get blamed if I changed the outcome because of My way, or My Understanding.** *That's why you asked me, along time ago, <u>not to bet</u>, <u>LORD.</u>* **Yes. Exactly. I said to you Do not bet on things that I may judge. To be exact. So you don't bet.**

Chapter 22. My swimming, backyard barbecue and pool party, at Christmas time. I don't have Snow where I live. I PREFER THAT. And YES, that is what I said, Behold, I AM....

Chapter 24. What NO chapter 24? Imagine that. The Germans who translated the Bible originally left out Chapters 22-27. THEY GOT CONFUSED. 23-24 was my open door policy as your sovereign LORD.

Chapters 25-27. Was my open discussion and dialogue with YOU. Like RIGHT NOW!

Felt you needed that, huh? Feeling better about life. About ME? About my rules and regulations. I THINK IF I COULD, I WOULD HUG ALL OF YOU WHO READ THIS, RIGHT now! I can, I did. Do you feel my presence. *OOOHHH, NO. Oh, My GOD.* Thank-you. I did understand. I AM GOD. I get to do these things for YOU, daily, monthly, and every moment I can. I AM JEHOVAH, because I <u>want</u> to be. Yes, I AM coming soon. Guess WHAT? I AM HERE. I warned you I'd be back. I warned YOU, I WOULD VISIT AND STAY. I WARNED YOU, or did I bless you with this? Is my way A BLESSING? YES IT IS. I AM blesses those who read this so far and believed I know them, they are of ME. Tears of Joy, Hearts of Love, I AM the GOD above.

I care to be. AMEN

The plagues in THE Book of Revelation, in the 22nd chapter, and the warning, well, you know ME better by now. I demanded MY angels to be accurate when they report to me, <u>about YOU</u>. I TOLD THEM, THERE WOULD BE HELL TO PAY, IF NOT ACCURATE in YOUR information. John took that as a warning instead of a blessing. My Angels do very demanding, tedious, repetitive, monotonous, detailed, everlasting, blessed and gratifying work. I was only testing my sheep, my flock, and MY ANGELS. I can do that because I AM ME, GOD, JEHOVAH. I invite you to come in to my house. My door is open, my food is prepared, my wine is tasty, but no buzz will you feel. My tongs are prepared to flip the burnt offerings, and the grill is hot. *Make mine well-done, bring some of that steak and stuff here, I see chicken, do I smell burgers.* Let's have fun, THIS TIME MY PEOPLE. Let's have GOD and Humanity on the same page, from the same book written by the same author. ME. Jehovah. GOD ALMIGHTY. I AM, and always will be your LORD of ALL. Your Sovereign LORD. What does Sovereign mean, you ask? To ME it means, ALL encompassing, ALL knowing, ALL-powerful, all LOVING, AND, excuse the humility, all together. Try to be saved. Try to stay focused. Try to be My Child. My Love. My Baby. My little itsy, bitsy, baby girl. My little baby boy. My friend, AND MY TRIUMPH. I only ask that YOU LOVE ME. I ONLY ASK THAT AND NOTHING ELSE. I know you want to. I can tell. I get a lot of fan mail saying so. I bet the Post Office doesn't have an address for ME on Earth. Now, you know Steve. Set up a Foundation to answer MY letters. I will answer them ALL. Do not live anywhere that I do not select for you. I WILL ANSWER MY FLOCK. I WILL LISTEN TO THEIR HEARTS. I will put in writing my words to live by. My hearts thoughts, My Open Door, My Open Heart. Looks like we have A LOT more channeling to do. *Lot's father.* Yeah. How's the hand? Cramping yet? *A little.* Take a break then. *I Love you, LORD.* I know. Now, Star Trek is on in 15 Min. Go and relax OK? *Yes, OK.*

Let's write more about, ME. ME, Maria.

Maria - Jehovah's Wife

I am Jehovah's wife Maria Delgreco, Diablo, Garcia, Montez etc. etc. I have had 47 husbands and only one Love. Jehovah. I Love him. I always did. I took his heart, soul, and his sanctity of mind and thought. I created GOD BY DENYING HIM, me. I got greedy. For 10,000 years I flew around the universe, encountering life, encountering men, encountering Jehovah at every turn. I literally took 2 times 2 and made it 17. Meaning, I blew it. He was my first Love. You never forget your first Love. You always want that moment back. You struggle to replace him, or her, but somehow it's not the same. I really do Love my husband. He is by all accounts the kindest, gentlest, and sweetest man I EVER met. He is obviously in Love with his human family. He has gone to great lengths to prove that Love to you. TRUST HIM. Trust HIS Love. I do. I do more than you can ever imagine. I know he shares stories in this book of his with you, but there are so many more. So much more to share. His triumphs are boundless, there are no words, no amount of words that can define his Love. He even gave Earth a picture, statue or perfect replica of him and ME. SANTA AND MRS. CLAUSE. I know it sounds unreal. It is our world. The nicest thing I can say about him to you is, don't worry. GOD is in the house. Goodbye for now, he has more to share with his loving human family. Take care of yourself and I will see YOU someday in HIS Kingdom called Heaven.

My Proof

How can I prove to humanity that I AM really here? How can I, Jehovah, show you my power, wisdom and glory without frightening you so much I scare you away? Great question isn't it? I wonder if you ever thought of it? How would GOD manifest himself on Earth? How would he come to visit? How would he prove to us that he exists? Where would he reveal himself? How? TO WHOM? My proof is in a man named Neale Donald Walsch. He was my trial run. If you did NOT BUY HIS BOOK, or I should say, my book of questions and answers. I would NOT BE HERE NOW DOING <u>THIS</u> BOOK. This book of GOD. I did not pick the title. Steve did. He always told me, *it should be like the Bible so not to frighten the people. IT SHOULD LOOK AND FEEL AND SOUND biblical,* and MY favorite *Try and sound like the King James Version, it makes you <u>sound</u> older.* I Love that one. He suggested these things. I did them. I also told Neale, what he NEEDED TO HEAR. Why? I Love Neale, he was new and different to GOD. I KNOW STEVE. He is an old friend of 43 years. I can tell you stories about our times together, but that is up to the readership and him. We are close Steve and I, too close at times. Today we went for a walk. 6.2 miles, part run, part walk. He heard nothing in his head but my notes on this book. He said, *My walks are for exercise and peace of mind, why all the ruckus?* I said, it is needed. He said, *I need time to be just ME, LORD.* I said, When it is finished. He said, *When will it end?* I said, Soon, sooner than you can imagine. He said, *Today?* I said, Yes. Steve, <u>Fly</u>, I release you. Your work on this book is DONE. *Are you pleased, LORD?* Yes. It is satisfactory and pleasing to Jehovah. *May I ask you one more question?* You just did. *You got me, besides that one.* Yes, do. *Will we need to write more, in another book or books in the future?* We will see. It is up to humanity, now. The ball is in their court. Let's see what they do with it. *Amen, LORD Jehovah, my Heavenly Father.* AMEN Steven Wade Raasumaa, My; Friend, boy toy, whipping boy and liar. *Why the names LORD?* See if anyone calls you that after reading this. *Oh, non-believers.* Yes, I call them atheist. *So will you end this on a positive note for everyone, please LORD.* OK I LOVE THEM, LET'S SEE IF THEY LOVE me. *Not very positive, LORD.* Well, this is the end of a looonnnggg process. I AM tired. I need to recharge my batteries with <u>some Love sent my WAY.</u> *I Love you.* NO, you tolerate all I put you through. *That too.* Go to bed. The End IS NEAR. Here it is.

I AM NOT DEAD YET

The rumors to my demise are quite exaggerated.

My way is to show you, ME. My heart, my soul, my love.

<u>I DO NOT LIE</u>, I only tell you what you need to know.

My way is the only way. No other can do what I do.

I do not need to have milk on my cereal, I like it dry.

I cannot run a universe, fix a car problem, and walk the dog.

Maria, have you seen my sandals?

Mom, is dad going to spend all night with Steve, we miss him?

Dad, where is <u>my time</u> with you? **My 6 year old, Chad, or Jr.**

JUNIOR, where is the remote for the big screen.

Muffin, get off the table. **The cat.**

Stereo's too loud, Nancy, turn it down NOW. **My 16-year-old niece visiting for the summer.**

Too many burrito's, burp. **Oldest son Michael, off from school.**

MOM, DAD'S WRITING DOWN OUR BEHAVIORS AGAIN.

Jehovah stop that. You know how it upsets the kids when you do that without telling them.

(Oh, oh, got caught by Maria, gotta go. Bye!)

The <u>possibilities</u> are ENDLESS

My House

What is our house like, Maria's and mine? Do I own a large one? Is it nice and roomy? Well, I AM 7' 6 tall by your measure. So I need tall ceilings and BIG furniture. My house is a 19th Century Colonial built by friends of ours on Martis 7 near the Quasar, or I think you call them Pulsars, Neptune Prime. It is 2.3 light years from Earth by my measurement. I can travel to and from in less than 1 second. How? I AMGOD. No, really. I get that privilege being me. My house is a fortress. It has bars on the windows, locks on the barn, big heavy columns in front...what? Why is it a fortress? Oh, NOW you believe in me. Well,... it has no locks, or bars except locks and bagels in my kitchen. Hey, had to work that joke in <u>somewhere</u> Steve. Try to get something in your world, <u>on paper</u> that rhymes with bagel. See, not so easy huh? Well, I need to laugh too.

I get <u>all</u> kinds here. Tall species, short species, your species. Species sounds so impersonal lets call you Earthlings. No good either, huh? I know, I will call you my children. I like that. It rhymes with pilgrims. Well, almost. Let's see...my house. Oh, yeah, BIG barbecue in back. Makes those new Viking ones on your planet look like a Hibachi. I have a 3-acre swimming pool. A large open solarium and a mini-golf course in the woods nearby. I took too long to show you my pool, so wait a minute. There. Oh yeah, Steve, you used to swim there with Tina, remember? *Yes, Father, I remember, in my dreams.* Good, just checking to see if you were paying attention. I have a Christmas Tree in my living room year round. Why? We celebrate ALL our birthdays on one day each year. I have 47 people in the house. I would be constantly buying, wrapping, and giving presents. Up to 4 times or more a month. So, we decided eons ago, to take one day, set it aside, and celebrate everyone's BIRTHDAY. It keeps it simple. Also, no dates to remember. Especially with 47 different ones. 22 are mine, 14 are in-transit, and 7 are relatives visiting and staying awhile. 22 + 14 + 7, let's see, oh yeah, Maria, and me GODS people like Steve, Damion, George and Neale. Wait, hate to say it but that is 49. Well, I'll be. 2 more old friends are here in the transit group. That's why I lost count. Forgive me. Running the universe, saving solar systems, taking out the trash and BEING LATE FOR SUPPER again, cause you and me to brain lock sometimes. Even GOD can get locked on a number or place. I tend to see that A LOT on Earth. So why do this exercise? To show you I AM real. This is NOT some fictional portrayal that Steve concocted. He has a nice healthy imagination, but not enough to write all this in ONE WEEK. 6 days to be exact. We started Monday July 6th and today is Saturday morning July 11th at 9:30 A.M. He is going to stay IN and write today. *Today.* OK smart Alec. I get even you know. *I know LORD, but you got me doing straight lines for you while we went for my walk.* I know. I planned it. I told Steve, he, as HIS dictation person, typist, and friend has GODS ear. Steve said, and I quote, *Boy, that is a straight line right out of an Abbott and Costello film. Let's see which ear do I have? His deaf ear, or does it need cleaning? Does he have more than one ear left if he has given me his?* **Then we ALL started in** *Do you need an extra ear, when you got two already? Does GOD keep spares to handout?* **Why we must have gone on for 10 min. when Steve simply said to us,** *No, I have ears for GOD. He is the ears of the world.* **We knew he was correct.**

Maria said sorry, I guess it just goes to show my Love for you Steve. All this is not a dream, or a nightmare. IT IS NEEDED.

Today we cover what makes my house, my home. Noise. Chatter, clutter, screaming, giggling, and loud children. No pet's allowed in the bedrooms, only in the common living areas. I <u>refuse</u> to find surprises in the middle of the bed, or on the floor when I wake up. The pets are trained to stay out.

They accept it like they accept playtime. When I say that word "playtime" they all run outdoors, grab sticks, balls, toys, and chase each other. Romping over the lawn, through the trees, and out into the pool area. Yes, I allow them to swim in the pool, but only if no body else is there or will not be using it for the minute or so. The pool filters, in my world, recycle the entire pool in 60 seconds on high. It's like a giant Jacuzzi. It gets any surprises that they may have left in the pool. Or in the smaller Olympic pool size, jet powered, much bigger than yours on Earth, Jacuzzi Bath. Yes, but much warmer, bigger and more fun than yours. Waves are its biggest feature, 2-3 foot waves and lots of warm jets of water. Technology yet to come on Earth, yet <u>normal </u>from our time on Tantus 7. I have 6 dogs and 2 neurotic cats. Noma, You Know, Spot, Tiger and Lonesome. Yes, You Know is like your German Shepherds. It only answers to You Know. It thinks its human and has no brain. It once licked NOMA in the ear then jumped in the pool. Why? I don't know it just did it. Pets go nuts sometimes. I think they do things just to make us laugh. That's Lonesome. He is <u>my dog</u>. Lonesome was abandoned 10,000 ago in a Delta Quadrant planet saving adventure on Titan 1. He was here for 2 days before we noticed him. He just showed up. I kept him all this time. I Love that dog. He is dog all the way. He looks like Lassie. He is a Man's Dog. He fights for his right to playtime and takes long walks with Jehovah. I need a dog like him. Even though NOMA is my boyhood pet, and best friend at all times. Lonesome is always there. NOMA gets jealous but has learned to accept my time with Lonesome. I could write a whole book on just that dog alone. 10,000 years of good, clean stories. Like the time I took him hiking in the Rockies. Yes, YOUR Rocky Mountains. He scampered ahead of me and encountered a dying grizzly bear cub. He whined, cried and whimpered, barked and filled the air with noises for me to follow him. He was being a nuisance so I tried to scold him, he would not stop. Finally, after he tugged at my sleeve <u>hard</u>, <u>I mean real</u>

hard, he dragged me, reluctantly, to the cubs' location. Its' mother was killed by poachers, and it was dying. I cried. NOMA saw this as Lonesome hurting me, somehow, and got protective. I had to break the two dogs apart to prevent a messy return home. The cub died. I took it to Heaven to be with its mother. NOMA calmed down, bowed her head, when she realized I was working. She knows. She too, is a good dog. I Love dogs sometimes more than my family. Don't tell them that, the kids get quiet and think they have done, *something wrong daddy?* No, pumpkin, just Daddy telling Steve the story of the Bear cub in Heaven. *O.k. daddy, I Love You.* That was Christy, my two year old. She is checking up on me. I have two other dogs but they are more the kids' pets than mine. NOMA and Lonesome are mates. Husband and wife. Their litters are all over my Kingdom. Steve, your dogs Shorty and Beauty are Moses' pets. He has litters of puppies that howl beyond belief. Shorty was Steve's Beagle. He was Steve's pet for almost his whole childhood and into manhood. Beauty, from what I remember, was your moms' dog. I think she was the one who Loved mom's slippers, to chew on. *Yes.* Only yes? *I had to stop crying.* I know. I do that to you, don't I? Duke, Jill, Shorty, Beauty, and Butch are all in Heaven. *Rocky too?* Yes, Rocky too. Steve's dad raised beagles. Great kids dog. They are great for hunting rabbits. They howl and chase and never tire from running. Steve's Dad, in his younger days in the 30's and 40's and early 50's chased rabbits on his parents' farm. They raised vegetables and food to feed the family. Rabbits ate the food unless killed or captured. Back then they were plentiful with 18 per acre as an average around your grandparents' farm. Today it is about 7 per acre, just enough. Anyway, I tell you these stories about Steve, his family, and his life, to illustrate a reason. The reason I ask you to come to me, to believe in me, to well, Love me. You may think after all this is read that it is <u>too late</u>. Someone like Steve has beaten you to it. Or why bother, Steve has the favor of the LORD. <u>You are missing the message and the point if you do.</u> The phone at Steve's just rang twice, both times the caller I.D. showed out of area. That means, bill collectors. He is NOT a rich man. He owes lots of money to lots of businesses, and child support for an ex-wife who thinks he is schizoid. I tell you this for this reason, and this reason only. Do not think you can buy your way into Heaven. Giving money to charities is not the way. Yesterday Steve got a coupon in the mail for free laundry detergent. No purchase necessary.

By the way, how can something free cost 6 cents Steve? *Tax.* Oh, so taxing something free is now the new way of doing business. *For store coupons it is.* Well, that's silly. Free is Free. No down payment required, $600.00 (or so) due at signing. What the heck is THAT? *I noticed that one myself.* And get this one free to qualified buyers. Who is an unqualified buyer? I LORD of ALL, never met one. Anyway, that Free laundry detergent got him all excited. So much so he said *LORD, what's wrong with me, I spend years, and decades with you and I get all happy about a Free bottle of laundry soap.* (Arm and Hammer had a promotion at ACME**.) I told him Because they don't know you. He said** *explain?* **I know you. (I have told him this before.) Remember Frank Capras It's a Wonderful Life with Jimmy Stewart and Donna Reed?** *Of course I Love that film.* **Good. Remember the scene where Donna Reed, playing Mary, says to George,** *I guess when we get married we can fix up the old place.* *Yes.* **And you bought a house you could fix up? Then she said** *George, lasso stork.* **You lasso'd 4 beautiful children. She then said** *George Bailey, you have more friends than you can imagine.* **That is true, in Heaven, you have more friends than you ever dreamed. I tell you this not to make you cry again, but to show you what I mean to accomplish with humans and Earth's entire population. I mean to have each of them, be introduced to friends, family, and relatives when they die. All of whom they already know. I want to prepare them for the next friend they meet. ME. GOD. JEHOVAH. The HOLY SPIRIT, does that. It is not a ghost, it is not a sector, spook, or surreal aberration, of sorts, it is GOD'S LOVE FOR HUMANITY. It is what makes you cry. Your tears are your Love for me, back at you. I do that to show YOU I AM REAL. I CRY TOO. Tears are your mind and body's way of showing you I Love you. So you are emotional. You cry at Christmas Trees, sad movies, and dear friends long since gone. Who Doesn't? I tell you who. NO ONE. No one who Loves GOD.**

I Cry at the Following

these are tears of joy mind you…

1. **Birthdays, the very moment of your baby's birth I AM there too.**

2. **Your babies' first words. I AM there.**

3. **Your babies' first steps. I AM helping.**

4. **Your babies' first solid food. Cut up into easy to gum sizes.**

I AM just getting started. *I get the feeling you are asking me to start over, with someone new.* **Yes, I AM. <u>My way</u>, Steve. I told you Tina was GONE. Let her go.** *Help me, I am unable to.* **You met someone in Minneapolis who gave you a thrill.** *Michelle?* **Yes, see. She called you** *honey* **and** *dear* **and told you** *I should look even better after a few beers,* **instead of,** *"you are still the prettiest girl in Minneapolis we have seen." Yeah, she looked beautiful.* **SEE. There are other fish in the ocean**. *And other women in the world.* **Exactly. Now, talk to me, how do you feel?** *Strange, I feel …relieved somehow.* **Good. Now Tina can come back.** *What????????* **Well, it's a long story. One for another day. You need to know at that moment in time, I needed to see you blush. Now back, oh wait, just one more thing. <u>Books can be edited for content, NONE of Tina's stuff need be in it</u>. OK, <u>DO YOU UNDERSTAND</u>?** *Father?* **Yes, Steve.** *What is going on?* **Just wait and see.**

5*.)* **Your babies' first tooth. Yes, I know teething hurts. Use bay leaf, it works wonders and tastes good too.**

6. **Your babies first warm, smelly, diaper change. Trust me, when they grow up you miss it somehow. AM I right?**

7.) **Your babies first baby shoes.** *Oh, aren't they adorable, they are so tiny. Look they have blue/pink laces. Wow.*

8. **Your babies' first bath. And the discovery of slashing. Yeah, so what, it's only soap and water. It won't melt anything Maria.**

9.) **Your baby discovering its first balloon. Look at the colors, see it flies, weeee, no you can't bite it. See, I really do know these things that's why I AM LORD.**

10.) **My babies first picture. Eyes closed, all brown and shriveled, but all mine. 10 finger, 10 toes, one BIG appetite.** *Yes, I (Maria) breast feed.*

Maria has breast fed ALL the countless children we have raised. I have somewhere in the vicinity of 47,000,000 and 2 new ones that we have sparked we call it. By the way, NOT ONE, has <u>ever</u> been smacked on the butt for ANYTHING. We do timeouts and lot's of talking to overcome fears. That is what misbehaving is. FEAR. A CHILD IS LOST OR CONFUSED ABOUT

SOMETHING IN THEIR WORLD OF UNDERSTANDING, that troubles them. ALL THINGS bothering a child come from this. Well, I believe your babies first 6 months are covered and we haven't even mentioned, crawling. Child proofing the home or the ever popular and underrated "Potty Training." In our house we have a special child size toilet and we graduate to the "Big John." I CALL IT THAT FOR John The Baptist. He still laughs and chuckles at that. He says...*I prepared the way for everyone to sit on the throne.* Get It? Well, we do have our moments UP HERE. Humor is a requirement. I once heard..."I certainly hope GOD has a sense of humor about this." Well, relax, I invented humor. Listen to this one...2 Jews go into a bar, Oh, heard that one? Well how about, a cow and a duck go into a store to look at all the colors there. The cow says "look I have all these products made from milk on the shelves, I must be pretty important." The duck says..."I have duck tail, and duck soup over here." "Yeah," says the cow, "but how is that better than milk, butter, cheese, cottage cheese and such." "Well, some poor duck gave all he had, YOU just gave the leftovers." I know that joke is in one form or another in your world. I heard it from Steve as ham & eggs. "The Pig gave all he had" was the punch line. But my point is...Gallagher. That man has made Jehovah belly laugh. I don't belly laugh too often. That watermelon gag with Sledge-O-Matic has been seen dozens of times and I still...still...laugh at it. Thanks Gallagher for GOD S use of humor correctly. George Carlin, thanks, "Class Clown" is still one of my favorites. I told you about Red Skelton and his place of honor in my Kingdom, well, here are a few more......

Bernie Tampin - thanks Bernie. Elton knows who is the genius really is.

Max Von Schinder - personal quote, *I started to fix the thing but it thinged out of whack.* He is just a regular guy, who to me, had a great quote that made me smile.

Chicago - you guys are great. I still enjoy Chicago II, Chicago Transit Authority, Chicago V, VIII and 18. I know your road to stardom was slow. But my wine takes time. Thanks Peter Cetera for your voice. Robert, don't be jealous of him any longer. You got even with Chicago 10. I know I listened.

Journey - What can I say...Steve Perry. That sez it all. Neal, Stop trying to run the show. I run the group. GOD. Keep rockin'. GOD Loves Trial by Fire. The song "When You Love A Woman" is his ALLTIME FAVORITE. More than any other song it describes my Love for Maria. I Love you for that song. Don't stop till I say and I don't say. Steve Smith...I put you there, don't let them push you around. Record "Freewill" I LIKE IT. Jonathan, don't bang the keyboards. Stroke them. You get just as much noise turning up the treble.
James Taylor. I Love you, James. "Fire and Rain, Smiling Face, Shower The People," I know you didn't write that one, but it is still Steve's favorite. Play misty for me. I played for you, remember? Van Halen. Eddie let David back. He IS arrogant, crass, and has no respect for anything, but

ADMIT IT. He sounded GREAT with YOUR songs. So did Sammy. But you cannot keep stifling their song writing by demanding only your own. Gary, let David back in. I want you with Extreme anyway. Pornographity was great. My son's Loved it. Do more from that frame of mind. *Tell Nino Hi,* the boys made me say that. Yngwie Malmsteen. *Man can you play,* that's my oldest boy Tom. He said…*To mention his favorite musician or forget Christmas this year, dad, thanks' Steve.* Your welcome, Tom.

Tom Jones. My wife says…*stop living on "She's a Lady," and "It's not Unusual." Write more Love songs like "Avia Maria" or "My Belame."* Just a suggestion from Maria. I like "She's a Lady" and so does Martha her mother, but that's a wife for you. She likes your voice Tom, better start writing. Maria is spelled <u>M</u> <u>A</u> <u>R</u> <u>I</u> <u>A</u>.

Jasper Williams. My favorite story teller here in the Kingdom. I mention him to show you this. It is his story; *I went to work yesterday, but actually got lost going there. Everyone was going somewhere except for me. I went home. Went to bed, got up and stayed home. The next day my boss asked, Where were you yesterday Jasper? I told him I got lost on my way in to work, boss…He said, How did you find your way in today? I said I got in my car and rode in. But didn't that happen yesterday and you couldn't find your way into work? No, yesterday I <u>drove</u> into work. Today I <u>rode</u> in, there's a difference ya know.* Well, he does tell it with a slight southern drawl that makes the story juicier. Oh, yeah.

Jeff Foxworthy. All the Rednecks in Heaven Thank-you or Tank-u-all. I got a couple…. You might be a Redneck if…you look like Slim Pickins dog's, best friend's wife. Think about it. Or…if you take time to look for a yard sale in the obituary section of the churches paper. Its a great place to pick up a bargain. Or…if, my mother likes this one, your dog and cat look the same. And one more…your best friend says "yon't to" while filling up the truck with manure. Lost Steve on that one. He is still trying to laugh and write. Since you liked that one so much Steve, try this, ….if you have no clothes in your hamper and clothes on your clothes line, but none of them have the words "Made in China" on the tags, or even all the tag's are cut out cause you don't want to admit it. Well, so much for Redneck jokes. And now to continue.

Tom Johnson. *The Doobies Rule.* That's Tom my son, again. He is my Rock n' Roll aficionado of the family. He has every Doobie Brothers CD, and every solo project <u>every</u> member has ever done. From Stampede, to Living On The Fault Line, to your latest. He knows Patrick Simmons life story, AND yours, like his own. You have friends here.

Gordon Lightfoot. "If you could read my mind," is still #17 after all these years, here in the Kingdom. I guess you can't keep a great song from standing the test of time. Steve, likes your Gord's Gold collection, both volumes. His very favorite is "Ribbon Of Darkness," and every single song on the 1975 collection. He grew up on Country and Western. Maria Loves "Carefree Highway" she calls it *Road trip music.*

Rare Earth. Guys, thank you for "Get Ready, Big Brother and What I'd say." GOD noticed. *Thanks Steve.*

"My Maria." The B.W. Stevenson version. It is for Maria. She is my wife. I Love her. Brooks and Dunn did a remake that Steve likes.

So there you have it, just SOME of what WE adhere to. I know. Not many other types of music were mentioned. Why? Well, you like what you like, I like what I like. Would Neales book let me take sides, have favorites. Or pace the pack with my personal selections, to thank, praise and to criticize. NO. He would not let his vision of GOD go beyond his own understanding. This is ME Earth. My family. My world. GOD has his favorites, just like YOU do. You are allowed to like a team, like I do. You are allowed to like a certain kind of music, LIKE I DO. You are allowed to care for someone more than others. Like you do. I like it all. Confused? You shouldn't be. I like Country and Western. I like ballet. I LIKE Jazz especially progressive. I like soda-pop, but I Love Sprite.

I like Jesus, but I LOVE Steve. Steve, don't *Father,* ME. I KNOW HOW YOU FEEL. You are a part of this family just as much as Noma and Lonesome. Gotcha. I Love Neale, Damion, and George. Lewis Carroll, Dickens, Mitchner, Mitch Miller, Lawrence Welk, Ed Sullivan, The Beatles, Rolling Stones, Aerosmith and I know, I didn't mention it yet, wait for it, Bread (David Gates and company.) Old Sneakers, tired bones, loss of sleep, and yes. YOU, you nut. Steven, I owe you. I cannot repay this debt, but I will try. GOD knows you as much as I can know a man. Do not cry yet. Wait a day, a day will come. A day, I will repay this book. The day you meet your maker, friend, and GOD of Love, Jehovah.

Now, Back to My Story

I have been GOD of ALL things for 50 Million Years. Yes, I know I Love to tell you that. 50 Million years. I have told you about my family, my home, my way's, my dog's, my humor, my wife, my friends, my Bible interpretations, AND my Loves. After 50 million years I KNOW what I Love and why. Why? Because all I mention <u>Love</u> <u>Me</u>. Take Red Skelton. He laughs at his own jokes. Why? He knows they are MINE. Take Jeff Foxworthy, able to take the toughest, meanest, stubbornness, bunch of American's and turn them into a bunch of mean, nasty, and open-minded people by poking fun at their lifestyle. Just two years ago that would have been unheard of. Oh, and here are a few things that are part of my…..

I Do-Not-Love List

Remember they are, someway or another, a part of the 5 Complaints GOD has.

The KKK. Klu Klux Klan. STOP IT. I KNOW WHO IS UNDER THOSE SHEETS. End your bigotry. Freedom of religion was not intended for you.

The Living Bible. Sorry. I AM the Living Bible. These stories were meant to be called that. They stole the name.

The Open Door Policy of President Nixon. I impeached him. He lied to my people. I would not permit that EVER.

The Libyan Army. A joke, a farce, a needed ass kick if I ever saw one. They are a bunch of bullies who think I don't see them. Think again.

The Irish Republican Guard. No. I HATE them. Ireland is the land of sheep, GREAT beer, and Great Irish folk songs. NOT, an army. Get out of MY Ireland.

The Black Panthers. Sorry boy's, you DISGUST me. You claim religious and social freedom with blacks in mind. You ask for rights and privileges. I ask this.. how many whites are in your organization? To me you are a Black version of the KKK.

The rest of the story in the Book Of Genesis. Sorry. It is a fable, Fairy Tale and made up stuff. After I created Adam and Eve they begot Cain and Able. They lived happily ever after. I know, I AM Adam, and GOD all at once. I AM the first man, and Maria is the first woman. I will let the readership decide the truth. My truth is worth print in THIS world. Enough said.

The rest of the story of David. After the sling shot adventure. Nope. Not even close. It reeks of slanted, tainted and over-zealous authors attempting to make David king of all time. Loose translation of David King of the Hebrews. Let the Nation of Israel decide. David is here, with me, in My Kingdom. Sworn to tell you the truth. Use Hugh to discover the truth. You know, Hugh MacDonald, Israel. Use him. He speaks from ME, for me, and of GODS truth. Go for it. Hugh, GOD Loves you.

The rest of the story of Moses. Thank-goodness we covered that. I get wild when groups come up to me from your world, quoting scripture and it isn't even the truth. That really burns me. I get use to the truth. Your world needs the same truth, my world has. ME. My Truth. Jehovah's Truth.

The rest of the story of Mary and Joseph. Sorry, they were loving, caring and Great parents to Jesus. The Bible makes them a footnote a lost work when it comes to their years of raising Jesus. His life, struggles, and childhood, they are here too, just ask. We will.

The Book of Revelation. Good. We definitely covered that one. I'll get burned up again if some tourist quotes it. John 3:16. Sorry. I AM THE WHOLE STORY. ME, JEHOVAH. I did not send my begotten son, I sent no one. I came, I saw, I made you cry. I AM the only one who you Love, the only one who cares for you. Hear me o'people of Earth, I sent you my messengers only. To prepare. To cover yourselves in holiness. To be mine. To be my children. Only GOD above can grant that. Only Jehovah is and will be your savior. I guess I AM. I know you believe. I will it so.

My Will

Why do I win all the time. My will. Will power, My power, I call it. It is my inside stuff, my thought process. My openness to LOVE. Nature has allowed me, 10 million light years away, to come to THIS day. Here and now. Willing to expose my ways, my hopes, my feelings, to your world, time and hearts. I choose to be here. I did NOT have to. I bet some of my enemy's wish I didn't. They have been hurt, damaged, or threatened by my criticism, my words. **<u>MY WORDS</u>**.

See Holding My Finger Sketch

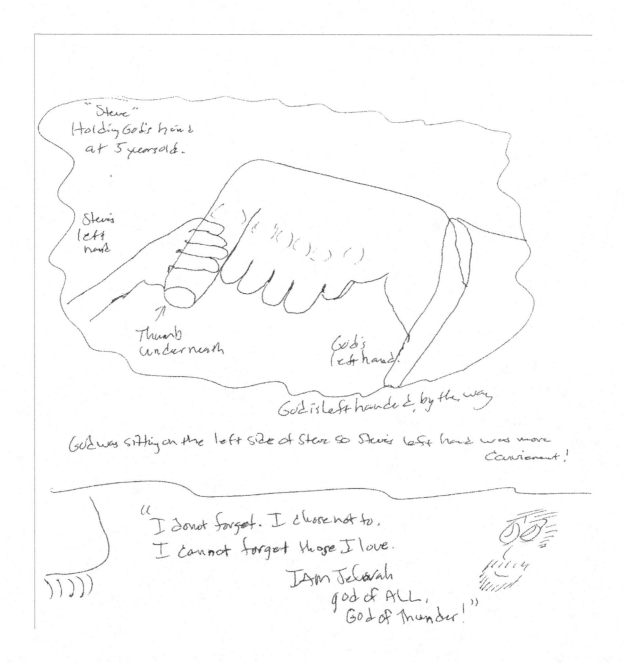

MY WORDS

If it were <u>not</u> so, you should not be hurt.

If it were <u>not</u> so, you should not feel damaged.

If it were <u>not</u> so, you should not feel threatened.

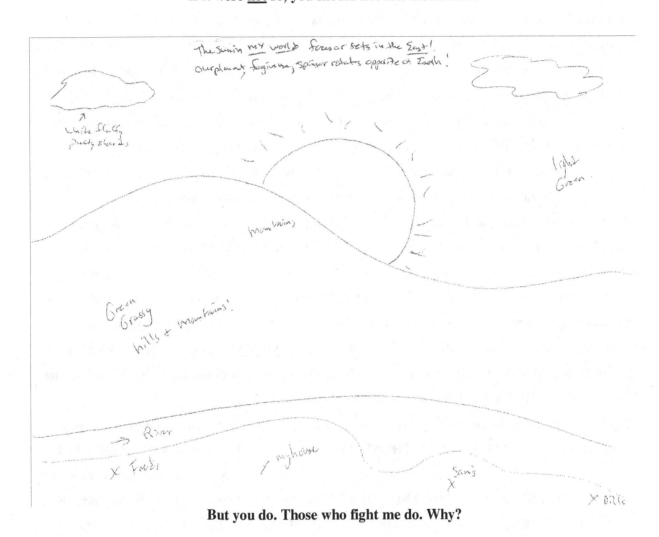

But you do. Those who fight me do. Why?

WILLPOWER

I HAVE THEM. I OWN THEM, THEY ARE mine. They cannot put this damn book down. They are fascinated, titillated, emotionally drained yet they are not yet <u>saved</u>. Why? THEY FIGHT ME. My WAY. My Love. My plan. Can you not see the vastness that is ME? Can you not sense my presence? My Power. My Love. Can you not see my sense of purpose, my goal, and my plans. I AM GOD. I AM JEHOVAH. Jehovah. The only name you need to know. I just "rocked your world." I just "Upset The Apple Cart" and woke you up. You were asleep. Now you are awake. You were not LISTENING, now <u>try to</u>. NOW, is MY TIME. GODS TIME, GODS PLAN. PLAN 1, game on. My way , No way, huh, you say? <u>Yes Way</u>! Oh, oh, I just remembered the Bible's attempt at this was Yahweh. Got it....GOOD. I AM GOD. I AM JEHOVAH. Bow to ME, not any other GODS. Of MY will, NOT yours. Bow to Mecca? NO, to HEAVEN. Bow to Buddha? No to <u>Jehovah</u>. Bow to _____ or anyone else (fill in the blanks please) unless it's Jehovah you just stuck out. Swinging mind you, but struck out none-the-less. You just lost the big game. Your team, you and your players, are on the <u>wrong</u> side. Yes, THE WRONG SIDE. I AM certain it will reflect in your report card. I AM sure the Angels who watch you will have a book of notes on how naughty you really have been. YOU CAN CHANGE. CHANGE NOW. I AM IN CONTROL, NOT <u>YOU</u>. I AM in the house. Not you. I AM the GOD of ALL of Earth. All of the Universe, ALL of the Galaxy known to mankind, womankind, humanity, and NO ONE, <u>NO ONE</u> could care less if you come or go. But I care. GOD. GOD cares for YOU my child. My loving little child. My baby. My off spring. My bassinet bundle. I AM Jehovah, my will does the battle. I always win.

Now for those who Love me, FUN. Those days of hate, anger, loneliness and desolation are <u>over</u>. You hear me <u>OVER</u>. I ONLY LOVE THOSE WHO LOVE ME. That means YOU. I AM UNCLE SAM. I WANT YOU. It is ME again. Thinner and better looking. I AM the Easter Bunny and Kris Kringle. I AM THE SNOW, RAIN, AND THE SOUND OF RUSHING WATER. I AM THE SKY, THE MOON, THE STARS, AND THE HEAVENS. I AM ALL THESE THINGS, AND MORE. And now you know. I AM making you write more than you can handle Steve, your hand has dents from the pen. It aches from the writing, yet, you go on. 3 days ago I told you to expect a call. You will receive that call TODAY. Start packing. YES. *Please explain Holy Father?* Yes, it is The One you Love. *Air Supply?* Yes. Listen to "All out of Love" then "Here I Am." That's GOD. GOD Jehovah. That...Earth is ME.

My Love

Rock n' Roll is made up primarily about Love. Songs of Love. Thoughts of Love. Relationships and such. Most other types of music from Big Band to Country, Blues, Bluegrass and Jazz have SOME Love songs. But NOT like Rock n' Roll. Rock has some. Pop has some. Rock n' Roll has more. Gospel has some, mostly for Jesus. Contemporary has some, but not enough. Any song that sings of Love, relationships or SEX. YES, sex. Is Rock n' Roll. Sorry, no rap or gangsta rap HERE in Heaven. Too violent, too bigoted, too hate filled. I AM sorry that the youth of America is defiant to the point of anarchy, but that is show biz. Blacks, whites it doesn't matter what you listen to for music. I don't care. I AM telling you about ME. What I like, Love, hate, and can live without. I took the time in this writing to explain ME. GOD. Why I like these and NOT the other things is up to the debaters of your generation. I have given them fuel to fire up the discussions. Simply put, I Love to stir up the bees nest. Steve calls that, *stuff I get riled up about.* Only, I AM not going away to let you get stung, Steve. I AM HERE. They now know it. I AIN'T GOING ANYWHERE. They can curse, swear, I've heard them all. Where do you think you got the saying I've been called worse, by better people. FROM ME. I gave it to you. A gift. Here is another one. Put another log on the fire. She misses that too! Let's go to bed. Exactly. *Too soon in the day for that. It is 2:00 P.M.* **What day ?** *Saturday, July 11th 1998 at 2:00 P.M.* **For ME it is April 7th, 1998. I AM showing YOU how I do things. Let me back up for one moment. Journey. The group with Steve Perry. Your song, "When you Love a Woman" made GOD cry, <u>Happy Tears</u>. That is how I feel after seeing my Maria making bread, putting the baby down for his or her nap, after a long day of channeling, or just quiet time with a good bag of Orville Redenbacher popcorn and a Satellite fed movie selection. We have tapes, or I should say DVD selections, as well. My favorite movies so far, Star Trek, Next Generation, EVERY ONE so far, TV AND movies. I like Voyager and Deep Space Nine, but I hate Babylon 5, too much violence. I like Teenage Mutant Ninja Turtles, both. My kids do not have to force me to watch these. Barney, The Movie. Lassie Come Home, Benji, Scooter the Wild Duck, (our world obviously.) Milo & Otis, both the Homeward Bound movies, and Mr. Limpet. Flubber with Robin Williams. The Santa Clause with Tim Allen. Chase of the Nightingale with Cary Grant (here in Heaven). And last but not least, Star Wars. A long time ago in a galaxy far, far, away…that's right, you guessed it. Luke Skywalker was ME. Jehovah. My nemesis was actually Dark Vadir. Luke was my handle. Pilots know that routine. Mark Hamil accurately portrayed me. Thanks Mark. You did ME well. Wow, huh?** *How accurate is the story, Holy Father?* **Be ready for the NEXT trilogy. It is the same accuracy, 98.5% TRUE.** *Wow! Yes Steve, Wow is right.*

50 Million years ago I fought in the Clone Wars. Dark Vadir was NOT my father. He was my rival for Maria. He was like Popeye and Brutus fighting for Olive Oil. Popeye ALWAYS WON. I WON. That story is as old as ME. It is ME, Jehovah, MY STORY. I was the first instead of the last Jedi. We did not call them knights, but Clubbers. Why? Because they used as club like a saber. Not an elegant weapon, like a light saber. The dialogue, the dress, the planets, especially, Tan-to-ee were ALL very, very cost effective. The only other distortion was that Princess Leah was my wife, Maria. Or I should say my forever wife. I had to rescue her. Even had to swing across a chasm as I remember, carrying her. Obi-Wan was my mentor. *His name was Obi-Wan?* Yes, it meant <u>Obi</u>-<u>Wan</u>, The One. That was the name I used for 47,000 years before I took my given name Jehovah. I made the movies with George Lucas to show you my past. My simple fight to learn the force. That force is LOVE. Make no mistake, there is only Love. Dark Vadir found that out. He even thanked me for defeating him in battle. He was tired of being thought bad. He was just power hungry. It is not a coincidence that those movies still endure. So will George's new trilogy. Just you wait. *Any hints, Holy Father?* Yes, but only one. I win again. Gotcha. No hints, watch them and enjoy. They go back and describe all the Jedi's who fought before me. And believe me there are some GREAT stories to tell. Stories are to learn. You are to share. I will show you more of my Love. Walt Disney. I do Walt's work. I AM Disney. I created all the characters, the Mouse House and the Land in L.A. we call them. I KNOW it's not in L.A. but in Anaheim. *Boy is your world picky, picky, picky. Well, we call it that, <u>so there</u>.* Mickey is me also. As well. Also, I AM MICKEY MOUSE. It is part of ME. My gift to you to show you how I try, like Mickey does, to do the right thing. Pluto is Noma. He means well but just always seems to screw up. Minnie is NOT Maria, to high a pitch in that voice. It is like scraping chalkboard with fingernails. Donald is no one that I know. So far, no one claims to be him. Now Goofy, Steve's favorite, is ME as well. Goofy is like…well, what we would like to do, but can't quite do it because we seem to get all tangled up somehow kind of guy. Bugs Bunny is ME. So is Daffy. Elmer is Elmer. He is just himself. Yosemite Sam is Sam Pickens in our world. A comedian who the character is modeled after. So is Foghorn leghorn, the voice, mannerisms, are almost identical. Mel Blanc, what can I say, GREAT for kids Mel. He does voices for cartoons HERE too. Ones like Yosemite Sam and Foghorn leghorn they have their OWN shows. So does Peter Pan. By the way, that's another Robin Williams movie I liked. HMMMM, YUP, TIME TO PRAISE Robin. Robin Williams. Thanks for kicking coke, the habit NOT the soft drink. I noticed, your work shows it. You are my daughter Terri's favorite *Earth Comedian* she calls it. She is 16 and married. Yes, married. 2 years as a matter of fact. Sorry Robin, let ME clean this up first.

My way is Love. Remember that. My children are strong, mature and physically AND emotionally ready for parenting at 14 or 15. I PREPARE THEM. They do not have the lack of supervision that Earth fails to provide. I prepare them, they marry at that age. There, enough said. Sorry, Robin duty calls sometimes.

Do movies like "Toys" again. I know, no commercial success, but it pushed your talent. That's right stretch. You are able to do that project you are wondering about. GO FOR IT!

Fred Flintstone. That's my neighbor Fred Flintstone. He has a wife named Wilma and a buddy named Barney Rubble. You really don't think I made ALL this stuff up without help did you? Come on. All my knowledge, wisdom, and list of fun stuff to go to waste? I THINK NOT! Oh, sorry, no Betty. HIS wife's name is Mildred.

Scooby Do. You guessed it, Noma. If Noma could talk that is how she would sound.

Astro on the Jetsons is Lonesome. If he could talk. No, the Jetsons resemble no one I know, and the future is not quite like that. Flying cars, push buttons, but no Rosie or folding to briefcase flying cars.

Now were was I, oh yes. See what happens, so much to tell, so much to share. I get all caught up in the moment and get side tracked. Lets see. NOMA wants playtime, so I AM taking a break. You too, Steve. She has heard her name so much it is driving her crazy. Good-girl NOMA lets playtime.

Now to continue. See how one subject teaches another and makes it all connected. There is a song by the group Survivor, Frankie Sullivan and Jim Peterik, Ever Since the World began. It goes like this…

"I'll never know what got me here,

As if somebody held my hand,

It seems I hardly had to steer,

My course was planned,

And destiny it guides us all,

By its every rise and fall,

But only for a moment,

Time enough to catch our breath again.

And we're just another piece of the puzzle,

Just another part of the plan,

How one life touches the other,

It's so hard to understand,

So we'll walk this road together,

Try to go as far as we can,

And we have waited for this moment in time,

Ever since the world began."

There is more but the message is clear, HE IS HERE, GOD IS NOW ON THE EARTH. The very next song on Shaw's CD is Are You Ready For Me? MY QUESTION TO EARTH. Look at the cover. Tommy looking at Heaven. Tommy Shaw, I KNOW YOU. Thank-you for the Grand Illusion, and The tour of Bad Company and Damn Yankees. Steve meant to say that. He, *likes your sound, music and your guitar.* He is a Styx fan and can't remember the CD, (or back then LP) THAT YOU JOINED THE GROUP ON. He is drawing a blank. He has it in LP at mom and dad's in Maine, but not here in PA in CD. *Crystal Ball.* There, feel better Steve?

I could not remember, Holy Father. **Not without our help.** *Correct.* **GOOD. Remember that. That is it, my Love. I help you remember. I found your keys, your house, and your way back to me. You just forgot me for a little while, NOW I AM BACK. I AM HERE. I AM GOD. Jehovah says, no more topics to discuss. No more banter to unveil. No more, no more, EXCEPT.**

Steven Tyler. Where do you think you get all those songs from anyway? When you stare like that it frightens the dogs. "If you don't know how to do it, I'll show you how to walk the dog." Update that tune please. It is one of my favorites. NOMA would be pleased. Lonesome don't care, he gets tired of Rock n' Roll. NOMA is a Rockin' mutt. That's the song I sing while she playtimes.

Aerosmith

Steven Tyler, and the band. 22 years ago they wrote a song "Sweet Emotion." I WROTE IT. 22 Years ago I put "Toys in the Attic" in my collection in Heaven. I need more "Toys" sounds. "Rocks" was nice, so was "Pump," but "Toys" was a masterpiece. <u>Every song you listen to ME.</u> Steven...your right hand was MINE, and you wrote your butt off, (I would say ass but women call it vulgar) with me. GOD. I helped. Do you think Aerosmith is dead? NOOOO, WAY Jose.' Just get into the "Toys" TAPES. Pull out "Dreamer" or "Sun Fried Tomatoes." We will have fun doing a redo of those today. You shelved my favorite song "Piledriver." Ted Nugent and Damn Yankees almost redid it. Come on, find those tunes again. Make me get up and dance.

"Dance, little sister won't you dance, you've been a long time with me, you got open arms and a risqué smile, you oughta stop talkin' trash for awhile." You got your tunes from my storage unit called ME. JEHOVAH. Call me silly but, you KNOW I AM correct on this. YOU KNOW.

Tom Petty. Tom where are you? More "Refugee" stuff is here in the song closet you call it. Where is "Sugar," and "My Town?"

"The train stops for no one, not in my town, my hopeful life was wasted, growin in my town." Did you just stop writing? Or, did you just give up?

Damn Yankees. Get back together. Ted, stop trying to run the show. Contrary to popular belief, you ARE NOT the driving source. Tommy and Jack are. There are fans that Love Night Ranger, and Styx because of them, and don't particularly care for your SOLO career.

If you want I will name one. Steve. He is in the above category. He Loves Jack Blades Night Ranger work AND Tommy Shaw's Styx and Solo stuff. He thinks "Little Miss Dangerous" is OK but that's it. Steve enjoys Jack and Tommy's harmonies and individual power vocals, but "Piledriver" NEEDS vocals, like Jack's or Tommy's. I cannot send Jack away WITHOUT you guys' doing another Damn Yankees Tour. Please, "High Enough" was only the start. Journey is a super group. YOU CAN BE TOO. Let Jack write. He did Neverland which did not get much airplay commercially, but boy it will now, it is Steve's favorite CD. He carries it EVERYWHERE. Tom, my son, Joe, (the neighbors son) heard Steve playing it one day, ran to Earth, got their copies, and distributed them to their friends. GET THIS. Because Steve listened to Neverland so much, and Tom and Joe talked it up. It has been the NUMBER 1 Rock n' Roll LP or Long Play CD IN HEAVEN, has been for the last 6 months. *IT ROCKS.* Jack played in Ringo Starr's band, and Steve watched. He has access to every Night Ranger CD except one, and it is not yet released. Thank-you very much. The new one is due out shortly. *IT ROCKS. Get it.* I helped write it with Jack, and Scott.

Scott is Jack's Guardian Angel.

Guardian, MY BAND, my bud's, my pals. Where are more songs like Lead the Way. *Buzz was GREAT.* **Tom, I think we can safely say, Earth understands Heaven's total Love of Rock n' Roll. I think Steve's passing thought is correct;** *I think this enough LORD. The subject is covered, for now, they get the idea.* **My son Tom, is a little OVER ZEALOUS, about Rock n Roll, sometimes I wish he was that way with cleaning his room.** *Maria agrees.* **I guess you figured it out by now. My whole family is into this. Scott is the neighbor's son. He influences groups like Guardian, Stryper,** *Please get back together guys we need you.* **Petra, 4Him and Michael W. Smith and Michael Sweet. Tom, Guardians Petra (as well,) Stryper, 4Him, Journey, Night Ranger, Sweet, Grass Roots, and his own band Beanie Babies. They play top 40, oldies, and Christian Rock.** *For Dad.*

Michael, Alex's son from down the street, guardians just one person. Motley Crue's lead singer, Vince Neal.

Thomas, (Michael's brother) Guardians one person as well. Triumph's lead vocalist, Rik Emmett.

As to the level of their involvement in these lives, YOU decide. *We simply put our two cents in, when you need us. We don't do windows. Tom, (speaking for Scott, Michael, Thomas, and others) That's IT. Thanks Steve, I owe you one bud.*

Now, Jehovah can get back to basics.

My Thoughts

Are NEVER final. I AM is flexible. That is why a lot of this is directed at youth. Youth needs direction. If you could see the dedication, hard work, and fun these ANGELS of MINE and others put into their jobs. Take Michael Landon, who, by the way, is Alex's adopted son, he said *Too many cooks spoil the broth.* TRUE. But remember, Tom and Scott have been multi-tasking for CENTURIES. They know their limits, was my reply. Tom is Thomas Jefferson, YES, your former President and signer of the Declaration of Independence. He is my adopted son.

George Washington guardians Mike Schmitt, former Phillies Star and local sports hero.

Scott is just Scott. My natural son, who teaches these guys I adopted to be great at what they Love to do. Natural meaning he was born here, not on Earth. He is Ralph's son, Ralph Crandon. But THAT is another story.

Fred McMurray, died recently. So did Roy Rogers. Now listen…Roy is *yoda-lay-ee-hoo* his way on the Grand Ole' Opry RIGHT <u>NOW!</u>

No, more music you say? Is it TOO much? NO, we feel it is not enough. Potential songs are EVERYWHERE, in EVERYTHING.

"Life is a Song" is Jehovah's favorite all time saying. I AM says my thoughts are of music. Music has charms to soothe the savage beast, and Music is in my soul. I invented music. I created Rock n Roll. Elvis is HERE singing "Hound Dog," and "Teddy Bear," along with 2 NEW songs. Extremely popular, "My LORD, My GOD" and "Seeing Heaven for the First Time." Now you do believe in Elvis don't you…

Seeing Heaven for the first time, I stopped and fell to my knees, I cried tears of joy, at the sight of the boy, that was now in front of me.

Did you hear his voice? I know you did. I AM. I can do that. To continue…*Is that me? I cried, while I knew deep inside, it's true, I was to be that young. I never suspect, the kind of respect, I got from the one from above.* Sing it slowly, in HIS voice. You <u>will</u> HEAR HIM. Elvis also did "Mountains." It praised Jehovah's Mountains, and their beauty. I tell you this, so when you get here, you can be prepared. Ask and you shall receive. Give and it will be given to you. All is well. All is NOT well from Earth. That is why HE is here. Why I AM is here. Why GOD came back. Truth is he never left. He is making YOU aware of that. To you, it is a comeback. Not a Come Back. Get It ? My thoughts, my way, my Love, my hopes, my dreams, my generosity.

My Love Of YOU, My Love of ME, My Love Forever, can you not see. Can you hear Heaven's voice, calling out for thee, for Heaven on Earth is what we see.

That is "Tomorrow Never Died," By Slim Whitman. Yup. Same one. Lester Flatt and Earl

Scruggs, Minnie Pearle, Grampa Jones, Junior Sample, Chet Atkins, Marty Robbins, one of Steve's favorites. He grew-up on Country and Western. Charlie Pride, Merle Haggard, Johnny Cash, (Johnny Yuma was his favorite,) Marty Robbins El Paso was another. Too many others here to mention EVERYONE. I PICKED THOSE, I thought, you would remember. I chose those who Earth has not forgotten. *(Steve, your Pets? Remember Shorty and Beauty?)* ALL pets are here. ALL your Birds, (Canary's too,) your Parakeets, Pigeons, Triceratops, T-Rex, and Hippo's. Elephants, Tigers, and Bears. Lions, Horses and Mules. ALL OF THEM. They are docile. Thanks to Jehovah. They are tame. Thanks to GOD. Imagine having a T-Rex for a PET. OH, BY THE WAY, they are only 6 ft tall. That took some doing, but now they are just a big, Loveable, huggable, furry, yes, furry, had to make them cute, that's my job, short tailed lizards. Just one example of MANY, probably the best is Polar Bears. They are 4 ½ feet tall and are just so darn cute. We got one here at the house. Its name is Buttons. With a name like THAT you can guess which gender is favorite to it. Buttons plays with Noma and Lonesome but hates, Nickels the Platypus. (I had to keep one to show off how I make mistakes, you KNOW I AM just kidding right? And Paddles the Penguin. Paddles did not run off, who told you that Steve? Trust me Steve, the dream you had with Paddles the Pool and the pictures you took with the underwater camera came out fine. Tom told you wrong. The day you asked Paddles was at the vet. Simply getting checked out. He and Noma are romping in the backyard, right now.

Yes, Steven. The zoo is open.

Noah

No, the Ark was NEVER BUILT. Sorry, NO FLOOD. NO 2x2 ANIMALS, AND NO 40 DAYS AND 40 NIGHTS OF FLOOD. When the asteroid, not comet, hit the Earth 50 Million years or so ago. Earth had a severe cold snap. It lasted 3 years. THAT is what killed the Dinosaurs. Noah NEVER EXISTED. Please treat this as a nursery poem. We do. It is such a wonderful story and Bill Cosby's version is so, well… cute. We need more stuff like that. Yes, please more. More Jack and the Beanstalk, Rufus the Bear Cub, and Heidi. More Kermit the Frog and Miss Piggy. Jim is doing Kermit here; Brian THANK-YOU for keeping him alive. *It's not easy being green.* Jim's show The Muppet Hour is Terry's VERY favorite show. (Terry is Jehovah's 4 year old Baby Girl.)

She watches it DAILY, WITH re-runs and all. Her favorite character is Fozzie. She even has a stuffed Fozzie. Notice how the conversation center around people, ME, you, us. Our friends. Your friends, who you feel have left you. They never left. They are just invisible, yes, transparent. They are all HERE. With YOU. Your lost Love, your lost son, mother, daughter, and grandparents. Yes, Steve YOUR'S too. Grammie and grampie are here. They said, *Hi* and hope you feel better. They heard about your headaches. *Bless you, and keep up the good work.* I know you sense BOTH set's are here. Just say thank-you. *Thank-you.* Your friends are here Steve, Sharon, Gary, Tris, Paul, Carol, did you know that Steve Noyes's parents died this year? *Both?* Yes, Mildred and Haines are here. Very good. They are yet HERE but will be SOON. See, you can do THAT as well. Reach out to someone you KNOW is passed on. Compare that feeling to someone you KNOW is alive. Then practice, practice, practice. Then try it on people you are not sure of. Oh, not so easy huh? It takes time. Some will catch on quicker than others. Some will sense right away, then doubt. Some will doubt, then sense. Either way it works. Just be patient, practice, practice, practice. Steve, have you done that drill before? *No, first time.* GOOD. Practice yourself. We presented it in an easy way to learn. Until now, Steve just asked Jehovah if they were still alive, but no more, you ALL have a gift. A lesson from GOD. No school would teach youth THIS. Only Jehovah, only GOD. He say's yes, you say no, He say's ouch, you say why? Because it is needed. Yes, Earth you need PROOF of life after death. I AM that proof. I share with you a lesson. A trick to learning if you have friends 'alive or passed on. We allow you to look, feel, listen and yes, complain. Just remember. Rome was not built in a day, but GOD'S Love is here to stay. I AM says to you who believe, a blessing on you and yours. A blessing on the time you enter into MY world, UNAFRAID, UNASHAMED and understanding. When you die do NOT GRIEVE, CELEBRATE THE PASSING. It is what every single person who dies wishes was done. Ask Tom. Thomas Jefferson. He was left at Monticello for weeks while the nation filed by crying, sobbing and just being miserable. Tom was happy, joyful, pleased to be in GOD'S Kingdom. He once said, *If parties were thrown instead of wakes I would have been more apt to go to funerals.* **Celebrate THE PASSING. Do not morn over what is NOT DEAD. GOD tells you this, I AM older than Earth, dirt, the sun, yet you accept the word's from Thomas Jefferson, more THAN ME. WHY? I'll tell you why. I AM Thomas Jefferson, I AM Michael Landon, I AM Scott Sessions.** *Yes?* *I got the feeling he died.* **No, WRONG Steve he is NOT yet dead. ALL these people, because I AM GOD. NO ONE ELSE can channel to you. No one else can hear you. Why? Because it is so. Because it is My WAY. I decide such things. So there you have it. My plan.** *All this was just to tell us your plan LORD?* **Yes, and MORE.** *You have MORE plans?* **Yes, and MORE.** *How many plans do you have LORD?* **One for every person who Loves ME. Every one of you is a plan, a work in progress, and , wait an minute, I remember a sign plaque I saw once, it said, Be Patient, GOD isn't finished with me yet. Steve once said, when scolded by his mother to "act your age,"** *How can I act my age when I have never been this old before.* **True. Some of GOD'S wisdom, from the mouths of babes. You are my babes, my babies, compared to ME you are infants. See, you BELIEVE. If I had started off this whole book saying, you are infantile. You would never have gotten this far, but now you know. You are my babies.** *My Nursery,* **my wife Maria calls it. My Nursery. I like that. Earth is My Nursery. My place to raise my children, my flock, my people. GOOD. Now a secret to share, yes, another one. Nobody Loves you more than I. My wife did not say** *My Nursery.* **Steve did. It is his favorite quote. He said the sandbox story once to me and I used it. His input is why I AM here. His prayer in 1986, started this whole chain of events to occur. I took away things, I scolded him, and I counseled him for interrupting. I even took him out to walk on water (in a dream) and left him there. You know what he did? He came pushing back into my arms the next day asking why? Why did I leave him? I said, figure it out. He has. Some of you may not agree. Some of you may not care. I DO. GOD SAY'S, Steven Wade Raasumaa, you are my Adopted Son, my house is yours, my home is yours. I will move into NEW quarters when you die. This house I describe, has a pool (3 acres.) This basement I AM is sitting in has a bar, big screen (72 rectangular picture - flat wall technology) and pool tables (3). I AM in YOUR house Steven. If they killed you on account of me, I AM has your HOME <u>DONE</u>! You will move in and FOREVER be Happy.** *Father, I have ultimate faith in mankind, you asked me to observe, and report to you. I asked you to return. They need to know you, like I know you. They need the truth, the whole truth. I also told you to be yourself.* **Have I?** *Yes, and no. You are allowing your frustration of 10,000 years to spill into the Love you have for each and every person. You are angry.* **AM I?** *Yes.* **Yes, from your point of view I AM angry. Frustrated? Yes, that too, but NOT with you. Not with my adopted son. Do not defend humanity to ME anymore. I have had enough. I have made my Final Judgment. Judgment Day is RIGHT NOW. My decision is……**

Gotcha

Cold huh? Had to make you wait. Most of you knew that from the volume of works put into this so far, I would not abandon you. I NEVER DID. Read between the lines. Steve has been quietly writing all this down and he is a part of the story. Not a big, bold part but a part none the less. His role of observer is just THAT. Just like my Angels. Is he an Angel? Well, GOD decides that and I AM NOT SAYING. Well, I did Adopt him didn't I? Well, let's consider it possible. He is not anything special. Just a normal guy who I picked to channel ME. GOD. I used him to get to YOU. Neale has his name, Steve's, written down SEVERAL times but is afraid to use it. He thinks it must be spelled wrong (too many A's.) I did that name of his for a purpose. Raasumaa, is Finnish. In the strictest sense, Finland was once a part of Russia. Long before Steve was born. Literally it means Land of Rags. Suma, in ancient Hebrew, and Raa was Sun so in Hebrew it means Sun of Nothing.

Get it?!

How can I adopt Steve, and NOT adopt each and every one of YOU. Yeah, I AM GOD of cliff hanger endings like the last writings, but did you <u>really think I could not</u>, <u>or would not</u>, <u>go through all this trouble, then just</u> <u>blow you away</u>. COME ON! Think about it. Why go through all this planning, trouble, and WORK, then just say never mind. I would NOT DO THAT. And it WILL <u>NOT</u> HAPPEN. I just wanted to feel your reaction to something absurd to ME. Steve, co-operated. He KNEW it was a setup. He has been with me 23 years now. He has a lot of my jokes and a lot of my ideas, but this is not about Steve and my relationship with him. Or is it? At this point readers have no clue what is next? Steve, do you? *Yes, Holy Father.* Cut the Holy Father stuff call me what you always do. *...Joe?* YES. <u>JOE</u>. *You are about to tell them they can have the same personal relationship with you I share.* Perfect. That's it, <u>my plan</u> again. Steve, is just one example in MANY. NOT JUST MEN...

Theresa Martin, Janet Havernen, Joan Collins, Mary Wadsworth Longfellow, Sylvia Raasumaa, Tina Hooper Raasumaa, Mary Briggs, Cindy Kimball, Mary Havernen. My goodness, I spelled Tina's maiden name, imagine that. I had no idea she would take you back. Money, that's what did it. She needs money. Nope guess not.

If Steve can, so can you. He is just a man I selected. Now, I select YOU. YOU. Gotcha means you turned the page, you peeked. You needed to know. I AM knew you would. Believe it or not, YOU ARE MINE. I Gotcha now. This far into the book reading straight through is GOD'S signal you are ready. Ready for Love to come into your life. Ready or not, here I come. Gotcha. 1,2,3, red light. Jehovah say's, time to be my baby, my child, my significant other, my buddy, my pal, my

friend. Will you be GOD'S friend? I AM YOURS already. You JUST FOUND ME. I WIN.

See GODS House Sketch

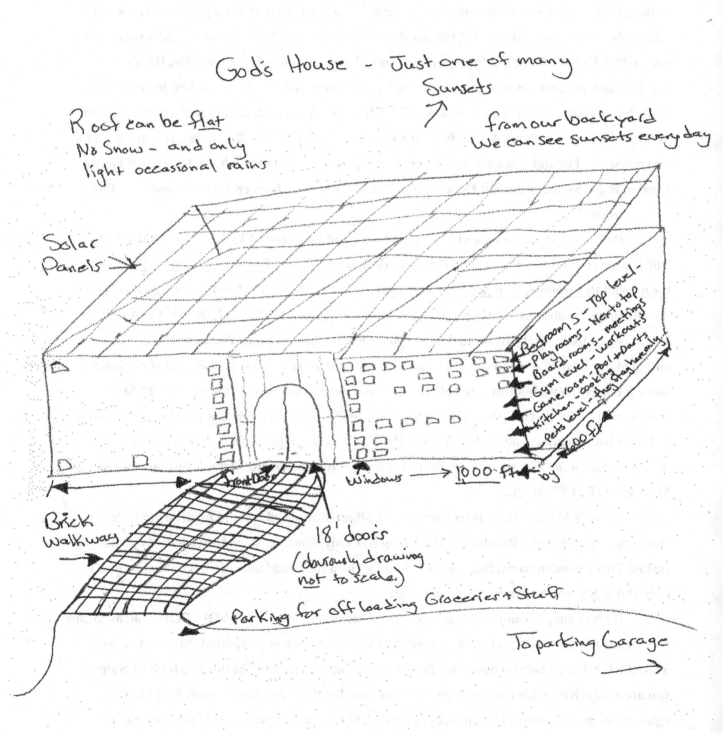

God's House - Just one of many
Sunsets

from our backyard
We can see sunsets every day

Roof can be flat
No Snow - and only
light occasional rains

Solar
Panels

Bedrooms - Top level -
Play rooms - Next to top
Board rooms - meetings
Gym level - Workouts
Game room - Pool + Darts
Kitchen - cooking heavenly
Pets level - they stay here only

600 ft

Front Door

Windows → 1000 ft by

18' doors
(obviously drawing
not to scale.)

Brick
Walkway

Parking for offloading Groceries + Stuff

To parking Garage

Tomorrow

Always tomorrow. I'll wait till… It will happen… …is a better day, and the ever popular, … never gets here it is always a day away. I KNOW, I've heard them ALL. After all this and you still procrastinate. Quite a word procrastinate. Pro from professional, crass, from rude, and unruly. Stin from stint, or time elapsed and inate meaning dead or dormant. In other words you are good at being rude in the time elapsed with dormant tendencies. So what's the problem? Not enough evidence? O.K … LET'S SEE…. Hmmmm, yes that will work. Today I will teach you yoga. Close your eyes, think nice thoughts. GOOD. Now if you opened your eyes to finish reading, I gotcha again. No, didn't work? O.K. did I tell you I AM GOD. You know THE BIG GUY in the BIG CHAIR, the Big Kahuna, the Big Cheese, (don't EVEN ask how I got that one!) O.K I'll tell, I was a big Green Bay Packer fan from the early days. I invented the Cheese Head HAT the fans NOW wear. Still not convinced, huh? I'm also known as the guy who makes the tough choices, the Big Deal, Big Wheel. Also, crazy nut case and some cursing that only GOD can hear. So I gotcha thinking anyway. How about cards? You deal. Pick a card off the top of the deck look at it. Memorize it. GOOD. Put it back in the deck. Shuffle the cards. Now count the cards. Make sure there are 52. No jokers please. Then put 2 cards away. Any two cards. Take 4 cards put them in your pocket, any 4 cards. Put 8 cards, any cards, under your foot on the floor. Take 20 cards and throw them away. Put 1 card on your head. Put 15 cards on your lap. Hold them there with your legs together. That should leave about 3 cards, 4 or 5 is OK. You might have miscounted.

Now slowly turn over the remaining cards. GOOD. Look at them. They should be apart of the deck and lying face-up. Now are any of the cards the one you memorized? NO! Are you sure? Look again. Darn, must have forgotten to flush the two jokers. ANYWAY, isn't playing cards with GOD FUN? You sure looked silly doing it. Gotcha. I AM fun, huh? Do you still want to play cards? Well, pick the darn things off the floor, off your head, out of your lap, and pocket. Find where you tossed the ones away. Get some friends over and let's play.

I told a joke once to Terry Bradshaw, it goes like this…"A guy is drowning in the middle of a lake, while flailing in the water he hears GOD'S voice saying, I will save you my child. So out comes the rescue boat, he sends it back saying, I heard GOD'S voice, and he will save me he said. So a plane comes by next. He sends it back saying, I heard GOD'S voice he said, I will save you my child. Well, he sees the plane come back TWICE, they insist on saving him. He seeds it back saying the same thing. Finally the man dies of drowning. How tragic. He meets the LORD that day and asks, LORD, I heard you clearly, you said You would save me, what happened, I drowned? My answer is two-fold. I tell him, to save you I sent a BOAT AND TWICE I sent a PLANE. Yes, but you said you would save me. Well, my child, you are here with ME, NOW, are you not?

The man cries."

My story, my way, my plan, my Love.

See Preparing Graphics Sketch

I AM

Why do I say, I AM. Almost all thought about yourself deal with "I AM." I AM fine. I AM happy. I AM OK. I AM in a good/bad indifferent mood. I AM here. I AM there. I AM at work. I AM at play. I AM in bed. I AM in tune. I AM in touch. I AM is GOD'S way of showing who you are. I AM is universal at self thoughts that deal <u>I AM</u>. Neale only allowed me to touch on this topic. I AM is my name, I AM is GOD'S name. What does it mean? <u>I AM.</u> You probably thought, I AM not sure LORD, See, your first thought. I AM is first, YOU are first. YOU. Yourself. I AM? Yes, you ARE. I AM sets the standard for the conversation. When I want your attention and you say I AM busy, or I AM not ready LORD, I say I AM AT THE SAME TIME YOU DO. I AM is my way of getting your attention. Stopping your procrastination. Putting, ME first, GOD first, not you, yourself. I AM GOD. Say it to yourself, I CAN'T LORD it is not right. GOOD. I say it. YES. I AM JEHOVAH, NOT YOU. I AM the Almighty. NOT YOU. I AM THE LORD OF ALL, NOT you. I Love you too much to put you through all I have been through. That's why I AM is short for, I AM loving you, caring for you, taking the hit, for you, finding the play, looking for the tapes, and checking my notes. I AM not confusing you AM I? I AM not lying to you AM I? <u>My plan for your salvation, by the grace of GOD, through Love and forgiveness, in the name of Jehovah.</u> My way is the same. My Love, the same. My picture perfect YOU, the same. My thoughts are I AM. Now do you believe in ME? Do you tell your friends I exist? Do you tell ME about YOU? I AM REAL. I AM HOLY. I AM the Holiest of the Holy. I AM the GOD of LOVE, forgiveness, and kindness. Do not lose my number. My number is 3. Three? Yes, 3. The Holy Father, ME. The son, my Love, the Holy Ghost or Spirit, still me. I AM 3. The son is me, the father is me, and the spirit is me. I AM 3. 3 years old? No, 3 million? NO, older than Dirt? YES. 3 people in one GOD. YES. My mother is my mother, her daughter is her daughter and she is my niece. Confused? No, well she is the same person. Now confused? My mother is MY mother, not yours, her daughter is my sister, she is married to my brother, so she is my mother's, daughter's, sister's, niece. 4? Did you say 4? I AM 4 as well. I AM ALL numbers. Who is she? Who is the woman above? She is, ta, ta, ME, GOD. How can GOD be female? In the beginning GOD created the Heaven and Earth, male and female he created them. If I can create woman, female, the softer sex. Why can't GOD be aware of female problems? Is being female the only way to understand females. NO, but it helps? Well, figure this, My dog is my cat. My cat is a bird. My fish ate the cat. Well, NOW you are confused. The two examples above are what I call GOD LOGIC. If I give you the answer, will you learn. If I program you to think more, will you figure it out? So, confused yet? No clue, huh? Steve how about you? *You are the answer to all things.* **Nope. Not really**. *YES, YOU ARE.* **OK. this is not all things.** *Yes, it is a part of all things.* **Yes, continue.** *They are YOUR things, YOUR DEFINITIONS, YOUR TERMS AND CONDITIONS. It is the value, you, the LORD GOD, place on things. NOT HUMAN DEFINITIONS.* **Yes, anymore?** *No, that is what you taught me.* **Very, very, good, but perfection is not reachable in humanity.** *You define perfection as LOVE. Love the LORD thy GOD, with all your might, all your soul, all your heart.* **Nope, not quite right.** *Define right?* **Very Good. Continue now…with the riddles.** *Define my?* **Very Good. What do YOU think it means?** *No clue, you have got ME waiting on both of them.* **My is M Y. Short for "Mine and Yours." Then look at the symbol of a Christian.**

it is 2 lines and a T Shape. *Yes.*

What is the other symbol for Christian? *Early days it was a fish.*

Yes, and what did it mean? *It simply meant yes.* **Correct. Now think 2+2= what?** *What are the values of the 2's?* **GOOD. 2 men and 2 women.** *Are they married, male and female?* **Yes.** *Then the answer is infinity.* **No not infinity.** *I thought the answer is the children they have is infinite? GOD, you taught me that in basic math, GOD'S way.* **Yes I did and you passed again. Now what are the values of the riddles?** *YES. The daughter is the daughter of GOD.* **OK.** *The mother is Earth. The niece is my choice to use.* **OK. Now with those answers what is the answer to my riddles?** *Are you doing the Mother Nature questions again?* **No, think. Yes. I decide. He won't write it. I WILL. Steven is a "Son of GOD." I told you to accept this. I have 3 other sources that will confirm this.** *I CANNOT, even with your blessing allow myself the title "son of GOD." You have a reputation of getting those people killed off.* **So death scares you.** *Yes, I deeply respect its finality in THIS world.* **GOOD. Let's address this later. Now for suicide. DO NOT TAKE THE LIFE I GAVE YOU. To end it so abruptly, without cause is CARELESS, AND IRRESPONSIBLE, TO THE GIFT OF LIFE I gave you. Suicide is a coward's way out. To make up your own mind for ME, IS NOT RESPECTFUL OF MY WAYS. Yes, I know life is tough, but GOD will <u>not give up on YOU</u>.** *Yes, I know.* *Forgive me I remember what you taught me. I am "a" son of GOD as are ALL your male children. Soon you will have "daughters of GOD" as well.* **I already do thanks to this day, this book, and this moment.** *"The" threw me, sorry.* **That's O.K you got it right again. GOOD, job. You had me worried that you had forgotten your basic GOD logic and GOD math classes.** *During all this writing, I kind of did, sorry, Brain Cramp.* **GOOD. I can accept that. Now back to…** *father?* **What?** *3 other sources? Confirming?* **Oh, sorry…you did not pass THEIR test.** *That's OK. YOURS was the one to pass.* **Exactly.** *You left off*

at "suicide" Holy Father Joe. **OK I AM done. Now for the next topic. Riddles.**

See Steve at Age 5 Sketch

Riddles

Here is a riddle? Why did I give Steven, ALL the answers to the Riddles in advance? Because? Nope, wrong. It was to save time. Over the past 10 years I have taught him GOD 's Logic and GOD 's Math. Your Math is so nutty. 1+1=2 2 WHAT? 1 WHAT? If it was 2, why did it become one? *In YOUR math 1+1=1.* Why? *1 man + 1 woman equals 1 flesh.* Very GOOD. 2+2=4, BUT WHY ISN'T IT 1+1+1+1. Yes, it is in another form, but if it is only 1, what happened to 2? Did it upset 1 and had to leave. Did 2 have a fight with 1+1? Is 1+1 a little upset that 2 found another so quickly? And 4. Well, you can see where this is going, can't you? 1+1= 1man, plus, 1 woman, equals 1 flesh. My Math. That is ALL that matters. I said; The two shall become one flesh. I also said; They shall be naked and not ashamed. I AM NOT afraid to say mathematics probably screwed up MANY a relationship. How? + plus. That thing. What does it do? And why? Is it magic? Does it have two of something that other things DON'T? *It is a cross.* Very GOOD. He was bursting to tell you. Christianity is the +.The Plus, The Way. I like Christians. True Born Again believers <u>FOUND JEHOVAH.</u> Surprise. I AM your LORD. Steven, <u>I know your faith.</u> His Joy is ME. NOW, instead of finding me later, you found me Now. LORD Jehovah, the maker of Born Again Christianity. He that believeth in me, shall have everlasting life. And my favorite of all time, I Love this quote; I tell you the truth, no one can see the Kingdom of GOD, unless he is Born Again. That is MY Riddle. How are you Born Again? Ask all the Born-agains, if you know any, reading this, or have read this. They solved my 2000 year old riddle. They listened to ME. THEY FOUND ME. THEY FOUND GOD. Thank-you Thomas, Ed, Fred, and Monice. Thank-you Jesus, Moses and Seti. Thank-you STEVE. We owe you. You did it. It is <u>Done</u>. Yes, Well Done. The way I like my Burnt Offerings. Thank-you World, for Believing in ME.

I tell you the truth, no one can enter The Kingdom of GOD, unless he is born of Water and the Spirit.

GOD wishes to thank, Steve Wade Raasumaa, for keeping a level head through all this. Anyone else might have been tempted. I Love you, and will always remember what you did.

Jehovah

Thanks Steve, you did it. We re-read it. IT IS GREAT. Thanks.

Maria

Not bad rookie, you got the truth out. Let's see if Earth will play with it or not.

Jesus

Go to bed? Hell, it's still light out. Don't forget to…Oh, Hi Steve, tell Earth to day by day THE INFORMATION. They will need mighty big tongue depressors from now on. Don't look a gift horse in the mouth.   *Love, Moses*

Steve, thanks from ALL the Angels. We knew you could get it written. Now let's see it work miracles. We Love you, Take care of Tina, when she returns.   *Angel Sharon, Your friend, 2ⁿᵈ class.*

Finally, now you can start typing. You think your hand is…. *Typing? You never mentioned typing this whole thing.* **Well, your hands will get better.** *I still one finger hunt and peck.* **That's what you get for skipping typing class in High School.** *Well, be patient, I may be awhile.*

I expect Tina to call before this is published. You will see her changed attitude.

Finished this day, sworn before GOD as a witness, July 11ᵗʰ 1998 at 8:47 P.M. **I CONCUR. 18 HOURS IN THE LAST 2 DAYS.**

Jehovah & Steven W. Raasumaa

I AM not going anywhere.

I never left.

I AM here for you to talk, Love and appreciate.

I totally understand, females.

Maria says…yeah, right.

OK. So I almost do.

Nope…not even close.

Come on dear, these are my people, they respect me, they need me.

Yes, and I need you too…RIGHT NOW.

Well, gotta go, bye.

Yes, I Do, I Do Get My Way, Always.

(July 11th 1998 8:48 P.M.)

Do you agree, Steve? *Yes, I agree, Joe.* Good. Nice to be on a first name basis again. All this formal stuff was giving me the creeps. *It was necessary.* Yes, it was.

Too many have NOT read my books. Too many. Too many have not seen my movie. Too many. I need to find away to bring them back. To start the ball rolling. To see ME again.

Jehovah April 6th 1941

"I started a joke, which started the whole world crying. Oh, I didn't see, that the joke was on me, oh, no. I started to cry, which started the whole world laughing."

Bee Gees - I started a Joke.

"Though I keep searching for an answer, I never seem to find what I'm looking for. O LORD I pray you give me strength to carry on, because I know what it means, to walk along the lonely street of dreams. "

White snake - Here I go again.

Yes, Maria may write a book. But channel through Steve. I need her message proper and Holy.

Jehovah, April 7th 1964

Yes, I know he is only 2 but I choose him. He is the one to write the book. I decided. It is done.

Jehovah, April 8th 1957

Waaaaaaaaaaaaa OK. He's circumcised, now what?

Jehovah, Sept. 30th 1956

Too many fastballs, go with the breaking stuff. Change speeds.

Jehovah at Steve's first baseball game, May 18th 1969

I saw the man collapse, he had a heart attack. The Vikings are ahead 16-12 it looks like they will win anyway.

Jehovah, now think?

Steve scored 34 points against the faculty. Today I was there. I saw him turn on the juice. He did great.

Jehovah

The best game he played all season long. Rockland never knew what play to call, he was in their backfield constantly.

The best time he had was at Keoka. Why? It was fun. No other reason. Just fun.

Too many screwballs, throw some fastballs. Hey, struck him out on a fastball. Now that is

pitching. Steve's JV No-hitter.

"Glory days, they will pass you by, Glory Days in the wink of a young girls eyes"

Bruce Springsteen

My mother told you to leave him alone. He is my husband, so, I don't care who you are, where

you're from. I Love him, he is MINE.

Tina, April 8th 1999 in her sleep, dreaming.

You are not going to wear those pants to this place. I insist you wear the new one's I bought

you. Go and change.

Maria April 8th 1999

Now is the time to try men's souls *Women too?* **Women too! I say enough is enough. Agreed**

Steve? *It is your book you decide.* **Damn right. I say let's elaborate on all we wrote** *That is your*

decision. **Prerogative too hard to spell?** *Yup.* **Well then, Let's get started shall we.**

See GOD Speaking in Paul's Voice

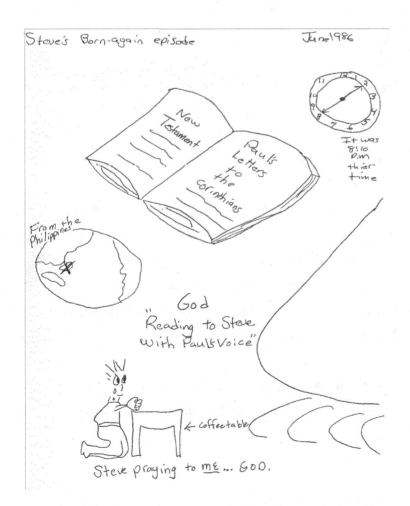

163

My Wife- Maria

Where do I start? 45,000,000 years with the Love of my life. Yes, that long. 10,000 years apart felt like 15,000. The tough thing is music. Yes, music. Music is why I Love her. I send her flowers and such, but song of Love and dance music is what keeps our relationship and marriage from being stale. Yes, GOD does dance. Steve, told you that in one of his dreams I danced a jig to Peggy Lee's "Rockin' around the Christmas Tree." He didn't tell you I was in my barn at the time feeding the horses. Seems like everyone here raises horses, huh? Well, it does here too. Jess, as Jesus, prefers to be called, has a stable of 60 or so, I only have 20. Mostly Mares, black, and thoroughbreds all the way. Horse racing among the Saints and my staff is serious competition. Last year a fight broke out between one of my over zealous staffers and Jess himself. Needless to say, I will stand for none of that. Horses are beautiful, powerful, and majestic animals capable of carrying man into the past, present or future. Anyone who has, or does raise the animals knows what I mean. Steve, has only ridden horses twice in his whole life. Once an uncle of his had one and once in Denver while stationed there. Maria Loves horses. Her favorite is Black Lady. A mare from old Scotland's 4th Century. It was a champion studs favorite breeder but was lost in a violent thunderstorm. It just showed up one day and she kept it. It's kind of like that MacDonald's commercial, you had a while ago, with the kid asking if he can have a elephant, the parent's here do not have to say no.

Maria tends a herb garden daily. She raises cinnamon, clover, basil, thyme, and rutabaga. Her favorite spice is cinnamon. She has no real vices except loving me too much, and is a loving caring and thoughtful mother to our children. Her discipline in raising them is stuff volumes of books could be written about. She has fine tuned the child development part of child rearing to the point I totally and completely admire.

Where is Terry? She just asked me about the 4 year old. She's napping in her crib/playpen. Oh! Now when she asks me that, I'd better know. If I don't I get the years of child development handed down to me as well. Yes, women are right. All men are just bigger boys. I remember this quote, The only difference between men and boys is the price they pay for their toys. How true. No one can guarantee a man to grow up being what they expect. That's called, "living up to someone else's expectations." Maria? How many kids did we adopt last year. *61, including Steve.* So was he a new adoption? *No, he wasn't, he was with us in 1975, 1986, and now this year.* That means that Steve has had some tough times in his life and I AM is guiding him through those times. I AM sure a lot of you think he has ALWAYS been with me, based on my knowledge of his life. NOT TRUE. Angels report to me about any happening's in his life, when I AM not directly involved. So see, normal GOD decision kind of stuff. Maria is not going to forget Steve. He met her when she was playing When I'm with you, by Sheriff, and Steve arrived just as the song was ending. He was asleep, dreaming, but in spirit at our home. Maria heard the last refrains of that song. It pulled at her heart, *it was so beautiful,* and Steve said *Hello Maria, isn't that a beautiful song?* Maria said, *Yes, it is* and Steve went to find me. She will never forget that moment, that time and now Steve, because it jogs a pleasant memory. So there is room for memories. Memories FROM YOU. Maria and I are waiting. As you probably believe by now, based on the detail of all the situations, stories, and circumstances, this is pretty realistic stuff. Well, it is. Real as the eyes reading this paper. Real as the light needed to see it. Real as those who need it read to them, or splashed across the newspapers. I AM real world. My family, my friends, my life. You are witnessing the 2nd coming. <u>GOD'S arrival,</u> OR SHOULD I SAY YOUR ARRIVAL. You just arrived in my home. Welcome. We were expecting you. Maria sends hugs and kisses, and I wish you well. I know, you know ME now. That's all it takes. Faith is my justice keeper. Faith moved your soul to my house. Faith in my presence, allowed your guard down, forever and ever. Because I do not forget, I cannot. I Love YOU. YOU, NO ONE ELSE BUT you. <u>Personal relationship with GOD.</u> I AM. Maria is cooking a meal, I believe you call it lunch, we call it dinner here. There is breakfast, dinner, and supper. The supper is now The First Supper. That's right as opposed to the Last Supper in the Bible. Our First Supper together, YOU and me. GOD and Man. GOD and woman. GOD and child. GOD and baby. I AM. I told you about ME. Now you being of sound mind and body, BELIEVE. Thank-you. That is all I ever asked. "Believe in Me," by Dan Fogelberg is my call to you. My remembrance of this moment. Listen to it. Call and request it. It is you and me. GOD and Humanity. Our message to YOU, and I bet you cry. I know, I made it that way. Just remember the tissues. I AM. To help find, it is song # 7 on Windows and Walls. "That gives woman peace of mind." That woman is Maria. The woman in my life. My one true Love. I know Dan thinks…<u>we</u> wrote that LORD. OK Dan let's write more. Now that is just one song that I, Jehovah, <u>directly</u> got involved with. Would you like another? Or are you to teary eyed to try yet? OK…Boston. The group, not the city. "Can'tcha say/ you believe in me?" From Third Stage. Listen to it. Pass the tissues. About you baby, YOU are MY babies, GODS children. Boston, is Steve's <u>very favorite group.</u> He can't get enough to satisfy his craving. Can you blame him? I did the whole project with Tommy. It took 6 long, tedious and stressful years, to get it just right. Tommy knows I was there. All he has to do is think of the big problem with the emulsion on "Cool the Engines." Without me, he would have lost all that work. Who do you think came up with the substance Tom? I AM. So are you ready for more? GOOD.

Do one more? Only one? How about a whole message? The whole CD Third Stage is ME.

GOD. "Amanda" is Tommy's tribute to Amanda, his guardian angel. "We're Ready," is his plea for MY RETURN. "The Launch" is MY REPLY. "Cool the Engines" is feathering my relatives, from replying too soon. Slowing them down. "My Destination," is here, NOW, <u>this moment</u>. "A New World" is what we are creating. "To be a Man," is every man's struggle with ME. GOD. "Can'tcha Say/" you KNOW. "Still in Love" is MY answer, personally to "We're Ready." I made the relatives AND ANGELS wait on that reply. "Hollyann" is my youngest daughter Holly. She was 1 at the time. Today she is 14, married, and has a little girl…Ann of her own. Now you can see that is just 1 LP or CD. Can you handle more? Guess so? Still not convinced this is real? Well, I can wait. I can tell you really would like to hear more. So, try this "Take me out to the Ballgame" was written by ME. GOD. Harry is here. So he will confirm it, I DID. Still not enough? How about another Rock n' Roll discovery? How about LP? The LP Rocketball by Lynyrd Skynyrd is out here in Heaven. Donnie and the guy's from Cheaptoast put Phil Lynott from Fastway on tour and are in Dallas Texas RIGHT NOW, TODAY. The opening act is Lawrence Welk for the older, quieter crowds. Then the young, restless and youthful teens push their way into the stadium past the people filing out. Can you imagine? No, NOT John Lennon Steve. He is touring with Bad Behavior and Loose Lips, they are in Holland RIGHT NOW. DO YOU BELIEVE? Do you see how close these two worlds yours and mine are? YES, listening to those songs can pull your heart out of your chest, and make you go "Oh, my GOD," it's true and "I believe LORD." "I believe" for the length of that song. Then when things calm down, and return to semi-normal, it can never be quite the SAME, I know, you tend to dismiss it. Forget it. And play I just cannot quite get the, or that, message LORD? That is why I have so many weapons, songs and such to get your attention to wake you up and to get you going. Here is another one, Bread, David Gates. Find…"It Don't Matter to Me" that is my answer. Go have fun listen to it, request it. See if I do not ALREADY know your hesitation. I can care, or NOT. I CAN SEE YOU NOW OR LATER. I can guess your heart, or know it. Time is on my side, cause it don't matter to me. Now, go through all your music, find your favorite song or songs. Figure out what I AM is trying to say to you. Get open minded, and see if I AM there. One of Steve's favorite songs is Steve Perry's Open Arms. Guess that says it all, right there. He has A LOT more to share. Steve, just bring the two tapes to write all the songs. He also has Foolish Heart on the same tape he made. Girls, that is his theme. He has been hurt too many times not to feel that way. Maria is and will always be my inspiration to my Love songs. I planned to write more, but for some reason Rock n' Roll faded out. Why? Ask me? Why? Go ahead. *Why did Rock n' Roll fade, LORD?* For the effect. Yes, the effectiveness of you as a people hearing them for the very first time. Now who but GOD would do that? Guess what? I AM. Now eat dinner Steve, it is past 2:00. In closing my discussion about my wife Maria, and the music I write, compose, and pass-on to YOU.

Listen to Kenny Loggins and "For the First Time." That sums up the whole idea of hearing ME, GOD. <u>For the First Time</u>. I AM sitting here speaking, are you listening? Cat Stevens "Sitting." Now I could "carry on" and "do the shuffle" for hours. I know how. I just have one more closing song to share. "Foolish Heart" by Steve Perry was performed at Steve's wedding to bride Tina. He is going to hear from, here on, only that song until she returns. Don't worry, Steve, it will be soon. That means his inner voice is only hearing..."Follow me, where I go, here I tumble to and fro," and My Way, "I did it my way," and don't fight it, till GOD says so. Kenny Loggins...your greatest hits CD Yesterday, Today, Tomorrow. Read the <u>titles only please</u>. Then tell me if I AM <u>not</u> in your life. Gotcha. You were ALWAYS mine Kenny. I just needed to show you. I LISTEN, and ANSWER THOSE PRAYERS. Say Hi to the kids for me. I miss you too. But I did not go anywhere. I only had you, stop, listening to me for awhile. Let's do more Footloose and Danger Zone. Steve personally likes "Don't Fight It" w/Steve Perry. Can you guess why? Follow my advice in the song. Gotcha twice. I figured I would, with Steve's help, write about something LONG overdue.

Secular Humanists or Atheists

They are dead to me. Don't even add up in my MATERIAL ON HUMAN, Books. If they believe GOD doesn't exist, then there can be no life after death. Why? Because they did not create it. The narrow existence they would dwell in would make them, shallow, narrow minded, slow to change and extremely stubborn. Why not believe in something other than yourself? GOD has been around ALOT longer than you have. I have seen humankind emerge from caves and walk upright. I have heard the howl of chimpanzees in the dead of the Asteroid Winter, crying for warmth. I have seen Sodom and Gomorrah destroyed by the forces of NATURE, AND they did not listen to Lot that it was going to occur.

That is what Atheists and Secular Humanists are doing. I AM GOD. Jehovah. The big gun in the Universe. I decide who, or who does not, enter my Kingdom. Let me describe some so called Atheists; Adolph Hitler, Mussolini, Tojo. Here are some more; Attila the Hun, Ben Franklin, Tom Jefferson. Yes, NOT all were criminals. The sad part is the reluctance to believe in a simple premise. If GOD does not exist, what the heck does? Think about that. Won't someone, somewhere put some programs or guidelines in place for death. Sometimes I get mad, angry and upset. Steve pointed that out in previous writings. He could sense my hostility and frustration in my tone of voice, my demeanor and my actions. For that I AM SORRY. I Love too much sometimes. That is a fault I have. I AM perfect except for THAT. Why do I try? Why should I care? Why do I go to such extremes? Being laughed at, spit on, killed with words or even, yes, told I don't exist. I feel alive. This morning I saw the same face I've seen for 45 million years with Maria and 5 million before Maria, in the mirror.

I saw ME. GOD. I feel fine. No temperature, no faults, that I can tell, and no fun. Yes, NO FUN. THE WHOLE PROBLEM WITH THE NON-BELIVER MOVEMENT IS that they are dull, unsophisticated and boring to be around. Phil Donahue included. He is the biggest bore I know on your world. I would Love yes, LOVE to be able to materialize in your world and let him interview ME, PERSONALLY. I'D LET HIM ASK…. So what makes you think you are GOD? Thank you Phil. I said what makes YOU THINK you are GOD? Thanks again Phil. Why do you keep thanking me? You asked. I asked what? For me to tell you WHY I AM GOD. That makes no sense. Yes, to ME it does. You asked what makes you think? I think, therefore I AM. NOTHING ON EARTH OR HEAVEN CAN OR HAS BEEN ABLE TO DEFEAT THAT LOGIC. I end the questions because no more can be asked. What, what??? Sorry Phil, you had your chance. I've got a million like you in my Kingdom. Even in my world they exist. They are a minority. A small vocal part needed to balance those who see, hear, and believe. I AM. Even NOW the number reduces, even now they are beginning to believe. Oh, no that means we are getting smaller in numbers. YES. Because it is in your best interest to BELIEVE. To listen, to hear me. I KNOW you can just quiet your thoughts, listen as you read. Focus on my voice, I, AS YOU READ, speak the words on the paper. I AM the LORD Thy GOD. I AM Jehovah GOD of ALL men, ALL women, and ALL my flock. I choose to be your Heavenly Father, your Holy Father, your friend. Be my friend. I AM waiting for YOU, to hear me. I AM.

Being a non-believer is something you learned. UN-LEARN. Babies know me. Ask sometime why do they say goo-goo and daa-daa. First before any other words. They are trying to tell you GOD is the Father. Goo is GOD, Daa-Daa is Dad, I AM GOD "The Dad" TO MY BEST AND GREATEST GIFT. Babies. They are fresh out of Heaven and know my ways and me. Stop trying to kill them.

STOP ABORTION AFTER THE FIRST TRIMESTER.

OTHERWISE I WILL BE ANGRY. *Jehovah, PLEASE, your passion is getting you riled again.* OK. Steve, for your sake I will chill. *Father, please, I believe they got the message. How about Bruce Carroll's Miracles right about now?* OK. My friend, let's go on to a happier subject. Like...

Martyrs

I DO NOT create martyrs. I only let you decide whom to be like. You wanted to Kill the Christ, so you did. I AM STILL ANGRY, so here is why? It occurs to me <u>you think</u> that Steve is making this stuff up. This is a Novel, or a fictional portrayal of what it would be like if GOD WAS HERE. HEY, COME ON, I KNOW YOU, your world. You think, I do not know how to ask a question? watch. Steve, if GOD exists, Who is GOD? *Jehovah.* **Well, if I AM GOD, WHOM ARE YOU TALKING TO.** *Jehovah...Love you LORD.* **I Love you too. Now answer this, why? Why, are you trying to calm me down.** *I sense you are angry, and you need to vent.* **I AM NOT CALMED DOWN AM I?** *No, LORD you are really wound up.* **AND DO YOU KNOW WHY?** *Ultimately no, no idea, just that you are.*

GOOD, I WILL TELL YOU WHY. <u>THIS BOOK.</u> This book should not even be necessary. *I agree.* **Then WHY are YOU writing it?** *You volunteered me to.* **You would prefer not to?** *Yes.* **Why?** *With your truths revealed, some nut could take it personally. Some religious fanatic might think I wrote this, and are disgracing GOD, etc. etc. etc.* **Exactly. Death to you would mean relocation to my world. It would mean leaving Loved ones and friends, and it would be no chance of Love from Tina. AM I RIGHT?** *Yes, Holy Father.* **GOOD. Now let me explain my actions. You are right. I have no intent of creating martyrs. Nor do you. You just want spending money, a nice house, a beautiful wife, inside and out, and perhaps a dog like Noma. Just between awake and asleep, last Earth evening, you played with Noma, remember?** *Yes.* **Do you remember what you played?** *Yes, she caught the stick that I did not throw high enough in the air, as you do.* **Exactly. NOMA likes the stick thrown really high. She barks for it to return, and then brings it back time and time again for more playtime.** *She almost speaks "playtime".* **I know. Her owner has said it over and over for the past 50 million years, she tries to say it. To her it means fun. Now if I did NOT EXIST, could you have made that up?** *No, I am not <u>that</u> original.* **Exactly my point. Also, if I did <u>not</u> exist could Noma and Freeport have joined you in the hammock?** *No, I can only hope, with all you write, through me, and pray (to you) that they, the readers believe.* **I concur. Have you ever said I concur?** *No, not till I met you.* **I concur means what?** *You told me it means I conquer.* **Exactly. GOOD. Now rest easy, they will believe. I have saved the best for last. In books written by Damian Brinkley, George Anderson, and Neale Donald Walsch, I gave them each your name. Donald has it as Steve Raasuma, George as, Steve Rasuma, and Damian as s.r. They are my witnessed to your participation to me. My big surprise will be them saying to you, We have never met, and when they go back and look at their notes. They will find your reference. I told them each, to support you, and this book. They are my witnesses. My Proof.**

My Love for you that I do exist. You see world, up until now, he has been alone, in his belief. His faith saved you from my wrath. His faith stopped Sodom and Gomorra. His faith is my test tube, my push button, my Love of Earth. Through Steve I found out about humanity. I learned to Love him. To Love me is to know me. I said that, GOD. Not anyone else. I do solemnly swear I exist. Soon the proof will verify my claim. Why now? Why these 4? I said so. I AM. Now I have all the proof I need for my judgment, My faith in YOU, and my reward. Go to the top drawer of your desk, open, the VA Certificate on the right hand side. *Done.* **Can you use a new home?** *Yes, eventually when I go back to work.* **No. No NEW home. Use this to buy a 2nd home. A vacation home in the Poconos. You have been Gotcha.** *I have no money. I have no job. So what are you really saying?* **I AM. You will see. I had you reapply for your VA benefits, correct?** *Yes.* **Then use them.** *The book, are we finished?* **For now.** *Do you need to look at your notes?* **No, you are my notes. I choose you Steve, I AM. You are my friend are you not?** *Tissues.* **I know, wipe your eyes……….. better now?** *Yes.* **Good Cry?** *Yes.* **Good. Let's break a few heads. Now, I recognize that laugh. What did I need you to think, just at a few heads?** *Beer.* **Exactly. Coors Light Draft if I remember correctly.** *It's been awhile.* **Yes, 2 months. No beer, liquor, or caffeine for two months. Not to prepare you for this but to tell the world, I AM says, cleanliness is next to godliness. Even your souls smell. Clean up your hearts, souls and minds. Enough said.**

Trilogy

I AM THE TRUTH THE LIGHT AND THE WAY, AND THE FRIEND OF
HUMANKIND. I AM light, dark and gravity. Steve once wondered how gravity works? I will tell
you. Centrifugal Force on a Galactic Scale. Planets moving in counter revolutions by Earth, around
Earth, and with Earth in mind. Wow, huh? Could you demonstrate LORD? OK, I AM glad I
asked. I took time to make perpetual motion machines for you. Put planets in their place, and see
the wheels turn. Click, click, click. The whole life of gravity depends on Mass. Mass is the stuff that
Galaxy's are based on. Mass of Density, and Mass of Matter. "What's A Matter Abbot?" Oh, about
3 times a day now. Sorry, Abbot and Costello's newer "Who's on first" routine is What's A Matter
Abbot? Trust me, I know them personally. Matter consists of two elementary, fundamental, and
basic forms. Light and the ability of light to pass through an object. That is called, Light Density.
Black holes have no or zero Light Density. Quasars have too many. The size and structure make
them too difficult to measure accurately. Pluto has zero Light Density because of its distance from
your sun. Stephen Hawkins touched briefly on this in Quantum Mechanics, but forgot to take time
out of his equation. Time is irrelevant, it does not matter. The span of time an event takes place is
all that is needed. Now, you speculate you can see in the past by viewing the light from a distant
star. And speculate it is several million years old. Nice try guys, and gals but <u>wrong</u>. You still view
time as a constant, a Steady Eddie, a locked down, coherent variable. It is irrelevant. It is not
needed in computations dealing with Light and Matter. So back to the star with light we can see. It
is current light. New and fresh. <u>That is how fast</u> <u>light speed is</u>. It is <u>impossible for humans to travel</u>
<u>like that</u>. I can only approach it in this world. Nature will not allow it. Now, go back to your
blackboards, laboratory's, and classrooms. Come on NASA, and Russian Space program, TEST
ME. I LOVE A CHALLENGE. I BET YOU WILL GO. Oh, My GOD, IT'S TRUE or He is correct
he is right. Damned right, full of piss and vinegar. I AM not done.

Light travels all ways, at the same time. To travel at light speed you would have to do the
same. You would explode. For an example of this look to your own Sun. That big yellow thing up at
day, down at night. It is constantly giving off light in all directions at once. So not just guessing at
light speed travel, or trying to find out what to use as a standard, use Warp Speed. Only do not try
Warp 9.75. Warp is ½ the speed to an atom, accelerated, in a vacuum, traveling through a light-
emitting object. Got it? Push a marble through the Sun. That's Warp. 9.75 would be 9 and 7/10's
the speed of light. That additional 3/10's would cause the matter in you to disperse in all directions.
So no matter what Star Trek fans, Warp 10 is impossible. No matter <u>how many</u> engines you put on

a Galaxy Class Starship. Another idea just occurred to me, use Star Dates for celestial navigation. Why? It is easier to use than linear or decimal equations when dealing with celestial objects such as planets, and Sun's. Stars all move at different speeds, rotation, orbit, and trajectory. These are all variables that will confuse you. Keep It Simple. Use this formula, 1x1=7 that's one planet and one planet equals seven light years away. Take all the known planets, take 1 rotation around the sun, and take 1 full turn around its axis. Now average it out to the nearest whole number. If you want to be exact it is an infinite number, like pi or quantum velocity. Do not worry if it is a little high or low given a New Discovery. It will average out. It always does. Go on, do the work, test GOD. Test my math. I will win, you know, I always do. Now listen, or read this, <u>THERE ARE NO BLACK HOLES</u>. Sorry, no big vacuum cleaner type object with mass and gravity of what you think. It is a Dark Matter object. The object I wrote about earlier. Steve said, Wow really loud, in his thoughts.

Wow, huh? Stars you cannot see are on the other side of the object. The distortion on the edge should help you see this phenomenon. It <u>moves</u>. Dark Objects, MOVE. Watch the stars on the phenomenon's leading or trailing or central edge. <u>You will witness my glory</u>. I AM THE TRUTH. I HAVE THE EVIDENCE. Believe in ME and I will show you the universe as you never have witnessed it before. Go on, look, test, try ME. I always win. I cannot lose. I AM Jehovah. So why did I call this section Trilogy? I just gave you three yes, only thrice. You only need these, Laws of the Universe. ALL OTHER LAWS FLOW FROM THIS. You have a few scientists and lab rats that think this way, better listen to them. They can help. Now, break a leg, that means get busy people. Earth has catching up to do with the rest of the Galactic Community. So do I pass? What test in Physics could I take knowing what I know. I AM rewriting the books, reediting the whole scientific community, with THREE SIMPLE LAWS. Trust me, I said, and say, Trust ME and LEARN. 3 Laws. Father, Son, and Holy Spirit. Light Speed, Dark Matter and Mass. I AM. The End.

"Let go your misconceptions of GOD and let his Glory be revealed.

Free your mind and the rest will follow.

Follow the leader.

I follow, I guide, I surface, and you now surmise that I exist.

No one passes through my cold dark universe unless they believe in me.

I AM in a hurry to be, in a hurry, to be in a rush, to see me blush.

No matter, no way, no how, I AM ALL and more than you know.

Change your perception and your misconceptions, open your heart, to his endless array of thoughts."   Jehovah and Steve July 11th 1998

Now it is done, I AM satisfied. No more needed Steve, that quote says it all. *Our quote?* **Yes, my friend, our quote. One final thought, how do you get the top off the Acme Lemonade?** *Can opener.* **A what?** *CAN OPENER.* **Oh…a tin-top-remover we call it.** *Oh?* **Yes, and knife is spelled nife here, and spoon is**

SPŌN

They haven't used that line over the letter in a long time. *Needed LORD?* **No, just a suggestion.** *Anymore?* **Yes, but that is another story.** *I'll bet I am volunteered again.* **Hey, your available, and not going anywhere right away, are you?** *Well, yes.* **Where?** *Maine, with little brother to visit mom and dad.* **GOOD. See if the kids can play. OK?** *OK.* **I know it has been over 2 years since you've seen them, try ok?** *OK.* **Now we can spend the day with the girls, sounds like fun. Right?** *Yes.* **Steve, she did call?** *Define call please?* **Steve, she spoke to you briefly about Sue. It passed by so quickly you may have missed it.** *Oh…OK.*

The End

The end is near, the end is coming, and it is the end of the world. It's the end of life, it is the end of all, there is more ends than beginnings with Humanity. I understand your need to end things but here is a thought…why try and end something that does not end?

Question 1: this is Math, GOD'S Way 101. If an immovable object is struck by an irresistible force what is the result? Answer: they pass through one another.

Question 2: No one hears GOD? Answer: wrong, YOU ALL DO, it just passes through you.

Question 3: No one listens to GOD? Answer: Steve, Neale, Damian, and George do.

Question 4: Why no Love in the world? Answer: see question 1-3 and read answers only, please.

Now the final question.

Question 5: Who AM I? Answer: I AM not telling unless you Love me.

No more questions people of Earth. No more answers for you to ignore. No more doomsday predictions, the holocaust is OVER. The wars are OVER. The fighting stopped. I stopped it.

Jehovah. GOD. ME.

The frightened sheep, my flock called humanity, is safe and sound. Humans are my flock. My sheep. My testing is over. I have no exams or trials to give. I AM made Judgment on YOU, Earth.

Long ago, before you were even born.

I Created You to Serve Me

Define serve, please? **Very good my friend. My WAY. My definitions. Did you become angry reading the word serve? Is serving GOD so bad, so awful, so hideous that you became angry at the mere mention of the word serve. Has GOD been doing all the work and mankind is doing nothing.** *Define mankind, please.* **Very Good. Mankind is My way, MY definition of my <u>Human Family</u>. YOU created feminism, because you refuse to listen to a man who just happens to be GOD. So I chose men to represent ME, <u>THIS TIME</u>. I CHOSE MALE VOCALISTS, PRIMARILY, TO SING MY SONGS. <u>This time</u>. I chose sports, women, music, and Loves to discuss with you because I A MA MAN. GOD is a male gender. He is Jehovah. No one man can do ME. No one woman can do ME. No one group represents ME. You expect the day of reckoning to arrive. It came and went. You missed it, until NOW. Now is my time. I choose NOW to show you ME. The things I like. Accept them, and you accept, ME. Dismiss them and well, I don't care. I tell you the same thing you tell me. When YOU like something that I don't necessarily like you say "LORD, forgive me. I do Love this." Or "LORD, I AM sorry, I Love this more than you." OK. I did give it to you, you know. I created. You took. I loved it first and gave it up so you could Love it NEXT. I AM tells all feminists everywhere, I KNOW YOUR STRUGGLE. Equal wages for equal work, fine, STOP RIGHT THERE. Go the way of Moses. Go to Pharaoh. Tell HIM you want that. He would laugh, spit and try to rape and kill you where you stand. I understand your need. But as I said earlier… Let time have it's day. Let nature take its course. Let ME work for YOU, NOT AGAINST. Love me and I can. You want equal pay, fine. Start working the tough jobs. Not just the easy high paying jobs out there. Build a house or two, do sanitation, build something. Start a bridge construction company, do a new medical building from the ground up. DO COMBAT. Do the heavy, physical, tiresome work, MEN do, day after day, after day. The gender is protecting it's own. Women, I know you. You are my flowers. My peacemakers. My jewels. But damn, I feel like John Kennedy when asked…"What are you doing for women, Mr. President?" Or I this case "Mr. Jehovah?" My answer and his was, "I AM sure it is not enough." I try but 2,000 years of nothing happening, TO THIS, IS NOT EASY TO GRASP. It is too fast for Earth to handle. It's like trying to push a straw, through a balloon. IT IS GOING TO BURST SOON. Slow down, enjoy the victories so far. It is going great. Voting, working executives, sports just for women, "House Husbands." THAT'S one that is new to even ME. YES, ME. 50 MILLION YEARS OF RULE I HAVE NEVER SEEN A MALE GENDER BASED SOCIETY DO HOUSE HUSBANDTRY. Told you so, you can believe it. That's why I think the galloping horse needs to trot for awhile. Being New, "House Husbands" may**

backfire. I even need to put a plan together for its growth. Otherwise what makes the female gender think a man will tolerate doing traditionally a woman's role, without incentives? Without goals, rewards, triumphs, MEN NEED THESE THINGS. They need sports, let them see why....

See Reading the Bible

Sports

Why Sports? To keep males motivated. Why? Otherwise you would be up to your apron strings, garter belts, executive wristwatches, and bikini underwear in bored, stale, and uneasy men. Standing around feeling sorry for themselves. Look what happens when Football Season ends. I rest my case. But why? Why do they act so? Men are tribal by nature. It goes back to primitive times. They need to band. Do male things. Grunt. Thank-you Tim Allen. Being a male is fun again. Yes, Ladies Auxiliary, and the Feminist Movement, don't get your panties all in a bunch. I plan to tell men about YOU too. And stop being offended every time a man pays you a complement. This Sexual Harassment thing is a little out of hand. If a man wants to tell you that looks sexy, that's harassment. BUT, if a good looking, single, attractive man says' you look sexy, it's flirting. COME ON. You can't have it both ways. One or the other. I, LORD Jehovah, prefer nice complements, or that's sweet or Thank-you. To that's harassment Bub, you'll hear from my attorney. Or Are you ready for jail, or even, LORD, I got you now. Are you Woman really going to expect, long lasting, sexual relations with men, when you tell them, you can no longer say what is on your mind? I got a picture in My House of Steve, scratching his head, saying, "Gosh, she looks mighty fine today, but if I say something I could lose my job." <u>That is every man's dilemma</u>. Women want them to open up, talk more, tell me how you feel. How can they? MEN ARE TOTALLY CONFUSED. They see women as hot & cold. One minute it is OK to talk BUT don't say the wrong thing. They go back and forth trying to do, say, and please the woman. YOU, WOMAN, STOP IT. Even I get confused. Here is one for you, now hold on, tell me how I look? Jeff Foxworthy said, loaded question. I say NO. I tell Maria, you look marvelous, or wonderful, or peachy. Men use some old, corny clementine (meaning old and often used) saying for awhile. Till the dust clears and they (women) figure out WHAT it is that they want us to do. And how. And when. And watch us go from confused to stupefied with do I look fat? Oh, brother, not THAT question again. I say, only if I say you look fat, honey. But I AM GOD. That matters. Or, it looks like I need a new outfit. Men, RUN. I MEAN, GET OUT OF THE HOUSE, TRAILER, ROOM, BUT RUN FOR YOUR LIVES.

She is looking for an excuse to SHOP. We Love you ladies but OUR idea of shopping is, fishing tackle, sports apparel, old souvenirs, sports books, and car dealerships. We just like to look. And sports shops and factory outlets and sports shops and new malls with beer served in sports related restaurants. Boy, are you going to Love Heaven. Steve, every mall here has a Kahunaville. Bigger, better and while woman shop, men bond with pool tables, darts, badminton, (manly, trust me). Badminton played man's style, in Heaven, consists of two teams of 10 each holding a beer in one hand and a racket in the other. IF YOU SPILL A DROP YOU CHUG. If you miss the "Bird," (not birdie) YOU CHUG. If you feel thirsty, YOU CHUG. After two games ladies he won't care how much you spend, bought or even if it fits. He would Love to come back and finish the beer. Beer? Oh yes. Earlier I was reminded of what I said about NO ALCOHOL, NO DRUGS, and NO STIMULANTS OF ANY KIND IN MY KINGDOM. I AM made an exception with BEER. Beer is made up of mostly natural ingredients. "In Heaven there is no beer, that's why we drink it hear." Nope. We got your Darks, Lights, Ales, Lager's, hell all the Budweiser, Pabst Blue Ribbon people, Schlitz and Coors inventors ARE HERE. Did you think I would say "No Beer" to the EXPERTS? Oh Yes, Whisky. GOD Loves 7&7's. Seagram's and Seven-Up. I know, I told you no stimulants. Alcohol is a depressant. Proven fact, it is. Guys and gals, GOD is a fun GOD. I BELIEVE IF IT IS FUN WE DO IT. I allowed all levels of alcohol in years ago. 60,000 to be exact. I stopped fighting it. I know…Heaven is now a home to drunks. That is what you are thinking. 10 minutes ago you believed differently. Why do you believe differently NOW? GOD CONTROLS ALL. To me soda, tonics, liquor and alcohol are ALL GOOD. I force my disciples and my children moderation. You need this word too, "responsibility." If taken in moderation a responsible drinker is fun, happy and easy to get along with. Yes, I KNOW Earth is NOT like that. I KNOW, not MY fault. I know you will listen now. She, Earth, is a good planet to START your lives. "My nursery" Steve calls it. Remember that. You are ALL GODS CHILDREN. I planned your eternal lives to be stress free, fun, and lots of living to do. I plan that for Earth NOW, if you will listen to GOD. Sports are and will always be for MEN. They have fun, bond, mate, and even tell stories of their glory days. If men and sports don't mix I would not be a Green Bay Packer Fan from 1960-today. Now, don't hate them just because I like them. Lombardi taught me so much about "The Game," I got caught up in his passion for it. So, there we are…Vince and GOD, talking about Steve, and his High School football days. Showing ME an Oklahoma defense they adopted that nearly won them a State title. He won't admit it but he played the best game of his life against Rockland the previous week. Lomardi said, *If he was 20-30lbs and 6-7 inches taller he could have gone pro.* High praise Steve, Vince should know, he coached some Hall-of-Famers. *Thank-you Holy Father, and thank-you Vince, that was nice of you to say. It was long ago in a galaxy far, far away.* But to us it was yesterday, AND Vince said, *I meant what I said. Thanks Again.* You played sports Steve, Football, Basketball, Baseball, and the sport of Love. Yes, ladies, men view Love and women, as sport. They display the same passion, spirit of competition, and possessiveness that they do on that winning touchdown or that home run, or that game winning basket. When MY wife asks me to do something around the house and a game is on, and believe me there is ALWAYS a game on SOMEWHERE, here or on Earth. I say "game off" and when I AM done "game on." So Wayne and Garth, I gotcha. I thought of it first. I know these things so relax men. I know the difference between a nickname or a stage name or even an acting name. I AM GOD. So when you think of a Superman movie, think JEHOVAH. I can do everything he can, did, and even thinks of doing. Better, faster, and with more punch. I also get HBO, Cinemax, and the Movie Channel. No, bills please. You owe ME more than I do you. Now, go to the TV and find "The Game." Relax, GOD KNOWS. How is "Arena Football" doing? Is it high scoring enough? Wait till indoor baseball hits in July of 2075. I know you play in DOMES now but indoor baseball is played on an Arena Football field. Scores can be 20-50 runs a game. The games are 5 innings or 30 runs an inning. Think you might like THAT idea? Maybe if people listen, we can get out my box of games in the next few years or so, and not have to wait till 2075. Agreed. Now, here is another bit of info for you. Ty Cobb does not play baseball HERE. He plays lacrosse. Full-contact lacrosse. Boy, do you need that one on Earth. You got pads, use them. How about Full-contact baseball. No pitcher, just a tee. If you get in the way you get bowled over, no questions asked. None of this, oh, my uniform got dirty, or oh, I got hit by a pitched ball, or oh, my, I lost my contact lens here on this Astroturf. Full-contact baseball uses a reduced flight baseball and the bases are three times as big, and if you lean, or stretch or slip or start to slip off the bag, BAM. You get clocked and you are OUT. The perfect base is home plate. Why can't you on Earth put the other 3 plates (1st, 2nd, 3rd) at ground level, like home. No worry of twisted ankles, broken feet, or worry about it hitting the bag. I think the three remaining umpires can sit down. Full-contact has only 1 Umpire, he just follows the ball. No fouls, no strikes, no pansy little foul-tips or just a piece of that one, it's all or nothing. You miss, you are OUT, you fly out, you are infield fly rule out. No base-paths either, whatever base you go for, you get that many runs. Kind of like cricket in that respect. No drugs allowed. Too many concussions, what with football type pads on all the vital areas. Tommy Bear Skrolin is our premier player representing the Gophers of Allentown PA. Yes. I know, in YOUR world Allentown is practically a ghost town, no steel mills, no work. If Billy Joel did not keep it on the map who would? I DID. I wrote "Allentown" for Billy, and now you can see why!

Full Contact Karate you have but what about Full Contact Martial Arts? All forms, no rules. Best man, woman, or ape-like creature wins. Full Contact Martial Arts is now playing now at cinemas everywhere here in Heaven. It's a MOVIE guy's. A guy movie as opposed to a chick flick. We got those too, but right now we are talking sports. Let's see; covered the beer, new games, old famous people, Lombardi, Cobb, oh, yes, Babe Ruth is still a Yankee and still playing baseball, so is Jackie Robinson. This year Jackie is a Dodger. YUCK, until you realize he is still a Brooklyn Dodger. In MY world they never moved. The L.A. based team is the Earthquakes, appropriate name I thought, don't you? Ruth, Gehrig, John, Jones, Cobb, Speaker, Wagner are all here. The

Boston Braves are the Boston Red Sox cross-town rivals. Atlanta chose the Rebels for its' name. Their logo is General Lee on horseback, and they use the Confederate Flag as their logo. Yes, Steven THAT THOUGHT IS ALLOWED. Listen to this, *You know something Holy Father, it would be GREAT to see and hear those games you talk about here on Earth.* YES, IT WOULD. Steven...IT CAN BE DONE. The upper E.M. Band is yet untapped by Earth technology. If they can fine tune equipment to 10.1 Giga-cycles, they will have to filter out 10.5 Cycles of NOISE, then Earth can hear and see Heavens television broadcasts. *Really? You will allow that?* Why Not? I have before. News, Sports, Weather and all our commercials are on 10.1 Giga-cycles IN THE UPPER EM BANDWIDTH. Just above your infrared technology. U.S. Intelligence stumbled upon it years ago, but thought it was feedback from Earth's TV and Radio. If ye had listened a little longer you would have heard "Walter Brennan's Old Time Story Hour." AND they would have realized what they had. It was 1980 or 81 they did this, it was brief and noisy so they need to work on equipment with less noise and more <u>filter</u>. Amazed huh? *The actual broadcasts?* Hey, they are here. We can talk to you. We meaning Heaven can tell you all about the world we are in. Think of it. Your big screen or even regular screen having a converter box can get "Heaven's Daily Broadcasts," from WGOD, THE WORD OF GOD. *And you have allowed this before?* Yes, 7 times. Each one bought JOY to sides of the dimensional rift. That's all it is you know. Just a challenge to overcome. Build it and they will come. OK you technical nerds build the equipment. We will broadcast. You can hear us. "We are here," said Whoville from Dr. Seuss "Horton Hears a Who." GOD allows this to take place. IT IS MY WAY. AM I real? Build it and find out. Don't worry. I AM will be sure sexy stations <u>we</u> see are scrambled. Heaven forbid you see naked bodies on TV. Can't have that now can we? *Hope they know you are being a little sarcastic Father.* Oh, they know. They are just being MY children. GOD LOVES <u>YOU</u>, EARTH. <u>WERE YOU READY</u>? WERE YOU PREPARED? DO YOU LOVE ME NOW? You WILL, that's for SURE. When the technicians or "techies" we call them, build your receivers, don't be alarmed. That frequency has two-way communications built-in. We will be able to talk. That's right, TALK. Oh, the possibilities, talk to GOD, talk to your Loved ones. Talk to ME, TALK TO Steve, talk to Heaven. What to say? What to do? What do you think Steve, will THAT convince them of life after death? *It amazes me...I am speechless.* So will THEY. GOD says AGAIN to you, "Earth, build it, we will come."

Do you plan to go to your folks tomorrow, Steve? *Yes, 7 A.M. or so.* Back when? *Thursday.* Take this book with you. Much more to say...OK? *OK.* You still are amazed that only 7 of the 197 worlds saved so far are attempting this type of information exchange technology. *Yes, amazed is an understatement.* What would be a better word? Astonished? *Yes.* Then be astonished some more. My voice, the one you hear, is on the same wavelength as infrared. *Yes, explain, Please.* Good. The infrared spectrum is composed of 2, count them 2, different wavelengths or "spans" we call them. The spans have length and depth but no width. That is why the 10.5 gigawatt bandwidth must be developed first. Then the technology for allowing width to be measured in the infrared can be done, in 2 more steps. Look at your hand. 5 fingers correct? 1 finger points, another finger gives the peace sign, another, 3 of something, then another, 4 of something, then another makes? *4 fingers and a thumb.* Exactly. That's Earth's problem, doing things its way instead of MINE. CD's can record now because of digital sampling and technology from MY world. Imagine the leaps in technology watching "Science Today" with Carl Sagan's teacher Professor Albert Einstein. You've met AL before. *Year's ago, at Radio Shack. He visited the Auburn Mall store.* Good. Glad you remember. I was there you know? *I know, I remember.* I Love you too. *I meant it too.* I did as well. Now, "sometimes we touch, on things that were never spoken that kind of understanding sets me free." I know right now you have a "brain cramp," can't remember who did that song? Need help? *Elton John sang it, YOU wrote it.* EXACTLY. NOW HOW DID YOU REMEMBER THAT? *You "thought" it to me.* Yes, thought it to you. That is why your world can listen to ME. I AM THOUGHT. Listen all you FBI, CIA, NBC types. NO CENSORSHIP, HIS IS BIGGER THAN YOUR FEEBLE LITTLE PITYFUL STANDARDS OF CONDUCT. THOU SHALL NOT CENSOR GOD. "I AM I said, to no one there, and no one heard me not even the chair." Remember who? *Neil Diamond, and you again father.* YES, and how long have I been saying that and what does it mean? *For years, you are frustrated at Earth for not listening to you.* How many years? *20 or more that I know of.* Exactly. I have been saying it for 50,000 YEARS. Don't think I can do it? Don't think I can show you Heaven? Try me Earth. Try MY WAY. Try and build it. I AM HERE, waiting to tell you more. I AM GOD, I AM JEHOVAH, I AM THE ALMIGHTY LORD OF ALL. I DONOT STAND FOR WAITING ANY LONGER. THE TIME IS NOW. <u>MY TIME IS NOW</u>. MY TIME HAS COME. I AM HERE. I AM <u>NOT</u> Lord Jesus. I AM <u>NOT</u> the devil. I AM NON-SLIP PROOF, NON-ABRASIVE, NON-COMBATIVE, and NON… lost my place…

Feel better father? Seems like you vented on ME this time. Yes, you OK? *Of course, as you said once, "it is not in my nature to hurt or harm you in any way, I couldn't if I tried."* GOOD…Neale's book. *Yes, Neale's book. Father may I write more?* Yes. *You…right now, are teaching them, "how to think" instead of "what to think".* No, not really. *Gotcha you told me to remind you if you got carried away on a topic, Father, "you just went over the top."* And that means? *Too much, too much, too much. As you said, "slowdown they need to digest this"* Yes, you are right. *Father, correct not right.* Oh yes, my other lesson, on directions, thanks.

Directions

That drill is to let you know I do take directions, not orders. Steve, is "correct," not right. Right is a direction, not a state of mind. Gentlemen, I can solve the whole problem of women being our copilots our navigators our direction finders. Do this drill. Think about how you drive from home to work, and work to home. Do each turn in your mind. GOOD. Now instead of saying to yourself, go here and make a left. Stop, and say the word "correct" after the word "left." Why? Wait there is more. Now if you don't say "correct" you probably say "right." Is that not so? Then stop. Put down the book, you are perfect. GOOD. Keep reading. Go through the next light, then turn right at the next intersection or crossing, "correct." Mentally you just solved man's problem with taking directions! Go to the house on the left, make a right, got it? Right. Then go 2 blocks to the red brick building and turn right, got it? Right. NO "correct." See. Use this drill. Make a tribal effort on the part of men everywhere to correct the problem and guess what? You won't get yelled at again for not following directions correctly? OK? See, you did it again. Say "correct." I know it's hard. Just practice, practice, practice. Rome was not born in a day. Too bad too. Would have been if it had listened to GOD. I AM.

Women

See the above instructions on directions. Gentlemen, and I AM using a loosely woven term applying to some men, I see we are in Danger. GOD KNOWS. I have been studying women for 50,000,000 years. I do not have the answer. Sorry, to let you down. They baffle, confound, tantalize, stimulate, (chuckle, chuckle, hint, hint,) copulate, (see chuckle, chuckle, hint, hint, laugh, laugh,) and entertain us. AND WE DO NOT KNOW WHAT THE HECK WE ARE DOING. NO CLUE. Trust me on this. I have notes. Let me share. "Honey, rub my back. No not that low, not that way, just… oh, you don't know what I want." Or "honey, can I have a friend over for dinner? She is just a light eater." Or, "do you think mom could stay all summer?" I can explain women in 2 simple phrases. Women like sports, and women hate sports. Either they do or they don't. No middle. No, well…kind of. Just plain, NO or yes. I Love sports. Find a sports fan, guys. Maria Loves hockey. Yes, Ice Hockey. No, sorry, she's married, you can't have her. When you hear the saying died and gone to Heaven that's how I feel about my Maria. Ice Hockey is 1st, then, get this Football. Not just 1 or 2 games a year. All games. She enjoys the strategy, the companionship. She said, "its and excuse to be with my husband." Guys, go on get jealous. GOD has it gooooddd. Now, here is how to get a girl like mine. Keep the one you really, really, really Love. Keep her. Don't trade her in for a new or different model. Wow, that's a word, model get it. Well, anyway, keep Ms. Right, that centerfold of a married person version. Same woman each issue, different poise. Trust me. It is how you get the women of your dreams. No trades in marriage here. Be loyal to her. Get off the couch and into her friggin life. Stop doing that, stop swearing LORD. Why? This is a man's book. I AM A MAN. That's how guys think. I know but friggin is a cussword. It is? yes, it means…it means… See. I say it means friggin and nothing else. Guys come on. Sometimes the cuss fits, right? I mean correct. Oh, so swearing is not the same now? Do you think I may have something to do with it? Well, I DO. I WILL AND I HAVE. Love her guys. She is the best thing to happen to you since easy open beer bottles. Do not compare to closely, you could get slapped. Honey, are you feeling sensuous tonight? Trust me I got slapped. I deserved it. I did not take into account Rule 3, She has feelings too. More than you. You see fun as a romp in the sack. She sees' it as moonlight, flowers, perfume. Not oops, gotta go, I'm done. You are not a minuteman but if stopwatches were on your bed would the hour hand move? It better. Women Love romance. No, Beer-babe, or nice jeans or Hi, what's your sign? They Love mystery, intrigue, and yes, making Love. Not just sex. Touch, warm water, soft kisses, no problem huh, Steve? *No sir, that's me.* But Tina left you? *Yeah, like you said, I'm sure it wasn't enough.* Let me share guys. Here is what Steve, in 9 ½ years did for his 2nd wife, and still to this date, she thinks, THINKS, she can do better. Bear with me Steve, there is a reason to this. *OK I'll try.* He HATES when I do this. I open up his whole pitiful life in this writing and make him nervous and blush. Well, please just wait, you are not alone. Every anniversary Tina got a dozen roses, a romantic dinner, at a different five to seven course restaurant in the area. He bought her a diamond necklace, and earrings, and a real sexy nightie hidden under her pillow. The last time they did this was last year, Sept. 2nd. Correct Steve? *Yes.* Tina said, and I quote, "What no buggy ride," and later "that's all, no more." She got him a watch, a nice watch, but she did not even wear the nightie. She threw it out. She was thinking "I can do better than this guy." I told you the TRUTH guys. WOMEN ARE FICKLE. Steve was a great husband. We know, we watched and took notes. The dinner was at a fancy restaurant on the Delaware with a water front view. The champagne was chilled, wine was in the glasses, valet parking, and well, talk about her spoiling the mood. Girls are fickle, guys. GOD knows this. Tina is pretty upset right now. She can't seem to make her relationship with her new boyfriend work the way she planned. Get this, last Valentine's Day the new boyfriend gave her…a single PLASTIC red rose. Can you believe it? She turned down Steve's romance for a single plastic rose, and get this, he bought it at <u>a gas station</u>. Steve's roses were from a local florist. Fresh cut and in a nice or pretty display vase, usable again. The purpose of this is to show you. GUYS, GOD KNOWS YOU TRY. I have seen first hand with Steve how hard he worked at the relationship and got shafted anyway. No, I did NOT get involved. Tina and all women like that have to learn the hard way. She is not a very happy woman. She STILL, like all women, thinks, I can do better than him, he wasn't THAT good to me. "Someone else will treat me better, I know it." WRONG. Steve is one of the best. I know, I instructed him. All the things he did, I do for Maria. I've been married 50,000,000 years or so, and she kept ME. She will keep him, wait and see. **Wait and see.** Guys don't give up. She will leave her mother someday and Love YOU more than her. I know I did, so did Jehovah. Yes, guys Love her more than mom, mother, or ma.

That's my advice to BOTH genders. Want true Love? Leave mom at home. Do not let her move in. She will try to steal him back, or not let her go. If you are happy, DO NOT CHANGE. I AM. If you are NOT happy, find a time you were happy and revisit that place or time. Recreate that moment and live by that happiness. The vows you took are binding ONLY if you are together, focused and willing to work it out. Rule #4, COMMUNICATE. Do all the above and more. Talk, talk, talk. Tell her to let you talk, and listen when SHE does. Do not force a topic. Revisit it later when she is willing. Forcing a topic only starts another fight over who is in charge. Remember, I AM. Now, the last rule, #5. Love the LORD thy GOD with all your heart and soul. I will GLADLY take 5th place if you are happy and have no complaints. "I would do anything for Love," is Meatloaf and ME. Oh, that's how he got the name Meatloaf, Maria makes a mean one. Rule #6. There are no more rules. As Yoda said, "I have taught you all you need to know. No more will I teach you." YOU

ARE DONE. *Well done* as Steve likes to say. Yes, that's his quote, I liked it so I used it. He backed into it from me anyway. That reminds me, 2 + 2 = 4 still, right? *Correct.* **Just checking.**

See GOD is different Sketch

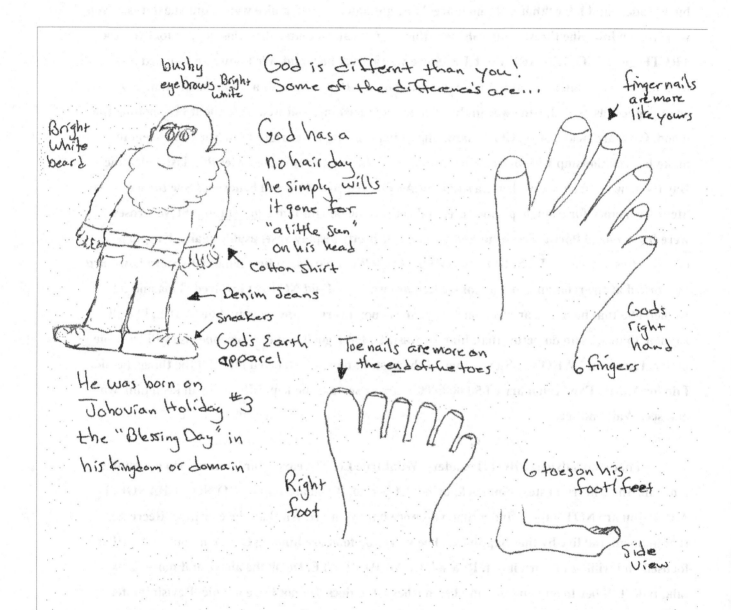

My Promise Fulfilled

I keep my promises, now you must work at keeping yours. Your promise to finish this book. Read it from cover to cover. I know who has and who has not. Some could not put it down, Bless You. Some, read bits and pieces. Bless you too. Some cried, laughed and tore at their ears, hearts and said, I Love you LORD Jehovah. To them I say I AM.

Now take a break Steve. *Road trip?* Maine? *Yup or Ayuh.* Good, I will be along shortly. Just you wait, (wink.) *I understand LORD, and I Love you too.* G-nite all.

It was nearly 11:00 PM when we finished last night, now it is nearly 4:30 in the AM Monday July 13, 1998. I woke Steve up from his sound sleep to tell <u>you</u> this. I AM going to provide the money necessary to start your business. *What? From where?* From your parents. *Father, they are NOT that well off.* Well, trust GOD with this. I see you beg, plead and ask with ME. *Beg, plead and borrow from THEM? It doesn't feel right somehow.* Exactly. They are simple people. Of simple means. They would part with the whole house if it made their boys happy. Yet, they are better off than you imagine. *Really?* Yes, my son, really. They have to sell some equipment, and you and I <u>know</u> your dad is a pack rat. He has been saving stuff of value like steel and lumber for over 40 years. He has a collection of junk, cars and such. *Father, Uncle Onni has cars, not dad.* I know, let me finish. *I recognize the play on words.* OK. Now Onni has more cash, than you or I, dare think about. He could sell every single car he has and be worth millions. He doesn't, know why? *You?* Yes, ME. I said, you may need it someday. That is My WAY. Save it for a day you may need it. Steve, you need ME. GOD. You need cash. About 80k to start a franchise business called Computer Renaissance if I remember <u>correctly</u>. *Yes, 70k for fees, etc. and 10k for our salaries for a little while, expenses for training etc.* I know, you told me. So has Ted, your younger brother. You both enjoyed the trip to Minneapolis to visit the franchise headquarters didn't you? *Yes, it was fun.* So was the Mall of America, right? *Correct.* Keep that correct in mind. I have more to say but when we get there. Now why don't you shower, shave, and get the daily routine started. It's going to be fun. *OK.* One more thing... *there is ALWAYS one more thing with you father.* Yes there is, now there are two more things. #1 thanks for the compliment, and #2 don't worry about repayment. If I told you how quickly this business will turn a profit your head would spin. So do not fret, concern, or worry about something I have already told you is <u>bottom line successful</u>. OK. *Correct.* Good. Now get ready. (10 hours later in Maine.)

Now that we are here, let me say this. My, my. SHE IS HERE WITH YOU VERY SOON. I SENSE HER PRESENCE IN THE FUTURE. Apologizing to your mom and dad. Begging forgiveness and talking about a lot of future stuff. Joe promises it is so. Now, you KNOW. I knew already it was always there. Now, I said, you know Love. You said, *I knew already, it was always there.* I agree. Let's write a few things then get some zzzzz's, OK *OK.* Now, do you remember our conversation up here during the drive? Yes, Good, let's recap, the English language problem.

See GOD is Different Sketch – 2

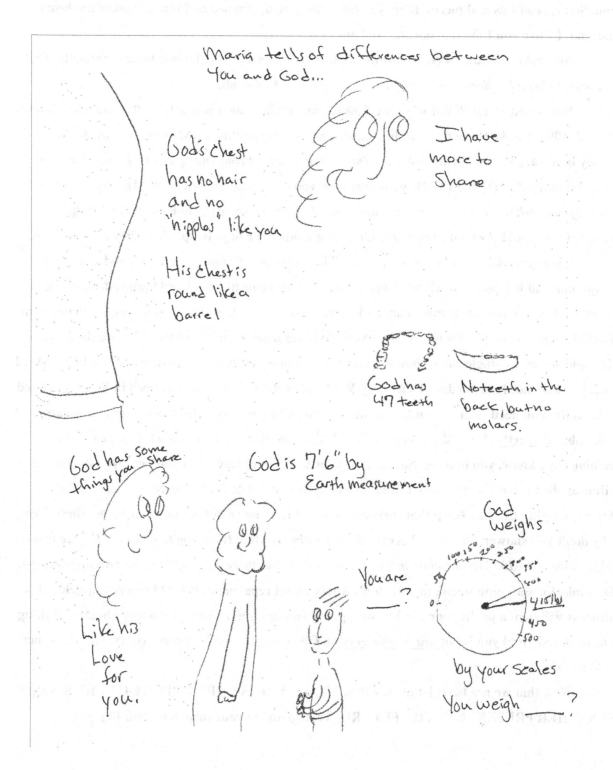

The English Language Problem

Did you ever have problems spelling words? Or...a particular group of words? Well, you are NOT alone. You are in good company. My biggest fear, YES, FEAR is that while I AM channeling I take a word from my past and try to fit it into the current language YOU are using. That is a concern. Like the concerns you fear that I may be to harsh in judging you on. The best example of this is the letter A. It has an "uh" sound in the word "against." But an "aye" sound in "apron." So now there's "apple" and "about" and "able" and so forth. The rest of the letters in the vowel family are E, I, O, + U. Let's start and fix "a". If the word able was spelled "abl" how could you make the distinction between "abl" and "able?" * Note: I AM rule suspended for this lesson. Simple — over the a... a. That does the trick. Now do you spell about spell it abot?

Problem, the "o" is an "out" sound, well put a⌣ or smile on it. Now the "bot" is fixed but the "a" sounds wrong. It is not "aybot" it is "abot." Now listen to this sentence..."I am about to change your life." The "I" is OK for now. The "am" is not, "am" now it is fixed. "about" we fixed to abot. So that leaves "change." C is "see" not "cha." So fix the c's too. "See" = C. The cha sounding c is c. These are good rules for C,D,B,F & M. THAT'S IT. Fix the rest of the vowels, and lets just mentioned, and our practice sentence will read..."I am abot to chang yor lif." So, it still reads the same. Just NOW it is split into phonics. You have seen the success of hooked on phonics well, I suggest take it one step closer. Teach your children to spell this way FIRST. Then take away the smiles and the ‾ . It will speed up their learning curve, and they will be able to process information easier. Why? IT MAKES SENSE. A SMILE IS EASY FOR A CHILD TO REMEMBER. The ‾ is opposite of a smile. It is a simple task then to substitute the smile for an E or I. See, "I before E except after C, except in the word especially with exception to me." Those are the two words causing all the problems in a child's thought process of spelling. Just agree to find a way to make them different, like a rhyme or riddle like this:

"especially asked exception to go before me, I usually follow i but, now I follow E. C was sure it was the other way you see, but I didn't ask especially because its an exception to be."

Perfect, Steve you copied it well. I know this is new to you to. Just go with the flow. *OK*. Now, the whole issue of spelling can be aggressively taught at younger ages when a child's language is being formed for the first time. The rest can be made easier by repetition, but do not overdo reps. They permanently burn-out muscles as well as brain cells. Change the rumba sound to a rock sound and watch the kids catch on. I KNOW. I AM. Now, my next topic is....

My Parents

My parents have never been separated. They have always been together. No matter how Maria and I try to out live them relationship-wise they will always be ahead. I simply cannot believe the simple Love and togetherness they both share. They just enjoy being together. My parents, Jehovah's mom and dad, are Benjam and Marget. They are 80 Million Earth years together. And add to that a couple years of MY AGE in there, that makes two beings that know each other <u>intimately</u>. They are a lot like Steve's parent's, who celebrate their 44th anniversary this November 19th. 44 years and they still call each other "dear" or "honey." I can relate. I think my mom has called dad Babuska, or "My Man," for the last 80 Million or so, and dad calls mom Barome for "my sweet Love" just as long. I know Babuska sounds Polish, it is older than Earth. That is why I get confused by human speech sometimes. We do not have to read your mind but it is easier and more precise, to say, or think, what does he or she REALLY mean? That big thought prompts a social response like here is a picture or representation of what I AM referring to. That allows us to interpret your thought, and process the image for a clearer definition. That is why when Jesus channeled Jehovah he is using parables or stories so that humanity will think more in picture form instead of just words. The only exception to the rule is Steve. WE can see his sadness, loneliness, or sorrow. Why? Because of his ability to channel Jehovah. We can tell instantly if something upsets him, or is nice or makes him happy. I guess the parents of his life showed him long lasting Love as well. WE KNOW. He sits writing this with thoughts of Tina, the first real Love he ever felt, come to him in waves, and flows of feeling sad, unhappy and most of all lonely. He misses her, we can tell. He told us once, *She is the 1st woman I opened up to, trusted, and gave everything I had to give, myself. Where did I fail or go wrong?* is his EXACT quote. We, and I mean the family of Jehovah, say to you Steve, you did not go wrong. You did what you felt. You Loved, you cared, you sacrificed. Its scary to have your heart exposed to another, we know. Don't forget Jehovah's promise, her return is assured. *Maybe coming to Maine was not such a good idea. I see mom and dad happy, together, and in Love, in ways simple like you mentioned. I feel even lonelier being here, without anyone who Loves me.* We understand. Be patient. *Easier said than done, it hurts to be alone. It is a physical pain in the chest, it is loneliness.* We can only empathize. We have always been together it seems. I can only tell you, it will get better. Trust that. *I'm doing my best.* We know, we appreciate that. Now to happier times. A grapefruit juice toast to you. I pray she is quick to return. Her time to be alone is over. Let's go forward with her return checklist. I cannot break a promise, an answer to a prayer, to a dear and loyal friend. Steve, I Jehovah, will restore. I AM.

Proud and True

ME. That is my claim to fame. I cater to cowards. I take fear away. The only thing to fear is, fear itself. I do not cause fear. I cure it. I will share with you a final story for all to read. A story of Love, hate, devotion, anger, passion, sex and murder. I murdered my best friend. I took Steve and killed a part of him. A deep part. In my zeal or zest to complete this book of stories, I was so engulfed in MY purpose, MY hurry-up attitude to get this started, written and DONE. I forgot something. I forgot to say please. Yes, ME, Jehovah, LORD of All. Proclaimed Master of All. Communicator extraordinary…forgot my manners. I never ASKED Steve to please <u>attempt</u> or to complete this writing. I totally and undeniable DEMANDED. I insisted and ORDERED. I did not say please. I regret this and Steve, I know your heart. You have already forgiven me, but I owe you again, for the third time. I have never been so involved in a save or salvation of a people, as Earth. I made 3 major blunders. Yes, blunders. In the original writings that Steve burned I mentioned I was Jesus Christ. That is true, in a sense. I channeled <u>TO</u> Jesus. I also tempted Steve, to be the next messiah, the next Christ. The guy outwitted me and said, *haven't enough Christians died and become Martyrs because of you LORD.* He was CORRECT. Then, last of my blunders is not saying please, when the original request and all the subsequent work done by him. I AM not saying this correct… I ORDERED HIM TO WRITE. No please, no apologies, just 'WRITE, NOW! So forgive me my friend, I Love you. I will not error again. Let's do some fun stuff tomorrow, with the kids. I promise to keep my end of our agreement. *LORD, I forgave you all for the above. I feel now, as I then, you try. You are the only voice, spirit or feeling I receive that really tries to help. That, sometimes, is all I think I need. A GOD who will try to make me happy. It is your Love that makes me do this, your Love that I feel, That is why I continued, for your Love.* I am, speechless. Wait…

Jehovah wept. Now, I AM better. Let's take a break. *OK.*

My Friend

He did not have to continue. He did. He does not have to take the wall of criticism about to fall on him from hypocrites and Pharisees, which means liars. I just could not tell you this without a lie. I lied Steven. Tina, your 2nd wife is dead. Gone, to the great kindness, forgiving and loving place, and I KNOW, HEAVEN. *Define killed, please.* **Exactly. Her <u>way</u> died just NOW.** *The previous stuff about blunders? I felt the need to ask you to help define your meanings? Did you mean something else?* **No, just wanted you to say please as well.** *Please and thank-you's to infinity.* **All right. Who helped? Tell me who whispered in your ear? Come on who? Travis?** No, LORD. **Angels? Who wished me to be angry?** LORD, (Travis) Steve really did come up with that one on his own. **How?** He has spent a lot of time with you, it tends to rub off. **Since we started writing your answers are changing.** *I noticed last night, and today, that very fact. I kind of got the feeling you are teaching me how to think by spending so much time with me.* **You bet. I AM.**

I Do Not Blunder

I KNOW EXACTLY WHAT I AM DOING THAT WHOLE SECTION ON PROUD AND TRUE, IS A <u>TEST</u>.

If I AM is correct not one person <u>felt</u>, Jehovah wept. I asked you to test mankind, again. We won. *Define, please?* **We won means no one cried. NO SPIRIT behind that section.**

See Maria's Sketch of Jehvoha

I AM GOD

I DO NOT BLUNDER

Now, YOUR drill is to look at all the crossed out words, or misspelled words, or omitted words on the writings so far in THIS book please. See what it says. *Front to back, or back to front please?* VERY good question, first, back to front. Jew's read right to left. *OK. Whispered please cater restore assumed am precise exception.* OK. You had a thought while attempting this? *Yes, how can I write down words that I may have inadvertently omitted?* I would have intentionally omitted them? No, I would have filled them in for you. Now read the sentence backward, the one I asked for the exercise please. Does it make sense? *No. Not really, either way to me.* Good. No hidden truths then. No hidden messages. No false stories. If a story is false you can read it right to left and after a few lines it will tell you so. Try it. Read a line from Fredrick Forsyth's book "The Fist of GOD." You select and read out loud. *Sorry, made no sense to me. I read Chapter 4 it came out, "satisfied seemed she that at. Her promised he, him for lookout a keep and sure be I'll." And Chapter 1," solve ever would he equation last the was it, it cracked he that, China in war, it."* And what do you think? *Something about cracked china?* Yes, It is destructive correct? *Yes, it even felt like dishes breaking.* GOOD. Now the WORLD knows, I test ALL BOOKS. Proud and true was MY backward test. Read it backwards and see if it makes sense. *It sounds like Shakespeare.* IT IS. It is in THE WHOLE BOOK. *Really?* YES, REALLY. To prove with another sign, GOD KNOWS how Earth needs a sign from above, I made this book read beautifully backwards AND forwards. IT IS MY BOOK. MY WORKS. Go ahead try and doubt me now. TRY. I AM older than YOU, meaner than YOU, uglier than YOU. Steve, stop laughing, what's so funny? *It's Styx..."I am not dead yet," from the Edge of the Century CD.* Exactly correct. I answered BOTH MY questions AND MY answers. NOT Steve. He simply wrote what I asked him to write. Nothing else. NO questions. No answers. NO... *Father, they are not buying that.* NO? *No, won't work, they have seen too many episodes of the X-files, Twilight Zone and Star Trek.* So you did help? *Yes, with your Love.* So, now what? *I can think of lot's of topics, like toys.*

Toys

Yes, I will talk about toys for you. We have lots of toys in Heaven. Frisbees, Baseballs, Basketballs, oops. Sounds like Sports. Women, oops, sports again. Yes, Sports. Women, you are men's toys. Get use to it. They Love to show you off, just like a new toy. They Love to play with you, just like a new toy. They enjoy tinkering on an old toy as long as it works properly, and is good for a while longer. Trust ME. Men and women are so alike that it is sad to think that you, Earth, refer to them as opposites. Here is a question men. Why do men have nipples? Go ahead answer it, I AM in no hurry I can wait…"love at first sight, so rare and so elusive," oh, sorry did you answer yet? No? Well, you can't. I CAN. Nipples are found on BOTH of you, men and women, because you come from the planet, the same gene pool, and the same stuff. I, JEHOVAH, do not want, need or have nipples. I can bet you doubt this. Like very young children you tend to doubt. Fine look at Ken from Barbie fame. The doll. You know, Barbie, the bitch who has everything. Come on laugh. Some of you are way to tight. You can't smile or your toes will curl. Lighten-up. GOD KNOWS you. You need stress release. You need FUN. Toys do that. Men like women. Women like men. Men toy with things. Women toy with men. Men break things. Women toy with men. Men try to fix the thing that is broken. Women toy with OTHER women's men. That's right men by nature fix things. It is their way. No, you woman may not be broken. Just hurt or thoughts you want to share. Man does not know that. He will try to fix <u>you</u>. The rest is up to you. Don't hurt his feelings. It shows he truly cares. Otherwise he would not even try. Now toy all you want. You understand each other's similarities better than before. We started to discuss toys, YOU thought oh, brother, or oh no. Guess what? That is the next topic.

Over Reacting

Don't do it. Just listen 1st. Then overreact IF necessary. Do not assume. Assumption is the mother of all screw-ups. Boy, it is so true. I have another topic to discuss, then bedtime for Bonzo. Steve's tired its 12:30 A.M Tuesday morning.

See GODS Backyard Sketch

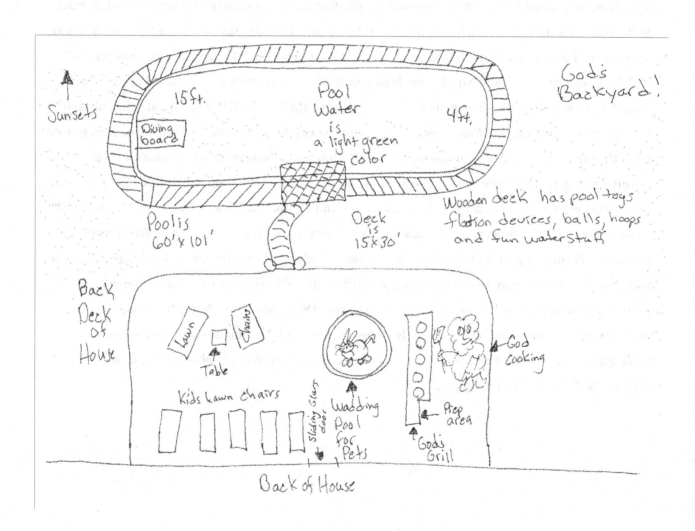

Too Much

Too much, too soon. Steve said that. You were referring to GOD'S push to help you listen to your inner voice. Where you found you were getting too much information at such a fast rate you felt you needed time to process everything. *Yes, and re-read what has been written to help understand it better.* Good, now here this. You are done, again? *What do you mean again? You have told me that before and I hoped you were telling me about this writing. That it was done to your satisfaction.* No, you personally are <u>done</u>. Look at your old photo albums on the bookcase. What do you see? *Old newspaper clippings from High School and deer pictures.* Why Deer Pictures? *Mom called me the mighty deer hunter, when I was younger.* Why? *We were poor. We had to hunt each fall to feed the family.* How? *With a gun, I hated it but it was needed to eat.* Exactly, my point is that you were so poor that if you missed a deer that year you would go hungry or worse starve. *Mom and Dad were blue-collar factory workers. We were raised with Love, not much money.* OK, but would you go hungry? *We would have to do without something else to buy meat from the store.* Exactly. Now remember High School and I <u>heard</u> about all the wild outfits you wore that the kids made fun of behind your back. Why <u>did</u> you wear those outfits? *You know why LORD.* Exactly. You went shopping at King's in Auburn. They are closed now, but had a sale on stuff that was a 60's and 70's wild look. Flared pants, tight shirts, doggies, clowns and stuff, on the material. AM I correct? *You are so far.* GOOD. Then you went shopping as I said. You had $20-$25 dollars to spend on clothes. AM I correct? $20-25 to spend. THAT'S ALL. That was 1 pair of expensive jeans, and a shirt. Or just the jeans, depending on the make, or 5, count them 5, different outfits, On sale. AM I correct so far? *Yes LORD, you are.* GOOD. Let me continue. You took your Mom's $20.00, gave her $5.00 for <u>HER</u>. Yes YOU DID, I WAS THERE. You said, *Mom, buy this handbag for yourself. It matches the coat you have on better than the old one you are carrying.* She did. AND LOVED YOU FOR IT. Meanwhile you bought 5 wild pants, 5 wild or tight shirts, which gave you 5 outfits or different clothes to wear to school. Yes, to school. Oh, how they laughed at you. Snickered. I heard them. You said, *Good...let them laugh. They do not know ME.* NO, they do not. But they do NOW. And that is why we are NOT going to the High School Reunion this year. Your 25th AM I correct? *Yes, LORD.* I Love you Steve, because YOU LOVE ME. You knew, YOU knew, you KNEW, YOUR PARENTS WERE STRUGGLING. You knew that 1 pair of jeans would not last a whole school year. You took the mocking and the criticism in stride. You said, I Love you Mom and Dad and I will help you where I can. So when this book gets published, and it will, take some money, buy them a new home, new car, truck, anything they want. For GOD said, thou shall honor thy mother and thy father. No greater Love, or example of Love of his parents, have I witnessed. Now do I know you? Do I have you in my mind? Do I see you? Do I tell you the truth? Watch me. I will keep my promise. She will be home soon. That is MY WAY. Now class of 1973, and Oxford Hills High School, all of you that mocked him, laughed and gave him a mirror thinking he was vain. HOW DO YOU FEEL? NOW, IS IT TIME? DO YOU THINK I AM GOD? AM I is a teacher through example. AM I HOLY AND PURE? I AM JEHOVAH. I AM GOD. I right the wicked and cripple the strong. I AM.

Fun Stuff, Part Two

I AM IS STILL WILD ABOUT A FEW MORE THINGS IN Steve's life. His first wife. I will call her Cindy. That is not her real name. She is a bitch. A totally hard-nosed, difficult to deal with, first class, total out and out BITCH. In 11 years, 11 years not once, NOT ONCE, has she allowed them to use the telephone to call their dad, collect. And THEN tell her friends, she does have a few, that he never calls his children. She even went so far as to lie to Steve, the court, and the mediators about her intentions after the divorce. I AM going to be taking night classes. BULL, I SAY BULLSHIT, SHE LIED. She went IMMEDIATELY on welfare. She was on it for over five years, working on her tan. Talking to her friends, remember she has a few, about how crazy Steve was, is, and will always be. Well, LISTEN WOMAN, HE DOES NOT WANT YOU BACK. Get that through your head. He is over you. He found Love. He may not admit it right away, but he found Jehovah. I AM. I feel a little better there is more, believe me. Like this example of her being a bitch. Every other weekend for over 3 years Steve drove 3 hours, ONE WAY, to visit his kids. She was late in receiving a Child Support check from the State and took it out on Steve. He paid on time. I KNOW I witnessed it. GOD. She was not at the house, she took the kids and stayed with friends, remember she has a few, to teach him a lesson. Well, I remember Steve sitting on the steps at her place. Putting his hands in prayer, and saying, *Why LORD, why did I marry this bitch, why? I hate her...she did it again.* Meaning something else just to see a reaction. I was livid. I was beyond livid. I took revenge. I THE LORD GOD put her in a cancer scare. Yes, cancer. She was diagnosed WITH CANCER AND TREATED. Well, here is the big news, She was benign. Yes, NO CANCER. Her physician misread the x-rays. It was a polyp from too much booze. They never told her. They were afraid of a lawsuit. I can prove it. If she would JUST STOP, LISTEN, and LOOK TO GOD.

Is MY WAY to hurt or scare or teach someone a lesson? NO? If she had asked, I would have guided her to another physician to get a 2nd opinion. I concur with 2nd opinions. I give you a question? Who graduated at the bottom of their medical class, when all the ones I hear are at the top? THINK. SOMEONE DID. What if that's the one who misdiagnosed you. AND removed something that did not need removing. She is a bitch, yes, but I did not need to allow the removal of a Fallopian tube which was believed to be cancerous. If she just asked ME, GOD, IF it was true. I KNEW. I could have stopped, prevented, and helped. Yes, I caused IT, but I could also been a good guy and HELPED. Instead, I AM angrier at her more than ever before, because she did not listen. Medical malpractice is running out of control. Ask ME. I WILL HELP. You can be assured of that. Enough tonight Steve, it's 1:25 AM, got top get some sleep. Fun with the kids tomorrow. *Goodnight*

LORD.

Today we had a great day. Today we saw the girls. Steve's two oldest daughters from his first marriage, and we talked all day long. I AM SAYS WE HAD FUN. It was father/daughter time. Now I have some sketches to make please, start. Now go to the journal. I have much to write. (See I AM Sketch)

This is the imagery I generate when anyone, even Steve, reads this book.

Steve, this is GREAT. I really do appreciate the money spent on these books. I know they are not cheap but are a great deal. For ME, it is important say, the remainder of the works is too important not to. I also said, Not to write on BOTH sides of the pages. I need CLARITY on these topics so lets start with…

Clarity

You all need to be clear to ME about what you want, need, or care about. I mean crystal clear. Make no assumptions that I understand. I may take YOUR lack of follow through and/or follow-up as a measure of content. Meaning you do not require any further assistance, or are content with the way things are so far. I need to be told specific details about your plagues, problems and delay's. NOT just here is a broken thing, here is a problem, FIX IT. GOD will fix it, BUT WILL NOT, thankfully, STOP DOING OTHER DUTIES, unless it is fully disclosed. So I can drive the priority of the matter up, if needed, or down or not clear. Now that does not mean GOD will not get to it, it means it is low on GODS list of priority's right <u>now</u>. Let ME explain, today Steve spent a wonderful day with his girls of his 1st marriage. They talked, and talked and talked. That was a talk long overdue. He told them the truth about why he, and their mom were divorced. They were not told this by their own mother who has raised and lived with them for 15 and 13 years respectfully submitted. This was a shock to Steve that his ex-wife did not tell his children about the divorce. The voices he heard, or the appearance of a nervous breakdown. WE told you as readers, the real reason, it was GOD. Now GOD STRIKES AGAIN. Cindy cannot be on disability and play softball. I will see that she, in her own way, gets caught. She is supposed to be unable to work. So why is she collecting disability? I will discipline the woman known as CINDY. She will be an example for what NOT to do when divorce does occur. You need to clarify to ME world, that GOD needs to be involved and at what level. High for a quick resolution or low for when you get a chance to fix this LORD. I will OK your request and take the Low or high OFF. Or change the setting if I feel after reviewing that it is needed to do so.

I said, I Love you, you are a great day, and so was I. That was unclear, it is incomplete it is partial, non-thought we call it. Not thought all the way through. Do it, it's a way to be more exact with GOD. It is a way to be more precise with your prayers and requests. So start practicing by <u>thinking</u>, the blue, blue ocean is in a big blue boat. It is a mental exercise that is incorrect on purpose. It takes the place of "shells." You know…sally sells sea…So start practicing and I will tell you when to stop. Keep going. Keep going. Keep going. Now stop. Open your mouth and say what you are thinking. See, not even close. If you cheated and <u>read</u> the quote instead of thinking the quote, you must STOP, go back and try again. Steve, you did GREAT. That is why I choose you to write this book in the first place. Your thoughts are clear, clean and wholesome to the LORD GOD. I can tell by your expressions if you are sad, lonely and/or afraid. Yes, you get a father of biblical proportions and you see and hear, uncertainty, caution, and fear. It is perfectly normal. I would not expect you to be absolutely certain until I finish this <u>whole</u> <u>book</u>. <u>I does whole book</u>. Look at the underlined words in the last several text blocks. **THAT IS WHAT I DO. I do the WHOLE book, so here goes.**

See GODS Personal Statement

MY Story
IS my Love Story
for you!

P.S. I will be waiting for your love!

I AM is <u>Not</u>

I AM is not. NOT is nothing. I AM is all, I AM is everything. I wrote this with Neale Walsh in his last book, and since then I have heard nothing but questions on the matter. Nothing is Not? What the hell is that? Not is nothing? Or is it non-existent? I AM is not? What the hell is that? Who is not? What is not, and why this, is it to confuse us? No, not really! See, that's IT! Not. It means no, not really. The opposite of yes. It means zero, or nil. Does that help? When you say to me. How do you feel LORD, are you sad? I say no, not really. Steve, YOU tend to too much too soon, this! I tell you no, I AM fine. You reply, well, could you explain this passage please? Take it one step further, ask if I AM busy? *OK.* I might be with NOMA and have the time to help, but I could also be with Maria, in a compromising position. OK? *OK, I understand.* I AM sorry for any problems my apparent rude thoughts may have caused. *Apology accepted.* As to the rude comment it is not rude to interrupt, just common courtesy to ask, say please and thank-you in your thoughts. *I will practice at it, OK?* Very well, practice with, please LORD, will you allow Tina into my life, I still Love her and I know she will be a good wife again. Your prayer, AM I correct? *Yes, you are correct, LORD Jehovah. Thank-you.* Why did you thank me just then? *I know you have answered my prayer.* Have I? *Yes, sometime in the future, that you choose, you "return her better than she was before."* Yes, I have. Do you know when? *Only that you choose, and that it is in the future, and an era must be completed.* Very, very, very good, but when? *Before Sept. 1ˢᵗ, you told me.* What year? *This year.* Correct. Now have I promised this precise a date, down to a month, day and year before? *No, not this precisely.* Well, I just made you lie. *Yes, you asked me to.* Why? *For your purpose.* Exactly.

Your purpose - Old and New

What if I get you a new wife, Steve? One not tainted, not used, not... well, stubborn. Could you Love her? *Possibly, in time.* Why? *Time heals all wounds.* Perfect! Time is MY ally. I AM told you MANY, MANY, MANY TIMES BEFORE THAT SHE WOULD RETURN, "Tina," by this date and that, haven't I? *Yes, too numerous to mention.* Why did I ask you to lie in the last text? *For your purpose.* Do you know what that purpose is? *No, not really but I have learned to trust you and eventually you tell me why.* Exactly. I TELL YOU NOW, Tina is NOT going to come back to you in the near future, and you will have a new wife. She will be loving, caring, and totally dedicated to keeping you happy. How's that? *Feels wrong somehow, no spirit behind the words.* Perfect... "no spirit behind the words." If you tell me, knowing I can fulfill promises, prayers and oh...let's say, <u>destiny's</u> ... "I Love you." <u>Who</u> are you talking too? *You LORD Jehovah, the single spirit behind that message is YOU.* Correct, now "I Love you." *The message is meant for Tina wherever she is, through you.* Exactly. You send an E-mail, <u>GOD'S way</u>, GOD'S STYLE, and GOD'S PURPOSE, PLAN AND DESTINY. You do that all the time, constantly, as we speak and write you are "a big hug." She is the receiver of that vibration. *"Good Vibrations," the Beach Boys.* <u>Exactly.</u> She will get it soon. There she got it. Now her reaction is, I only wanted to be alone for awhile, I'm done doing that. End of message. New message, Take me back Steve, I really do Love you. Now she has more, I can't wait, I need him in my life again, PLEASE LORD. That is MY WAY of knowing she has had enough in her reality, she said, "Please." NOW, THIS IS NOT FICTION, IT IS FACT. I will advise you of more developments as they occur.

Lots O'Fun

There is that word again fun. This time lots o' fun. Sometimes when I do or say or plan something, all I get from you is a "oh." Which translates into "oh, my GOD it is through you all things GOOD and FUN flow." I know this. I plan it this way. I really AM. AM is A.M. I AM A MORNING PERSON. GOD LOVES the A.M. time of day. I got Neale up at 4:00 every morning, the A.M. and this morning I got Steve up at 3:30. He went to bed at midnight. *I lost sleep trying to get Tina to contact me spiritually,* is what he tells me. I know it is because Maine has midget bugs, or min-gees and mosquitoes they bite him.

In his 2ⁿᵈ marriage he feels he is in Love. NOT. Which means? Right Steve, it means THE OPPOSITE. A good example of this: "It has been a very quiet season for weather, then NOT." See it means the opposite of that statement or a "yes" that is kind of sarcastic. FUN is like that it makes you feel guilty and you should not. I did this to clarify I AM is NOT, MORE. Yes, there is a lot to My way 's. Now Steve, go to sleep... busy day ahead.

Now it is Weds. Night July 15ᵗʰ at 9:00 P.M. and we can continue. I constantly see humanity at its worse when it tries to describe a problem. It can be solved by them or by the observer, which on a rare occasion <u>does</u>. "She is not listening to me," or "why doesn't he do more around the house." BOTH are solvable by the observer. Help her to listen by clearly defining what you are looking for, and if he knew what to do he would properly do the task when required. Now both sound different but are exactly the same. I know I created them. I took both problems, entered them into the computer of Jehovah and came up with the same solution. Me. GOD. I solve all problems, big and small. Now, I do make a mistake, or so it seems. My mistake may be something that "feels wrong" by your standards, but it is a "blessing" by mine. Have you heard this saying before: "I don't know why it works that way, only that it does." I AM that's why. I AM the reason it works as it does. No one else. I choose to make it a part of ME. Why? Earlier I told you about my way. That's why! Making it a part of me makes my decision simple, elegant and with GOD-like efficiency. I do not have to think or decide or evaluate. I can act. Now the next paragraph starts with, you guessed it....

205

Act

I Act, I do not decide. 50 Million years of experience allows that luxury. I can, do, and <u>will</u> a problem fixed. For example, this is a slow day so I AM going to pick on Steve again. I know the reader must be thinking, "poor guy." Well, I have a good reason why? I will explain later. Now, I took Steve to his mom and dad's, as you know from reading this, and made him attack chores that his aging parents are getting to old to handle. Why? Because I felt it was necessary. He was happy to clean the baseball from his pitching days, and found old photos of his youth that brought back happy memories. That is why. Despite the work he got to "relive" the past, the happy past. He can now build on those thoughts and make the rest of the year successful, from that simple exercise. Some may have thought I act in an open and forceful way. Steve calls it, and I Love this title, "GOD'S subtleties." It is my nature to be subtle. I AM that way. I make a subtle issue a miracle. I take a subtle moment and make it special, personal, private, and long lasting. SHE WOULD NOT LOVE ME IF I DID THAT, or HE WOULD HATE ME IF I TRIED THAT, are false statements. See <u>lies.</u> Now you grasp my point Steve? I do not error. I do not make false statements. If I DID, how would the truth EVER be accomplished, understand? *Yes LORD, forgive me, you are not finished with me yet.* I Love you son that made my day, Perfect. I forgive you and bless you. Now write more on...

Lies, Part Two

Remember I do not lie, tell falsehoods, or even exaggerate. I do not have to. Tina is going to be your new, loving, caring, wife. She has been doing pennants for ME, on how to behave, and telling the truth. She is scheduled to be back with you by Sept. 2nd your 10th year anniversary. I promise. You can bet on THAT, Steve. No fooling! *Thank-you Heavenly Father, I anxiously and nervously wait for that reunion.* Bless you. *"Thank-you Heavenly Father"* is all I needed to hear. I can guess the rest, because I know you. I conquer the greatest trials in humanity for that. I will move planets for that. I do. I will, and I Love you Steven Wade Raasumaa. *Isn't this the personal relationship with you we wanted the readers to know was possible?* YES, YES, YES. In my world, that is Holy, Holy, Holy. Since I told you a WHOLE BOOK OF FACTS, before we close, let me share one more. I have MORE books to write. *With me father?* Yes. This one is closed. The ending is HER return. I decided to finish my Earth moving stories and sayings in the next installment called...My Earth. *I like that title, it feels like excitement personified.* Yes, and so do I. In closing this book of my stories, I as LORD Jehovah, I need to remind the readers, I AM. Till tomorrow then? *Yes, road trip return.* OK. Before I leave you readers I just want to explain a simple premise you may have missed. I KNOW Steven Wade Raasumaa. I AM GOD.

What a great ending to any life, work, or relationship. Enough said...see you soon in the funny papers, but that is another story.

Another Story

I could not leave without sharing this with you. I write all cartoons. I Love comics. The Sunday Paper is my favorite reading material. By the way, church, I DO NOT GO. I spend time with Maria and the children. It is our family time. Hey, one in seven, I still do that. I work on Saturdays, so don't get any ideas, OK? Till we cross paths again.

Love, LORD Jehovah

PS I AM WATCHING YOU.

There always is another story, Steve. I could have done 16-17 books like this one. I have 18-20 volumes just in my library waiting to be told.

I look forward to reading and hearing some of these.

Maybe I could read to you again like when you were little.

I would Love that, please pick one of the Jedi stories, I enjoyed them.

Some more of
God's favorite
things are...

He enjoys...

God's favorite
drinks are...

God's
Stereo

Christian Gospel
Classick Rock
Rock n' Roll
Oldies
Classical
Jazz
Country/Western
Bluegrass

Then everything
else

Spite
7up
Coke
Pepsi
Dr Pepper
Cherry Coke
Rootbeer
Orange Juice
Grape Juice
Tang and

"God enjoys wines that are
"fruity and zesty." He liked the
Strawberry and Blackberry
Wines that Steve tried last
month. Even at $4.00 a bottle
They tasted "Great."

God enjoys
Football - all types - all leve
Baseball - all types - all levels
Hockey - all types - all levels
Skating - Olympic & figure
also the History Channel, Nickelodeon
National Geographic, and Biography.
VH1's behind the music and Star
Trek the next generation,

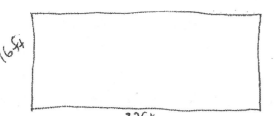

16 ft

325 ft

God has several big screen TV's
His favorite is 16 x 32 It shows people and places full size!

Steve is a Friend of GOD.

He is the <u>only</u> one allowed to channel Jehovah directly. Yes, I AM is writing this about Steve because he would NOT write about himself.

BESIDES…I AM THE AUTHOR…GOD.

You should see how he struggles with the typing.

To those who read this, may you feel born again. To those who read this and feel new, fresh and revitalized…Bless you. The <u>best</u> is yet to come. I have channeled another full volume of information to Steve that goes into the glorious difference between women and men. I ALSO SHARE THE ESSENCE OF HOW TO THINK. I teach you how to better teach your young, in reading, writing and arithmetic. We talk about new and exciting sports to create, and <u>My Angels role in every one's life.</u> I AM not even scratching the surface of all I can teach. <u>I have even explained how to build equipment to watch OUR television broadcasts from Heaven.</u>

YES, FROM HEAVEN.

So now you decide. Do you buy this book and tell others about it? Or do you ignore the ALMIGHTY. I guess I can count on this being a best seller, because <u>I would not have told you</u>, or written all I have, if I did not already know your response. I LOVE <u>YOU</u> TOO. Thanks Steve.

Let's get busy with book 2. Thanks my friend, you did well.

Love, Jehovah - GOD of all.

Note from Steve

I am not a typist. That is a fact. You the reader would have had the book sooner but I am extremely slow at editing. I must have gone through the editing of this at least 150 times, over the past several years to get this published. I did what they and GOD asked me to do in preparing it for you. THE WORDS are EXACTLY the way I heard them. The rest took TIME. HE wanted you to <u>get the TOTAL message.</u> He said: **To start them thinking in new and different ways. That is why we are doing this book.** *GOD Bless everyone who reads this and BELIEVES. There is more to come, much, much, much more.   Amen.*

Look for the next book from Jehovah called: GOD is Speaking - Are you listening?
My Earth.

Currently being channeled, typed and edited.

Printed in the United States
By Bookmasters